I Ran Into Some Trouble

I Ran Into Some Trouble

Peggy Caserta
and Maggie Falcon

Wyatt-MacKenzie Publishing
DEADWOOD, OREGON

I Ran Into Some Trouble

Peggy Caserta and Maggie Falcon

HARDCOVER ISBN: 978-1-942545-82-8
SOFTCOVER ISBN: 978-1-948018-08-1
EBOOK ISBN: 978-1-948018-20-3
Library Congress of Control Number: 2018937835

©2018 Peggy Caserta and Maggie Falcon.
All rights reserved.
No part of this book may be reproduced in any manner without written
permission except in the case of brief quotations embodied
in critical articles and reviews.

Cover design by Wes Wilson and Carolyn Ferris.
©2017 Wes Wilson and Carolyn Ferris.
www.WesCarolynArts.com

Special thanks to the editing team:
Marilyn Whitehorse, Lisa Romeo, Cindy Muntwyler,
Howard Lovy, and Karen Kibler

Special recognition to: Sheila Weller, for the introduction
after an interview for *Vanity Fair*.

Photos of Peggy and Grateful Dead at Mnasidika, and Janis Joplin with George
©Herb Greene. Used with permission.
Special thanks to Herbie Greene and Anne Morrow.

Photos on stage at Woodstock ©Jim Marshall Photography LLC.
Used with permission.
Special thanks to Jay Blakesberg.

Some names have been changed for privacy.

Wyatt-MacKenzie Publishing
DEADWOOD, OREGON

Wyatt-MacKenzie Publishing, Inc.
info@wyattmackenzie.com

*Dedicated to Mom and Dad.
You tried so hard.*

✳

Foreword

By David Dalton

Author/Co-author of twenty-four books and a number of biographies on James Dean, Jim Morrison, Janis Joplin, Sid Vicious, the Rolling Stones, Steven Tyler and Andy Warhol

PEGGY CASERTA is a genuine wild child of her time. You follow her adventures as you would a character in a picaresque novel. It's a rush. You open the book and you're on a roller coaster ride. Right off you sense something feral and out of the blue is coming at you. Oddly enough, however, nothing in her Ozzie and Harriet family background could've predicted the wildlife to come.

Peggy started out the all-American girl: beautiful, popular, the homecoming queen, but there was something about it she didn't care for—quite a few things, actually. She didn't want to get married, have kids and live the split-level, cocktail party, pool-in-the-back-yard, suburban American dream. It didn't seem all that idyllic to her. She needn't have worried. As it turned out there was never even the remote possibility of the normal course of events ever intruding on her life.

If you wanted to take a walk on the wild side, Peggy's story, as a plan for life, is pretty close to hair-raising perfection—including, of course, a few things *not* to do under any circumstances. It's heart-stopping stuff. As thrilling as watching something unexpectedly fall out of the sky. She handled it well, although often she was too wily for her own good.

She's like the heroine of one of those old Greek romances where a series of increasingly improbable incidents start with a phrase like: "*And then Fate began her game . . .*"[1] Each of her galloping adventures seems to have been conjured up by some wickedly mischievous imp of Chance—which after all, is just the fool's name for Fate.

i

Like, for instance, how did she happen to set up shop, the legendary Mnasidika, at the very center of the action just at the moment the Great Lost Hippie Kingdom of Haight-Ashbury was born?

Jimi Hendrix shows up at Mnasidika, his manager wants Peggy to get him a gig at Bill Graham's Fillmore. She helps Bill Graham get his start in show business. Also God. Seriously. Just the other day I spoke to the guy who physically brought God (Swami Bhaktivedanta) to San Francisco. Okay, so God's ceremonial cart broke down on his way into town. Maybe he hadn't heard that they'd stopped making wheels out of wood. But, hey, she had a hand in Levi's bell-bottoms trend (I'll forgive her for that), went on to become a hippie tycoon and then threw it all away. We expect nothing less of our heroine.

Peggy Caserta is a character out of Tennessee Williams teleported to Haight-Ashbury and that's just the beginning of her runaway-train adventures: among them resurrections, pirates (okay, pot smugglers) coming back from the dead, frying steak with Mr. Clean, miraculous escapes, premonitions, strange potions, prison and prison breaks—breaking out five pot smugglers from a federal prison in Mazatlan being one of her classic achievements. There's even a nurse Ratchet from *Cuckoo's Nest* in here. And who would want to miss the time Peggy and her girlfriend Kimmie in a single engine plane buzzed a nonplussed Janis Joplin as she's driving across the Golden Gate Bridge . . . or the time when she's tooling along in her Shelby Mustang and the steering wheel disappears? Did I mention she was on acid at the time? But still . . . .

Then there's the subterranean-junk-sick-blues-again sagas. Hustling doctors smitten with her, running on Santa Monica beach with sixty skinny snivelling shirtlength junkies for her daily hit of Dilaudid. There's outrageous business of getting her friend Dee to cop drugstore dope *dressed as a cop*! Or hiring limos to score at pharmacies (junkies with money are always welcome), mastering the hybrid hieroglyphics of forging prescriptions—part Latin, part alchemical symbol, part doctor's scrawl. Who said being a junkie wasn't hard work? And scary: hiding in dumpsters, escaping from a randy pig (on the chicken farm work-release facility) who wants to fuck her with that scary-as-hell corkscrew penis, and then writing her way out of prison with the play, *Ain't Love a Bitch*.

At various points her exhausted guardian angel wakes up alarmed and says, "What the hell has she got up to now?" From time to time you're not going to be able to resist yelling—as when watching a thriller—"Jesus, Peggy, whatever you do, *don't open that door!*"

Whatever life throws at her, she recounts it in her droll delivery that runs through the book like "Duck" Dunn's bass on a Stax Volt single. Note the wry, sly tone of voice in which Peggy spins her tale. If you call Peggy on the phone, an entire Southern panorama comes to life in the background. The forlorn whistle of a train chugging down the tracks, a hound dog howlin' in the distance, a rooster crowin', fish jumpin' in the bayou and then—to explain some improbable occurrence—Peggy'll tell you in her languid cat-on-a-hot-tin-roof delivery, "Honey, I cahn't help it if I keep throwin' sevens."

Peggy was an acid-eating, pot-smoking, let's-fuckin'-change-the-world hippie but, like Janis, marinated in Southern molasses, and one of the beauties of Peggy's book is her affectionate portrait of Janis as the sweet, funny (and unintentionally hilarious) person she was. She's right here, alive and glowing in her boas and mocking melancholy. You don't need to read a Janis biography (well, maybe mine) to know the brilliant, prat-falling, warmhearted woman that comes through so heart-breakingly in her songs. It's touching that as much of a force of nature as Janis was, she was also such a hoot.

I Ran Into Some Trouble is a kind of fairy tale told out of order, but with a touching if heartrending conclusion where the good-hearted daughter pulls herself out of her funk, goes home on the Louisiana Mississippi border, and redeems her bad self by taking care of her long-suffering mother for the last 12 years of her life. The two sentences with which she ends the book are just *precious* (to use a Peggy word) and couldn't sum up her wild and radiant life better: "I remembered the impossible was possible. Again."

Prologue

IT SOMETIMES HAPPENS when I'm out and about, in the supermarket, at doctors' offices, and other places when I hand over my ID or write a check. Someone—a devoted Janis Joplin fan, or maybe a student of the counterculture—asks if I'm *that* Peggy Caserta. I'd be lying if I said it wasn't somewhat flattering, and depending on how I'm approached, I'm happy to smile, say "yes" and chat a few moments. But I realize that it isn't about me; it's about my connection to Janis.

    The other requests, the more formal and professional ones—when some intrepid intern or a determined documentary maker manages to find me—never end, and they almost all begin with: "Can we interview you about Janis Joplin?" Sometimes, I'm called upon to pontificate about Haight-Ashbury in its heyday, about hippie fashion, about the 1960s, and sometimes about having survived heroin addiction. Occasionally, I have acquiesced to these requests, and answered the emails or phone questions as best as I could, and less often I have even allowed a well-meaning make-up artist to dab powder across my wrinkles, and faced interviewer questions on camera. When I think they are treating the subject and legacy respectfully, I'll talk—why wouldn't I want to reminisce about a wonderful time and a person who meant a lot to me? We had fun, meant no harm; when I talk about Janis and those days, I can do it with more joy and fondness, and with less of the pain and heartache that dogged my spirit for years.

Though I am often less than thrilled with the final edit, I've come to realize it to be the nature of the beast. I've appeared in an *A&E Biography*, on *20/20*, the BBC, and Reelz, and more recently on the American Masters' *Little Girl Blue*. But more often I say "no"—politely or not, depending on who's asking, and how.

After all these decades, I simply want to be alone with my rescue dogs. I find it alternately odd and comforting that a particular six-year period in my life, that took place nearly fifty years ago, is what I've come to be publicly defined by.

What's been written about me, in books and on websites—and here I'm talking mostly about my association with Janis—should be read with a healthy dose of skepticism, or at least an eye toward how the information was obtained. Much of what others have written is conjecture, opinions defined by a particular agenda. Many of these folks have a need to paint Janis as a lesbian, or to define her as straight, to woe her demise as a hapless victim of personal associations and to minimize or inflate my role as fits their narrative. Sadly, that includes some who knew both of us. Many were employed by her, so perhaps friendly business, but not simply friendship. Or, worse, the information came via hangers-on who weren't actually privy to the truth, those who, after Janis's death, assumed a stance of having been in her inner circle when they weren't. I have encountered these people over the years, and it is truly sad. We once heard of an individual who would hold court in Hollywood on the anniversary of her death, claiming to be her "secret friend" that no one knew about. To be clear, the same has been said of me—that perhaps I didn't even know Janis; that what I say now differs, sometimes dramatically, from what I supposedly said to the writer of a book published in 1973 at the peak of my grief and addiction. As I've written here, *that* story began as a look into an innocent phenomenon I was a part of, but ended as a way to feed a drug habit. Though I made no false statements, what I did do was allowed myself to be taken advantage of by unscrupulous people while I was addicted to heroin. Nobody's fault but mine.

But the root essence of it was true: we were close friends, lovers, dope-shooting pals. No one from the early days of Haight-Ashbury, who knew us both, has ever denied the friendship we shared.

And forty years later, that hasn't changed. I've been clean for over twenty years, and the past seems far more clear than it did even then.

If my own accounts in this book you are holding in your hands, or listening to right now, were inauthentic, if all these years I had been exaggerating our association and its meaning, then why would people who want to learn more—in some cases, Joplin scholars—continue to track me down? (And by the way, that's not easy even in the day of Google; I live quietly and mostly off the internet grid.)

Here's what I think: nostalgia always wins. But then we want more than just nostalgia. We want to know from someone who was there, up close and personal: what really happened? That's what I've attempted to do in these pages: tell what really happened, to the best of my current ability.

I won't ever outrun my ties to hippie culture in The Haight in the early sixties into the early seventies, and I don't ever want to. That was my life, the most interesting, exciting, formative years of my life. Had I never even met Janis, and had the exquisite experience of bearing witness to her explosive talent and the dynamic changes in rock-n-roll history, it would have still been just as indelibly etched into the very fiber of my soul.

Yet I'm also proud of what I accomplished with Mnasidika—how my dream of one little store not only grew into a tiny empire of many stores in several locations—but that, even as a neophyte in the business, I had the ability to spot emerging fashion trends, gamble on them, push them further, and make a few million dollars selling just the right kind of jeans to enough hippies, musicians, and wannabes to fuel change *way beyond* our little corner of San Francisco.

But Janis and I did meet, love and laugh. Oh my God, did we laugh!

When the emails and phone calls come in now, asking for a little bit of my time, what they're really asking for is a little piece of her heart, and since that is not mine to give, the answer is often "no" to them; but for you the reader, the answer I have is this book. How I went from an innocent baby in the Bayou, to Homecoming Queen, to the heights of The Haight and descent into the madness of addiction. From the inexplicable redemption on a street corner in Monterey, California to caring for my mother. I found myself. I'm still here, rockin' on a porch somewhere deep in the South after all these years; here to tell you this story, *my* story . . .

Part One

IN THE SUMMER OF 1964, a twenty-something, nondescript young man popped his head in through the open door of my study partner Adrian's apartment.

"Hi, I'm Steve, I live down the hall," he greeted us as he sauntered in, gesturing vaguely over his right shoulder. "What are you ladies up to?"

"We're studying. Why?" I asked, looking up from my homework.

"What's up? What're you doing?" Adrian piped in.

Steve walked over to the window and looked out on this foggy, gloomy night onto San Francisco's Panhandle, a broad strip of ground between Oak and Fell Streets, starting at Stanyan Street, just east of Golden Gate Park and running several blocks to Masonic Street. It was a lush bit of nature maintained by the city, with large trees, mostly eucalyptus, flourishing in the constant mist of the San Francisco air.

Steve turned to us and said, "I have a pill . . . two, in fact. If you take them, it will greatly enhance your learning abilities and I guarantee," he paused a moment, a wry grin formed as he reflected momentarily, "it will be an experience like never before."

"Whadda ya mean . . . enhance our learning abilities?" I asked.

"All I can say is that it's a *trip*! Ten dollars a pill and I promise you, you'll never see things quite the same."

"Ten dollars? Why is this pill so expensive? What could be worth ten whole dollars?"

Adrian was quiet. I was the curious one.

He looked at me and said, "LSD-25."

Adrian apparently didn't like the sounds of it and quickly said, "I don't want it."

Suddenly I remembered having read an article in an old movie magazine, *Photoplay*, I think, which said that the movie star Cary Grant had, under the care and guidance of a psychiatrist, been experimenting with a mind-expanding substance known as LSD-25. I remembered the article well because I had been so fascinated by the idea.

"Wait a minute, Adrian. Let's think about this for a minute," I said.

"What's to think about? Sounds strange to me . . ." Adrian said.

"But wait . . . ya gotta figure something here. Think about it. Cary Grant is taking it. Cary Grant! Do you see anything wrong with him? I damn sure don't! He's rich, handsome and famous. He doesn't look like he's suffering any!"

"Well, that's true, but he's always been rich, handsome and famous. I'm sure the pill didn't do that!"

"Oh Adrian, you're missing the point . . . the point is that it doesn't appear to have hurt him any. I'm gonna take it. Come on, let's do it together."

"Ten dollars?"

"Oh, come on." I turned to Steven. "Here's my ten. I'm in."

Adrian pulled her ten out right behind mine. I guess she didn't want to miss anything, just in case it was good. He took our money and handed us the small, plain whitish, capsules. As he was leaving, he turned, smiled. "Have fun! I can say that without the chance of being wrong, you'll never forget this experience."

We sat there for a few moments, looking at the pills and each other.

"Well?" I said to Adrian.

"Well what?" she responded, sounding slightly exasperated.

"Well, we bought 'em . . . I guess the next thing to do is swallow them."

"I'm not sure I want to do this . . . a magic pill? Sounds a little weird . . . suppose we don't like it?"

"All I can say is that I cannot fathom that Cary Grant is stupid! He didn't become successful being stupid. And furthermore, why would he continue to take the stuff if it was hurting him? Why?"

The "Cary Grant logic" seemed to convince her. I went into the kitchen, got a glass of water, and like two babes in the woods, we looked at each other, swallowed the magic pills, went back into the living room, picked up the books and resumed studying, as though nothing had happened. Unknowingly, we had just embarked on our first acid trip. It was to be, in fact, the catalyst that would change my life in more ways than my twenty-three-year-old brain was capable of imagining.

After about ten minutes or so, Adrian looked up from her textbook. "Well? Do you feel anything?"

"No, I don't. Do you?"

"Nope, not a thing."

Now bored, and restless, studying seemed a thing of the immediate past.

"We've been ripped off!" Adrian exclaimed. "I knew I shouldn't have bought the fuckin' thing! Shit, ten dollars!" Then she asked, "Wanna go get a beer?"

Disgusted, I said, "A beer? No! Why would you want to go get a beer?"

"Oh, I don't know. Just felt like getting out for a little while, get some fresh air, anything. That's right, you're not much of a drinker, are you?"

Few of my friends understood my aversion to alcohol.

"Not particularly. It just never appealed to me that much. Makes me kinda woozy in the head, and then I have to pee too much. Frankly, somehow, swallowing that much liquid seems to be hard for me. But I'll go for a Coke."

Books set aside, we put on jackets and left the overheated apartment. At the nearest bar, sure that we had been burned by the guy with "the pill," we ordered a beer and a coke. Then I noticed that a plant in the end of the back of the bar seemed to start growing—I could see it grow, or at least it appeared to be growing right in front of my eyes. It grew so fast that it ran up the side, and then framed the mirror behind the bar. I turned to Adrian to ask her if she noticed the bar was becoming a jungle, when, oh my God, Adrian's entire face was breathing in a pulse of melting illusion. Then suddenly Adrian wasn't exactly Adrian anymore, but had taken on the form of an animal-human *something*. Everything started changing, but with enough time still left to grab onto some kind of reason I whispered, "Adrian? Adrian? Are you still there?"

"Where?" she asked, her tone bewildered.

Oh, thank God, she's there—somewhere, I thought to myself.

"Eh, something is happening, really happening. Do you see what I see? Everything is changing fast." My words spilled out and then materialized as balls of energy going into Adrian's head.

Finally, Adrian said, "I don't know what you see, but something must be happening from that pill . . . everything's movin' and the whole place is filling up with people and they're in Technicolor. I want to go home."

Good idea, I thought, and we both darted for the door. Once out of the bar, the ever-changing spectacle continued to kaleidoscope about us. Wow! A world out here. Sidewalks that moved. Cars with large, bright beacons for headlights and the most unusual thing of all—mist everywhere. Water falling right from heaven. Where? Why? Which way was home? Adrian seemed to have an internal compass and I followed. She knew which way was home. Yes, she did, but once we reached the Panhandle, which had been only two blocks from where we emerged from the jungle bar, it seemed to then take days, instead of twenty minutes, to reach the block of her apartment. The trees were so friendly, they smiled down on me, the bark breathed and wiggled and suddenly I began to feel that the world was at peace and everybody was happy—except Adrian. She was especially not happy when I got down on all fours to climb the steps to her apartment—they were so steep, I had to hold on. The acid seemed to affect me more. Once inside, I heard water rushing.

"Adrian! A pipe burst somewhere . . . I hear water . . . pouring, rushing."

"Yeah, I hear it, too."

Oh thank God, she heard it. That proved it wasn't my acid imagination. We followed the sound and found nothing but a candle burning safely where we had left it. We both stood staring at the flame—God, it was beautiful, like none I had ever seen before. Adrian was as captivated as I was, so I knew she had also come "on." The melted wax started to drip, or pour, down the side of the candle and that usually imperceptible sound was now so clear and loud, it sounded like rushing water—we'd found the "broken pipe."

We spent the next eight hours or so in a world of changing patterns, colors, sounds—none of which scared me, though some appeared to frighten Adrian. I spent an eternity walking from the mantle to the window, where I wanted to gaze at the trees. An overall sense of well-being, of being at peace with myself and the incredible world of nature, descended on me. I saw a dog in the Panhandle and remember thinking, "What a phenomenal creature, four legs hitting the ground separately, loving and all covered with fur—God's creation." I sensed that the world was getting calmer and that truly peace really would guide the planets and that love surely would fill us all.

Unbeknownst to me, the advent of the "psychedelic revolution" was fast approaching, and what I was having would soon become defined as the classic "good trip." Not so for Adrian; her experience would be defined as the classic "bad acid trip."

We lost contact after that day. We hadn't been bosom buddies anyway, just fellow students thrown together in the same classes, studying partners. I'm not sure if the acid that day changed Adrian's life. I know it changed mine.

Even days later, basking in the aftermath, remembering some of the revelations and awakenings, I still felt calm, loving, and at unity with the universe. I hopped into my car and took a drive through Golden Gate Park. I parked near the lake and watched people, who appeared to take great pleasure in being in the paddleboats, leisurely moving themselves about the lake.

Watching the paddleboats, my mind drifted back to that time my father and I had floated together in the hand-crafted *Peggy C*, and he warned me of the shackles that working for a company could bring.

✳

I could hear the sound of wood being hand sawn. A concentrated rhythm that would go for a minute or two, the sound of a piece of lumber hitting the concrete floor of the garage. As I rounded the corner I could see my dad, his dark hair slicked back as he worked slightly bent over raking the triangular-shaped blade back and forth across the grain of the wood. I approached quietly, the scent of freshly cut wood hit my nostrils. I stood waiting for a break in the rhythm. The last stroke easily and decisively separated the pieces; my dad brushed the sawdust from the cut end.

"Hi, Baby Girl," he said as he stood up and grinned at me.

"Hi, Daddy," I said as I smiled back and then glanced down at my slightly brown toes. Part spring tan and part child's grime. I walked up and touched what looked like a lumber rib cage. "Whatcha doing?"

"Well, Baby, I'm making a boat," he said, a note of pride in his stance as he surveyed his progress.

"You're making a boat?" My eyes widened and my young mind filled the boat with adventure, my tiny self, swashbuckling and catching huge fish all at the same time.

"Yes, M'am."

"When ya gonna be done, Daddy?"

He wiped the sweat from his brow with a handkerchief, squinted and said, "About three weeks, I reckon. After work and on the weekends."

"Can I help you, Daddy?"

"You can keep me supplied with iced tea," he said as he handed me an empty glass. "You gotta make it real good, though."

"Oh yes! I can do that!" I said and ran towards the kitchen, glass in hand.

Sure enough, about three weeks later, I went out to the garage to help my dad and the boat was gone. I called out for him and heard him answer from the back yard. He had a hose draped over the side of the boat and was filling it up.

"Isn't the boat supposed to be on the water?" I asked, confused.

"Yes, Baby. But if it can't hold it in, it can't keep it out," he said with a chuckle. "This way I can test it before we get into the water with her."

"Oh." Then I queried, "How do you know it's a her?"

"Because she has a girl's name. Prettiest girl I know besides your mother. C'mon over here and have a look."

I wandered around to the back and gasped. "Peggy C?!" I exclaimed. "Like me?"

"Just like you, my darlin'. If she holds the water, you want to come fishing with me next weekend?"

"Yes!" I gushed and hugged him with all my little girl might.

The next weekend my dad got me up early. Seems the cicadas and crickets had finally gone to bed and the sun hadn't awakened yet. My mom had packed us a nice lunch the night before, and my father had a big thermos full of coffee.

The Peggy C eased into the water at Bayou Bogue Falaya with me in it, my dad climbing in handily as the back of the boat cleared the muddy shore.

"When are we gonna catch a fish, Daddy?" I asked about every ten minutes, patience never one of my virtues.

"Well, it's called fishing for a reason darlin'. It ain't called catching."

"That makes sense, 'cause we sure aren't catching!" I giggled. For all my fussiness, I was ecstatic to be spending time with my dad. Presently some fish did bite, and we reeled in enough for dinner. The sun was quite high as we made our way back home through the swamp.

"Ya know you'll never get anywhere working for someone else, Peggy. If you can, your best bet is to work for yourself. It's the only way to really get ahead in life," my dad offered, looking past me deep in thought.

"Well, how come you don't?" I asked somewhat perplexed, then exclaimed, "I know! You could make boats for a living!" in a self-satisfied tone, sure I had just turned the tide of my dad's working life.

"I can't risk losing a paycheck at this point. I'm lucky to be working for the Postal Service. It has good security, and that way your mom and you will be cared for if anything ever happens to me."

I suddenly felt uneasy. I felt that maybe my mom and I were the reason he couldn't start a business. He could not pilot his own ship, so to speak, nor could he launch his own business because if it didn't work out, how would he take care of us? I loved my father, and by his tone I knew he wanted something different for me. Though too young to imagine a life without my father and mother, I stored the information in a "very important to remember" file somewhere in my subconscious and scampered into the house.

A flat-line life, no peaks, no valleys, no dreams. Something had been touched in me in this first foray into altered consciousness. I couldn't color between the lines anymore. I wanted to live colorfully. Exuberantly. Cosmically. Without regret. Or apology.

I kept thinking and thinking about the acid experience. *The Experience.* Everything seemed clearer now, visually and emotionally. The trees were more splendid, the water unusually spectacular, more so than I had ever remembered it. Surely the acid had worn off. Yet within me I could feel a deep change. A rearrangement of some kind, swirling and gnawing at my soul. A gnawing to be free. To drop the constraints of a regular job and do something that would allow me to move about on my own schedule. Work, but work with a flare, a love of the art so to speak, of doing what I love. Didn't seem like an impossible dream or an unfair wish. I had only to make that dream real.

I thought of opening a small business, a clothing store or something. I kept thinking, "I'm young, energetic, reasonably bright . . . I can do this, I can do this." I called Mom and Dad, who still lived in the house I grew up in, on the North shore of Lake Ponchartrain near New Orleans.

Mom picked up. "Hello."

"Hi Mom, what's up?"

"What's up? What's up with you?"

I got right to the point, "Mom, I want to start a business." I knew she'd gasp.

"You what . . . start a business?" She did gasp, then relayed to my father, "Sam, it's Peggy, she wants to start a business." Turning back to our conversation, she asked me, "What do you know about business, Missy?"

"Nothing, but I think I can . . ." Before I could finish my sentence, she called back to Dad, "Sam, she knows nothing about business." I heard him say, "Well, at least she's thinking." She handed the phone to him.

"Hi honey. What's on your mind?"

"Dad, I'd like to take a gamble on the possibility that I might be able to make a business work. I'm not exactly sure how, yet, but I thought that if it was with just enough money, that even if it didn't work out, we could sustain the loss, well, at least, I'd have tried and, who knows, maybe it'll work."

"Sounds reasonable to me. How much is the figure that you feel *I* can sustain losing?"

"Oh, about fifteen hundred dollars." I did not have a clue what amount of investment I would really need, but that sounded like a good figure.

With surprisingly no friction, Dad said, "Ok, how do you want me to send it?"

I was thrilled! Dad was a good man, even when I wasn't asking for something. With my parents, I always knew I had their loving arms to fall back upon. If something went so far awry that I couldn't deal with it, I could always come home. That always kept me feeling secure in my choices, even when I made reckless ones. People have sometimes said that I am good at business because I took risks, but the truth was that my parents were always my safety net in case I failed.

The sensible thing to do was to scout my own neighborhood, close to where I lived. That was the Haight-Ashbury district. I walked the street from Masonic Street to Stanyan and found an empty storefront about 35 to 40 feet off the corner of Ashbury, at 1510 Haight. Without any trouble, I rented it for $87.50 a month. Scary, but exciting. Later, many people would marvel at how smart I was for picking that spot at that time, but really I didn't know that much. I was looking for cheap rent and was just tripping along Haight Street, saw the place, and never really focused on the fact that it was right off the corner of Ashbury. Haight and Ashbury meant nothing at the time. As I began to put my clothing store plan into action, I didn't dare give up my day job, working for Delta Airlines, because even *I* knew that businesses generally don't turn a profit right away. I'd have to do both. This all seemed a bit tricky, but being naïve, I thought it might work. The word "overhead" was foreign to me, but common sense told me I needed to keep the expenses low . . . very low. Back then, Delta allowed its personnel to fly for free, but it also allowed us to send freight by air for free.

Mom was a crack seamstress, and although reluctant to believe my venture would succeed, nonetheless she was a team player, and agreed to make a very specific kind of clothing for the store. She was a virtual sewing machine, the Haight-Ashbury version of Rosie the Riveter. Mom designed the clothes without a pattern, based on my general ideas. We began with blazers—double breasted with decorative piping and fully lined. A tag was sown into each one which read "Made especially for you, by Novell." When she completed an order consisting of two dozen or so items, she'd box them up, and Mom and Dad would then drive across the Lake and send it via Delta Air Freight and I would pick them up at the San Francisco International Airport. I was lucky to have such reliable (and free) help, and even though Mom couldn't make enough clothes to stock a small store, her touch of originality initially branded my inventory with a unique flair. The rest of the stock, I kept simple, mostly jeans from wholesale suppliers in the Bay Area, and deep-colored sweatshirts that doubled as sweaters in the chilled San Francisco weather.

![Mnasidika sign]

I named the store Mnasidika pronounced (Nah-SID-Eh-Kah) after the lover of Sappho, the ancient Greek poet from the island of Lesbos. My initial idea was to cater to the local lesbians. I knew enough of them personally, and relied on their word-of-mouth advertising to steer others to the store. At the time, in 1965, it was uncommon, and in many cases borderline scandalous, for the average woman to wear blue jeans outside of a ranch or similar outdoors environment. Skirts had to hit below the knee and the hair on a young man couldn't touch his collar, else he was suspended from school. The popular actress Mary Tyler Moore, fought to wear Capri pants in her role as Laura Petrie on *The Dick Van Dyke Show*, instead of pearls and crisp dress. Many might be surprised to learn that in San Francisco, now recognized as a stronghold for LGBT rights, it was illegal for more than 100 years to cross-dress in public. In 1863, as part of a broad anti-indecency campaign, the city adopted a law that criminalized a person appearing in "dress not belonging to his or her sex."

San Francisco's law remained in effect until July 1974.[2] This was all rapidly changing, however, and I could sense that—there was an errant thread in the conformity of conservatism that the youth had begun to pull on. It was about to unravel the whole damned ensemble.

Obtaining additional inventory was not easy, as I had little additional money to invest, sales were slow at first, and I had virtually no credit history aside from the car loan I was paying. Undaunted, or maybe naïvely, I simply showed up at supply houses and begged. Amazingly, it worked. I would just bluff and say, "Please give me a chance, I know what I'm doing. Believe me, I'll pay you." I truly meant that last part. If all else failed, I'd work overtime at Delta to pay off the debts. Perhaps I looked truthful and too naïve to be devious. I know I was bursting with enthusiasm, and of course, it was a different time. The vendors, including Landlubber and Roughrider in Napa Valley, with their beautiful corduroy straight leg jeans, seemed to key off my energy and said, "Ok, we'll try this, but the first time you're late, or worse, make us come after you for our money, it's over!"

I was blown away that I had actually gotten these manufacturers to take a chance on me. I was sure that I had bought the right items, that customers would materialize, and that I would pay those vendors in full. I was getting a rush from the self-propulsion.

The store opened in late '65 to little fanfare. I worked the early shift for Delta, then opened up at 3:30 in the afternoon. It didn't bother me or make me tired. I was having fun, knowing that *my* effort had actually manifested itself into a business. I was also quick to realize that the "overhead" word was coming into play; expenses had to be kept way down. One way to do that was having a pay phone installed instead of a private line. Pacific Bell installed it for free and there was no monthly bill. Anyone using the phone had to drop a dime into it every time they wanted to make a telephone call. Even me. It was a great way to monitor and control at least one expense.

Being in the store, observing and chatting with everyone who came in, and hanging out on the street in front of the store, it wasn't hard to get a feel for this encroaching trend: super casual, colorful, and inexpensive. I learned that even "inexpensive" adds up if you sold enough of it. A pair of Levi jeans and a sweatshirt was within most people's budget, and boy, did we sell 'em. Later I sold tie-dyes but I never was very big on those. They were being dyed by hippie chicks who could only bring in a dozen at a time. Mom's early creations, fully lined blazers in denim or Madras print, were a huge hit. Matching pants were available, too, but the blazers were so popular she concentrated on those. Mom never quite understood that she'd started a counterculture fashion trend from her little sewing room in Covington, Louisiana. Later, I tried to tell her that. I said, "Mom, you have no idea how the clothes you made helped define the look of a generation." Many iconic '60s fashion trends were born in my mom's sewing room, traveled to my shop in Haight-Ashbury, then moved on to the rest of the world. That never mattered to her. She was simply helping her little girl. To me, she was an artist who produced supreme quality clothing, launching my boutique and contributing immensely to a fashion revolution. Man, she was something. She *hand made* that many clothes, that quickly, and with so much care.

I purposely walked around on the street every day because I was watching everyone, trying to guess or predict or influence the next hip fashion fad. Observing the cast of characters, I felt like Alice watching Wonderland materialize in front of her. The tightly woven, relatively hidden little neighborhood was about to explode and become nationally visible. When Doctor David Smith moved in (God love him) with his free medical clinic, that did it. Now, no one had to leave for anything; we were self-contained, with Jerry Sealund's Far Fetched Foods, the A & P up on Waller Street, and now, we had our own medicine. We were complete. And if it hadn't been for the need to travel in order to keep up with Mnsasidika's inventory needs, I would have hardly ever left the neighborhood.

I loved The Haight. There was this unusual feeling, a spiritual camaraderie, everywhere within its bounds. No need to leave the realm. But, as more young people poured in and never left, the public image of The Haight projected on TV screens all over America was something different. Rather than the friendly, casual, trusting, peaceful people we thought ourselves to be, we were being judged as a bunch of lazy hippies without jobs who did nothing but take drugs and hang about constantly having sex. We were beginning to be scorned outside of The Haight radius, and people were starting to react harshly to us. Our style caused concern and speculation. And it's true, many factions among us *were* upheaving the status quo.

Then it got worse because we were objecting to the Vietnam War. Imagine that. Scorned for wanting peace, labeled unpatriotic. At the time, I couldn't understand how that label applied. Call us hippies, stoners, idealistic dreamers—whatever—*but unpatriotic?* Because we objected to a war where the death count rose by the hundreds on the nightly news. Our brothers were dying and even they weren't clear as to why. Maybe it was because some newscast somewhere reported that one random hippie spit on a G.I. as he was walking through an airport and that ridiculous gesture supposedly spoke for all of us? For God's sake, what activist group doesn't have at least a dozen or more loose cannons? What was unpatriotic about not wanting thousands and thousands of young boys to die for some improperly defined mission? Did we have to agree with every decision our government made, even when our gut told us it was wrong? It seemed clear to us that we weren't winning. And even if we had been winning, what exactly was the prize?

I remember a conversation with my conservative-leaning uncle, who was my mother's half-brother, about Vietnam one afternoon.

"Well you know Neesy, I was in the 7th Air Force Recon, Cam Ranh Bay, Vietnam. We flew hundreds of missions up the Mekong Delta."

"I didn't know you were in actual combat, Uncle."

"We were told we would soon be hitting the main supply route. My superiors kept telling us any day we were going to go in and end that war."

"Did you?"

"We kept waiting for the orders. So many of our troops were getting annihilated by the guerrillas. We knew exactly where we could fly in and cut off the North Vietnamese's supply line. The morale deteriorated as we began to suspect they didn't want us to win. They didn't seem to want us to end that thing."

"You all really felt that? You guys knew what it would take and you couldn't do it?"

My uncle swallowed hard. I could see that it took effort to speak.

"We, we . . . gawd . . . we could have spared so many. So many lives on both sides. . ." He looked at me and I could see his eyes were misting over. "You can't imagine . . ." His mouth tightened, his eyes were so sad as he struggled to contain his emotion. I could feel a tightening of my breath.

"I'm so sorry Uncle Billy, I'm so sorry for what you had to go through."

His shoulders heaved up and down and he wiped his tears with the back of his hand. There are no words for this type of sadness.

※

While Mnasidika was getting off the ground, my "landlord," from whom I rented an actual closet as my living space, was easily labeled as one of the early "hippie" girls. Judy Dugan had started sewing a paisley triangle of cloth into the bottom of her boyfriend, Richard's, Levi's, thereby allowing him to be able to pull them down comfortably over his boots. I thought that was clever, and asked her to do that to some of the jeans at the store. She could use a few bucks and I could use the gamble. I asked; she did it, and soon lots of folks in The Haight were wearing our altered jeans. I didn't really care for the contrast of paisley to denim however, so I asked her to just open up the bottom and sew in a piece of matching denim instead. These bouncy, flared jeans immediately became more popular than the ones with paisley inserts, and Judy grew grumpy with the increased demand. Then it hit me, Levi Strauss & Co. was located right in town, just over on Mission Street. Maybe, just maybe, I can talk them into making some jeans to look like these. It was a long shot I thought, but what the heck?

I made an appointment, and arrived in a mini dress, with hair down to my waist, and too many strands of hand-strung beads around my neck. The meeting didn't go well at first; the man I met with looked at me sideways.

"Miss, uh . . . what is your name?" he said. "Who do you think you are that you can improve on the world's most popular jean? Puhleez, Miss . . . you are wasting my time."

His dismissal was so final and condescending that I was going to leave without a fight. Then the head of Levi Strauss, who remembered me from when I had first visited months earlier (begging for store credit) arrived on the scene.

"Hey Peggy, what are you doing here? Ordering? You want something?"

"Yes, I do, but . . . " I turned to his underling. "He says, 'No.'"

"No to what? Tell me and let me decide yes or no."

This man probably hadn't heard that I was paying on time, but I realized he probably would have heard if I wasn't. So I took my shot.

"I want you to make altered pairs of Levi's. I want the bottom slightly flared out."

"Can you draw it?" he asked. I was never good at drawing, but I drew a pair of stiff little straight legs and made a triangular shape from several inches below the knee area downward to form the "bell." He picked it up and grunted, then said, "Let's take this downstairs."

On the factory floor, we encountered a woman in a hairnet, who appeared to be the head of the sewing team. She took a look at the drawing I had made, and when asked if she could make a pattern, she said, "Yes."

I was surprised when the executive turned to me and asked, "How many of these pairs of jeans are you talking about?" I must have just stared at him slack-jawed, because quickly he asked again, "How many?"

Could I be hearing right? They were going to do this? I knew that if I asked for too few it wouldn't be worth their time. But if I ordered too many, how would I pay for them if I was wrong and they didn't sell? But I swallowed and tossed out an ambitious number.

He must have sensed my nerves. "Can you pay for an order that size?"

"Not upfront, but if you'll take a chance on me and extend the credit line to cover them, I'll pay you for them even if I'm wrong." I was almost certain I wasn't wrong, because my customers already liked the ones Judy had made. Now I'd be selling the professionally made flared-leg blue jeans, and Levi's at that! I was ecstatic and scared at the same time, but told myself business is a risk anyway, might as well take it.

I honestly don't remember exactly how many pair were in the order, so much time has gone by, but I do remember taking it a step further, recognizing that he wasn't as sure of the product's success as I was.

"Since this is more or less a trial order, how about you don't ship these to anyone else but me, say for at least six months?"

He smiled. "Since no one knows that this jean is in our line anyway, that'll be okay."

I nearly fell over with the excitement of being the only store on the planet having these jeans. Could be big, I thought. The rest, I can say from a distance of five decades, was bell-bottom history.[3]

※

Living in The Haight, in the mid-1960s meant living among musicians. Rock musicians, blues musicians, jazz and folk and bluegrass musicians. Then, they weren't stars or celebrities. They were simply our neighbors, the guys and gals we saw on the street, strumming and strolling along the sidewalk. Putting on shows in ballrooms, halls and free concerts in Panhandle Park.

There was a kind of frantic energy in motion, the music swirling through the rapidly changing fashion, the protests, changing attitudes, acid, and free love.

And I loved it all.

Among those in my closest crowd were my girlfriend Kimmie, Bobby Boles, Judy and Richard, Ned and Stella, Cindy Lee, Rock Scully, Danny Rifkin, and five other guys. I was introduced to Ned and Stella, who happened to be marijuana smugglers, in front of Mnasidika one day by a mutual friend. Ned looked at me said, "Nice to meet you, Samantha." I started to say, "My name is Peggy," but it was clear that he *meant* to say Samantha, and from that point forward I was Samantha Lockhart when in their company. When Stella first looked at me, there was also a palpable connection. I knew she was an Earth Mother—not that I was looking for one, or that it even mattered—but I could feel the warmth exuding from her. She would turn out to be one of the most brave, most kind, and most generous people I'd ever know.

The five guys who made up the rest of my inner circle were a scraggly bunch—Jerry, Bobby, Phil, Pig Pen, and Bill—but more on them, later.

Long before Mötley Crüe, these guys were the original motley crew, but when I met them, they were the sweet boys who lived up on Ashbury Street, 710, to be exact. Stella and Ned lived at 734. Kimmie and I lived in an apartment right around the corner from the store on Ashbury, 635, directly across the street from a shared flat that housed Joe McDonald, who later became famous as Country Joe and the Fish, and a female singer who had just starting fronting a local band, Big Brother and the Holding Company.

Her name was Janis. She was from Texas.

✶

Bill Graham ran the San Francisco Mime Troupe at that time and one day he came in and said, "I'm going to put on a dance." He was going to have bands play, and charge a dollar to get in. "Too much?" he asked. I told him no. He said, "What about two dollars?" I said I didn't think so. He said, "What about three dollars?" It was the 1960s, and three dollars was the right price.

When Bill gave his first dance at the Longshoreman's Hall, it was packed and wild: strobe lights and day-glow chalk drawings on the floor, and of course hundreds of people taking acid. The next day he came in and he said, "Do you know what happened last night? I made three thousand dollars." Until that moment, from what I understood, he had been broke. I had heard that his family had been killed in the Nazi German occupation, and he'd had to make it on his own. "Do you know what I'm going to do?" His eyes were twinkling.

I said, "Let me guess. You're going to have another dance?"

"That's right." He smiled, then asked me if I would sell tickets at Mnasidika.

Instantly I agreed, knowing it would bring lots of hippies into the store and many would need a pair of Levi's. That was the beginning of the rock ballroom scene in San Francisco.

If you look at the early psychedelic posters promoting Bill Graham's shows, designed by Wes Wilson, on the bottom where it says "ticket outlets" you'll see it lists Mnasidika. I sold his tickets for years. When you handle Bill's money, you get to know Bill. That was the beginning of a very profitable relationship between him and me.

In those early days, Bill was driving a mechanically questionable Karmann Ghia. One afternoon he was about to set out for Los Angeles and his car was sounding like it might not make it over the next hill. I said, "Bill, that Karmann Ghia isn't going to make it to LA. I've made that trip many times and that car will not make it."

He broke down in Salinas and called me. "You were right," he said. "The Ghia is on the side of the road . . . smoking."

"Go to a car dealership and buy a car."

"Are you sure? Maybe I could take a cab?"

"You can't take a cab from Salinas to LA. Go buy a car."

"What should I buy?"

"I'm inclined toward Porsches, but you? Buy yourself a Jaguar."

He bought a brown E Jaguar and ended up keeping it for the rest of his life.

Most of us who worked in Haight-Ashbury could barely rub two nickels together. I was the first that I knew of to start making some real money. Nobody had career-type jobs and places like McDonald's had not yet cornered the worldwide teen job market. We were creative. We created income for ourselves in ways that didn't involve the typical drudgery.

*

My days were busy, balancing my job at Delta with running the store. By day, I'd dress in a starched white blouse, navy blue blazer, navy blue skirt, and navy-blue pumps. In the afternoons, I tossed beads around my neck when I opened Mnasidika for the day. When I attended what were called "Rag Shows"—sales exhibitions where retailers could see and order the latest offerings from clothing manufacturers—I wore Peck and Peck suits. I figured if I wanted to succeed in business, I better look like business. The schism between the average business world and my business, though, seemed to widen by the day.

As the store sales grew, I became ecstatic with the thought of easing out of the day job. I began to unpin my hair now when I got to the store, as the little bit of traffic coming in was not so coiffed, pinned or pressed. Haight Street's personality was burgeoning. The people showing up on the street were, well, different.

The first character to stand out was a guy who turned up on the street every day wearing a blue cape with a red satin lining; he was the first of what we came to affectionately call "tumes"—people who constantly showed up in costumes. He sounded normal until he got to the part about being Merlin. As unusual as he was, he was just the first of an array of odd characters that would find the street and practically live on it.

Next was a guy we called Beast. None of us ever learned his real name. Beast never talked—never—but he did make some sounds, sort of guttural grunts, but never a word. He showed up in the same clothes every day: jeans that were too big for his slender waist and too short for his spindly legs. These were tied with a piece of rope through the belt loops. A grey saggy, baggy T-shirt, with the funk of days on the street. Brownish hair, long past his ears and growing longer each week. Those sweaty strands twirled and bobbed with his gyrations. He understood everything you said to him. You could ask him to stop dancing in front of the store and he'd stop, glance at you, grunt and start dancing in front of the store next door. Dancing in no recognizable form, just some rhythmic motion, for hours. By then, I'd become friendly with all the other shopkeepers, and we could never figure out what was going on with Beast since none of us could have a two-way conversation with him. One day I gave him a T-shirt and a new pair of jeans. He stopped dancing, and looked at me so sincerely. I told him they were for him and he seemed to understand. He gave me an enthusiastic grimace and disappeared with the clothing. The next day he showed up in his new duds. The jeans fit better than the previous ones, but he still had the rope tied through the belt loops. And yes, Beast still danced.

The Mad Hatter materialized every morning with the exact hat as the fictional Mad Hatter and said, "I'm not Mad; I'm GLAD! And why, you ask?" (We didn't.) "Because I took the magic pill!" He'd break into a maniacal laugh and skip on down Haight Street. Before the Mad Hatter, there was, among a myriad of other tumes—a woman dressed as Little Bo Peep, parasol and all, who would look at you and say, "If you have to ask you're crazy." Apparently, she had lost something more than her sheep.

No one in our little neighborhood doubted that the weirdness was likely fueled by acid. An uncanny number of musicians, artists, writers, designers, entrepreneurs, and other diversely talented people had moved in and hunkered down. Mix this with the energy of the times and the availability of LSD, and what unfolded in front of my eyes made Alice's adventures in Wonderland pale.

Bob Stubbs had opened an incense shop over on the other side of the Panhandle, but quickly pulled up stakes and reopened as the Phoenix on Haight Street, a block and a half down and across the street from Mnasidika. He was selling incense, Madras bedspreads, imports from India, incense holders, and beads—all the inexpensive and groovy accouterments to the LSD-tripping youth cavorting around the area. With his store's presence, we had the scent of patchouli, sandalwood, and marijuana wafting in the air. The scents of home.

Like the spores of mushrooms that appear overnight after a rain, the cast of characters grew and in ever greater numbers multiplied exponentially. The color, scents, and human activity grew in volume and intensity. The Haight was no longer a tucked-away little neighborhood. We were fast becoming a national curiosity, and new people arrived daily. It couldn't last.

*

I was looking around the store in the spring of 1966, and felt the interior was, well, drab. Just then a couple of friends happened in.

"What's up, Peg?"

"I was thinking the store needs somethin'."

"Like what?"

"I dunno, like maybe some paint."

"What color are you thinking?"

"Black, white, green, purple . . . I know: Acid! I need to paint the walls on acid!" I turned to the girls, "Y'all with me?"

They looked at each other, grinning gleefully, and nodded. "If the acid is free, we're in! When?"

By this time, I was using acid regularly, but rarely during the week. I didn't need to continually "trip." I had gotten the "message" and was trying to live it through my store and the experiences I had with my fellow adventurers in our little enclave. I had several hits of acid stashed up under the desk in my office. I grabbed three and we all dosed.

We ran over to the hardware store a few doors away, knowing we only had about thirty to forty minutes before the effects of the psychedelic drug would kick in. By the time we got back and popped open the lids to the white and black cans of paint, the sinus clearing and slight brightening of vision indicated we were "coming on" and ready to launch. Brushes in hand, we began on one side of the store, painting alternating black and white stripes on the walls. We completed most of one half of the store when it all seemed to unravel. Painting in a linear fashion seemed too arduous, trying to control the paint was laughable. Hysterically, gut wrenchingly, hilarious. Then serious. Then mysterious. At some point, we all agreed on purple and spent several hours creating swirls, and free flowing arcs of purple on purple. At another point a flower took form. More colors, more laughter, and when it was over Mnasidika was dressed just right for the upcoming counterculture ball.

San Francisco, being on the cool side climate-wise, meant clothing stores sold a lot of fleece-like wear. I bought a line of sweatshirts that were snuggly, cozy, and 100 percent cotton, dyed in beautiful deep colors. At one point, it got to be hip to be in the store when the jeans would arrive. They were shipped in big cardboard boxes. We would pop the steel shipping belts off and the hippies would buy the jeans right out of the boxes before we could get the clothes on the shelves. It became our thing, a promotional event.

*

Mere weeks after my not-so-grand-opening in 1965, I had just picked up a box of clothing from the airport, unpacked it and then I stood just outside the doorway in the crisp fall air. I was hoping someone would notice the store and maybe come in and buy something. A group of guys caught my eye as they sauntered down Ashbury Street in my direction. Jostling and jesting they made their way down the sidewalk to the entryway of Mnasidika. The scent of cheap wine and marijuana accompanied them, each one looking rather disheveled. All were attired in thrift store chic, hair in various lengths past their ears. The first one to enter was a dark-haired guy with what may have been a cowboy hat, crumpled and customized by what looked to be accidents and mishaps, pulled down low on his forehead and adorned with a tattered hat band and large metal pin. He had a bit of a paunch, a confident swagger, and a deep intelligence to his eyes.

"Hi, I'm Ron," he said. "They call me Pigpen." He tipped the brim of his hat and nodded as he entered the store.

My first impression was "Pigpen"? Really? Who would introduce himself as that?

The next one bound in, looking a lot younger than he was. "I'm Bobby, they call me Bobby." Next was a shorter, stocky guy with dark frizzy long hair whose gait was slower, head down, ruddy and tattered. As he made his way through the entrance, he glanced up and grinned. I noticed an intense gleam in his eyes that contrasted with the ultra-casual, furry, and in-no-hurry demeanor. "Hello," he whispered, then softly said, "I'm Jerry."

The guys milled about, we exchanged pleasantries and somehow knew we had all ridden that same cosmic train known as the "LSD Experience." Though Pigpen was not into it as much, as he preferred drinking. They told me they were a band called "The Grateful Dead"—which meant nothing then—and after lingering awhile longer admiring some of the leather jackets, they left as casually as they had entered. They all came back the next day, and the next, spending more and more time hanging out in Mnasidika, talking and telling me stories. I liked having all of them in there because it looked like something was going on, so even more people came by to hang out and see what was happening. I suppose everybody thought everyone else was buying something, and eventually some did begin spending money. In the meantime, the Dead's managers, Rock Scully and Danny Rifkin, showed up and we all became friendly. Rock even queried me for a loan to buy Jerry an amp. I wondered who would ever hire these strange guys to play their music, but I liked them as people, so I couldn't help but say "yes," paying forward the good faith that so many clothing vendors showed in me when I needed it.

To me, their gentle manners and quest for the ultimate "experience" embodied the core of something that we didn't even know we were a part of, yet. As a favor, the band did some modeling for me—photographed for an advertisement—and in return I loaned them leather jackets and such for their band photo shoots. They

THE GRATEFUL DEAD IN FRONT OF MNASIDIKA
DRESSED FOR SUCCESS, WEARING JACKETS FROM PEGGY

wouldn't be the only rock musicians—or even the *most* famous—to find a home at Mnasidika. But I didn't know that yet, either.

The first musician to come in and spend some real money was Marty Balin from Jefferson Airplane. Following him, Sly Stone from Sly and the Family Stone bought five of everything that he wanted for his band. Things had begun to hop.

Unbeknownst to us we were poised on the very edge of the end of innocence.

✸

BOBBY BOLES, HAIGHT-ASHBURY SHOEMAKER EXTRAORDINAIRE

A young woman came into the store one day and told me that I needed to look up a talented leather worker named Bobby Boles who could be a great asset to the store. So, off I went to Carl Street, to a small flat and knocked on the door. I was met by a handsomely disheveled wiry young Italian man with denim-blue eyes.

"Hi." He flashed his beautiful smile.

I smiled back. His space was dominated by hides in various states of process and a single mattress on the floor. Bobby came over to the store with me, felt it was a match, and dragged his leatherworking materials with him. He very quickly made a wooden sign with old-timey writing that read "The Haight Street Leathersmith," hung it on the wall in the back of the store, and began making custom sandals right in the shop. It was an instant success. Bobby would have a customer stand barefoot on a piece of cardboard, trace around each foot, and within a few days they would have one-of-a-kind original shoes—mostly sandals, but sometimes boots. His talent and reputation became legendary and drew more customers to our burgeoning quadrant of San Francisco.

Jeans, sweatshirts, blazers, and sandals. LSD, marijuana, cheap wine and sex. Somehow there were more people in the neighborhood as each week passed. Whatever had once driven me to aspire to be a stewardess, now compelled me to dive in completely to this next phase of my life. With fear and exhilaration, I wrote my resignation letter to Delta and gave the obligatory one month's notice, and set out to work the store full time. It seemed the moment I did that, the floodgates opened. By now, my hair was down, it wasn't set with hairspray, and I hardly wore any makeup. Women were leaving their bobby pins behind. It seemed almost everyone had a guitar and the strumming sound of acoustic folk songs in front of the store on the corner started to seem normal.

The disregard for convention, the manner and dress, the increasing numbers of inhabitants to the previously sedate and nondescript neighborhood, unsettled the Old Timers—merchants who had been on Haight Street for years. Several times, older store owners would approach me and ask, "What's going on here, Peggy? What's happening?" I couldn't tell them because I honestly didn't know, though I did understand that something was "going on."

There is a very telling picture of Herb Greene's, included in *The Book of The Dead: Celebrating 25 Years With The Grateful Dead*, that depicts the barber (seen looking out the window in the earlier photo) standing on the street looking at the band standing in front of Mnasidika. The barber is scratching his head as if to say, "What the hell?" It's an iconic moment in Hippie History. I was so sure nobody would hire the scraggly group looking the way they did that I loaned them the jackets—the ones they are wearing in the photo—in hopes of giving them a chance.

The barber came up to me, "What's happening here?"

"I don't know."

"Oh yes, you do. You know . . . you know."

"No, I don't know."

"Well it didn't start until you came here."

"I didn't bring this."

"Well, I think you did."

I'm pretty sure that it was at that moment he said, "I'm not going to be cutting anymore hair it looks like."

I asked, "Do you wanna sell the Barber Shop?"

"Yes. If you write me a check right now . . . "

". . . you'll take your scissors and leave?" I finished his sentence for him.

"Yes."

And that day he was gone.

It might have been $5,000—I don't remember for sure—but my spontaneous purchase even included the barber chairs. And just like that, my floor space expanded.

I was glad for the barber chairs because I foresaw that Bobby and I could use them as a hip, comfortable way for trying on boots. People could sit in the barber chair and put their feet up on the footrest. Following is the famous picture of The Grateful Dead, posing in those barber chairs in the early days.

At first, we called the second store Haight Street Leathersmith, but later it became known as the Barbershop Bootery, then ultimately The Boot Hook. Bobby's little sign hung underneath the Mnasidika sign, which was perpendicular to the building (rather than horizontal, like all the other signs). Bobby had hides of various sizes which hung in rows like you'd hang shirts: reds, browns, blacks, and wilder brighter colors that he dyed himself. I often fussed at him to make sure the dye wasn't dripping onto the floor.

HERB GREENE HERDED THE BOYS INTO PEGGY'S NEWLY-ACQUIRED BARBER SHOP FOR A PROMO SHOT

In the early days of the Psychedelic Revolution, we rarely had anyone stealing from us. People had just caught onto "Karma" and its implications upon their life, so most people in the early days weren't willing to incur any of the "Bad Karma." However, on occasion, someone would decide to try and grab a leather jacket and run for the door. Bobby had a knack for sniffing out those who were so inclined, and the moment they exited the store, he catapulted over his sandal counter, right out the door, down the street, and tackled the thief. If they resisted at all, Bobby would give them a pounding that was unbelievable. Then he'd come strutting back through the entrance to Mnasidika, as if he were returning with a "kill." Casually he'd hand it off to one of the guys behind the counter, and go back to his sandal making hardly missing a beat. He was truly remarkable. We had a great time . . . working, laughing and succeeding at what we saw as our respective arts.

New, youth-culture businesses were cropping up all over The Haight. The Thelin brothers—Ron and Jay—were some of the new kids on the block. Their store, The Psychedelic Shop, was the first place selling pipes and other drug paraphernalia and enlightening literature. If there was any question about from where the weirdness was coming, the popularity of the products at The Psychedelic Stop put an end to the speculation.

The weirdness emanated from folks taking acid. The drug was very easy to buy—as easy to buy as Coca Cola, and a lot more interesting. By this time it was only a buck a hit, provided by friendly, local, acid distributors—which, at one point, included me. People were trippin' and getting weirder, and odd as it may sound today, it all seemed harmless then. Sure, some folks could get a little bewildered at times, but generally everyone was happy, gentle, and helpful.

The old barber was right about one thing—Mnasidika was ground zero, an epicenter. This is where hippies were named hippies, after all. A San Francisco reporter who had come to write about our subculture coined the term—specific to *our* social movement—while in my store.[4] This is where Jimi Hendrix's manager, Chas Chandler, came looking for a job for him. This is where Janis Joplin walked in to put fifty cents down on a pair of jeans (that story comes later) . . .

※

Everybody stopped into Mnasidika, because for a long time there *was* no other place to hang out. Things started happening—I mean fast. We started hearing more about the Sandoz corporation (which made the original LSD-25), and about Augustus Owsley Stanley III who made acid for the Dead, and about Richard Alpert/Ram Dass, and Timothy Leary. Bands were forming right and left, and halls were being rented for dances and concerts, even on weekdays. Other early bands on the scene were the Charlatans, George Hunter, Dan Hicks (later of the Hot Licks), Quicksilver Messenger Service, the little known Final Solution, the Ace of Cups (an excellent all-girl band), the Jefferson Airplane with the ever-so-talented Marty Balin, and the beat went on . . . and on. Other bands and artists of all types rose and fell within weeks or months. Ideas flowed through doors in minds flung open by LSD-25, splashing out into the street in psychedelic exuberance. (A footnote: Ace of Cups has re-formed and are recording in 2017!)

Though the population was rising, by 1967, we all still knew each other. We knew who had taken acid the night before and who was down in the Panhandle playing music. The musicians would play music, the rest of us would take acid. Seemed like a perfectly natural arrangement. From the inside, from the vantage point of my 20s, it all never seemed quite as weird as it eventually got depicted. People were dancing and exhilarated. We started calling these gatherings "Be Ins" because we were just gonna go *Be In*. Then, in '68 or '69, along came "Love Ins," which started attracting too many people on too many different trips with too many agendas pedaling too many different drugs. In '68, it was heading out of control. By 1969 it was getting ugly. By 1970 it had blown up. I never took anything but acid and never smoked anything but pot in those early days. The times, they definitely were . . . changing.

Slowly, people with hifalutin educations and cash began to show up, wanting to look like hippies, and they came to Mnasidika for all the requisite attire. Leather jackets then were costly, at $150, but the newer arrivals could afford 'em. The latter wave of kids, though, showed up broke. The Haight attracted so much attention that they hitchhiked from Kansas, Iowa, Indiana, and all kinds of places, wide-eyed and without a place to stay.

Some of my best customers were Super Spade, who was buying

for his girlfriend, and Spade Johnny, buying for his girlfriend—those guys were shopping, and, of course, dealing pot. Wes Wilson was making his now-famous psychedelic fonts ubiquitous and culture-defining on the posters he designed and sold. Mouse was also making posters, and Bob Seidemann was taking pictures. People were selling macramé and dream catchers. And beads. Lots and lots of beads were being strung together. I would walk down the street and someone clearly flying high on LSD, pupils ablaze, would come to me, smile, and slide a beaded necklace right over my head, or hand me a flower and utter a heartfelt, "Love." They would stare into my eyes for a second and then drift merrily on down the street. It felt like a precious time, a feeling that love really *was* all you needed. Maybe it could change the world. It certainly was changing ours.

*

The San Francisco fog was rapidly being replaced by color. What we were experiencing in our minds on LSD spilled out onto the streets. Posters on light posts and telephone poles oozed with a psychedelic hum. Where the Beat generation was fading, with its black and white minimalist cool, this new phenomenon was electric, loud, inescapable, and absolutely palpable. The revolution was beginning to hear itself and wanted to keep the conversation going. A generation ready to relay Martin Luther King Jr.'s message, and herald the "Black Movement." Betty Freidan's book *The Feminine Mystique* inspired women into owning their sexuality. The advent of birth control made many women feel for the first time that it was not only possible, but healthy, to enjoy sex outside the marriage covenant. And without threat of an unintended pregnancy. The illumination of Rachel Carson's book *Silent Spring* spawned a generation of ecologists, and created an awareness of the land as something to be tended to, rather than dominated. The Free Speech Movement started on the University of California Berkeley campus, then reverberated through other institutes of learning, and ricocheted around suburbia and the corridors of urban streets. The illusion of everything being alright was unraveling at every turn.

For me, business rocked, I was having so much fun making money that I took less acid and got more serious. And, pushing me forward was the image of my father and his warning to me that I would never get anywhere in life working for someone else.

There were also all kinds of "hippie industry" happening all around us. There was money being made. Owsley had an army of people who were selling acid (like I said, including me). He was a short, stocky guy, with wild brownish hair. At that time, The Haight was still a somewhat sleepy enclave—it was still early on. Probably 1966.

The small neighborhood Bank of America was near the corner of Haight and Clayton. Its doors were open to the street on warmer days. The loan officer could see my store from his desk through the plate glass window. I once introduced myself in order to ask for a loan and he said, "Hi Peggy." I had never spoken with him before, but he was aware of the buzz of activity at my store; we did more business than the bank! I asked him for a loan of $5,000. He said, "Sure. Just fill this out." He handed me a one-page document, then looked it over and said, "Sign it. Then take it over to the teller and you'll get your money." And just like that I had five grand.

Back to Owsley. One day at the bank, I was making a deposit when I heard a rumbling and saw him pop a partial wheelie on his motorcycle, bump up over the curb, cross the sidewalk and ride right through the doors of Bank of America. He ended his entrance with a flourish, his back tire skidding in a semi arc as he killed the motor and dropped the kickstand. He walked over to the teller, took off his helmet, and tipped it over, raining down cash all over the counter. After the money was counted, he shoved the deposit slip in his pocket, hopped back on his motorcycle, started it up, and rode out of the lobby, off the curb, and down the street. The amazing thing was, no one batted an eye. They simply watched as if it was the most normal thing in the world. And truly it was—in our little Haight-Ashbury world.

Next to the Civil Rights movement, none of the activist groups were more visible and vocal than the anti-war movement. Vietnam, half a world away, covered by jungle, hot and miserable. Why were we there? Along comes Country Joe McDonald and pens the greatest anti-war song of our time. Along with the Fish Cheer, the "Feel like

I'm Fixin' to Die Rag"[5] turned people on to the reality of war. This song, when he sang it at Woodstock to thousands upon thousands of people, whipped us into a virtual anti-war frenzy.

The draft in place at the beginning of the Vietnam War meant the Selective Service was sending off thousands of young men. Beginning as early as 1964, American male students began to burn their draft cards and flee to Canada or Europe. Local draft boards seemed to be targeting poor and lower middle-class men, who comprised the majority of non-volunteer draftees. The conservative elite complained of draft dodgers, meanwhile protecting their precious sons with loopholes. Televisions began to show the young men of our generation coming home from Vietnam in body bags. Our brothers. Our sons. Our sweethearts. Our friends. That triggered rage, and, galvanized a generation into a common, visible, and vocal objection to the war.

By the time our generation converged onto Yasgur's Farm in upstate New York in a little-known town called Bethel, we were ready to unite into a single voice. Who knew I'd be there, too, huddled backstage with Janis Joplin, who sent a helicopter to airlift me into the festival.

When I looked out over a virtual sea of people (some reports estimated over a half million) waves and waves of them began to stand as Joe and the Fish wailed about the war. It was chilling. From my vantage point, with Janis, everybody seemed happy, or at least happy enough to be schlepping through mud, enveloped in something stronger, much stronger than ourselves, and our music.

How I went from selling clothes in The Haight, to standing next to the biggest female rock star in the world, makes up the most complicated, and also the simplest, story of my life. And while those years were intense, and important to the outside world, perhaps the most curious and interesting thing is they were only *a part* of my life.

Four years that ripped my world apart, and also made it whole. Showed me things, I would have missed otherwise, which, depending on how you look at it, would have been both a blessing and a tragedy.

Part Two

GROWING UP IN THE SOUTH, outside of New Orleans, in bayou country, besides being humid, was all in all pretty innocent—a kind of *Happy Days* experience. I had great parents, no siblings, some friends, and plenty to do. These were the 1950s, and my teen years coincided with the advent of rock-n-roll music and kids with cars. The world was still flat—at least my scope of it. I mean really, there was Texas, Louisiana, and Mississippi, Alabama, Georgia and Florida— the Delta Belt. That was all I knew. Flat, flat, flat and flat. The topography, both physical and cultural, was restrictive and predictable, which incited in me a yearning to break free. To drop the yoke of convention and hop on the train of possibility. Explore new terrain, to have a more tactile, visceral experience of life. Something in me just knew there was more. Deep, wide, dimensional, expansive.

While there was nothing wrong or terrible in my life, I knew I had to escape the South. It wasn't that I hated the South, but seeing how my father felt he could take no chances in life, so he could take care of my mother and me, set me on a path toward escape. I wanted to get out of the South not because of a bad childhood, but due to a wanderlust that was inside me, propelled by a feeling of lost opportunity if I did not get out. I wanted to have control over my life. I needed control. I did not always succeed. But in my business, in my relationships, and even in the midst of my heroin addiction, I longed not for escape, but to experience it all with a child's sense of wonder and a feeling that whatever happens, whatever I suffer, I can seek my own way out. And in my darkest days, I always found a way to seek light through the knowledge that my parents were there with open arms for me to fall back upon, or through my own will to move forward. My generation wanted to get away from their parents. Not me. I wanted to escape the South, but never my parents.

But, for now, my pre-escape days were filled with chasing boys, driving in our parents' cars up to the Dairy Queen for an ice cream custard, and listening to Elvis and the Platters. Fats Domino had found his thrill and Louie Armstrong wanted "A Kiss to Build a Dream On."

The longest overwater bridge in the world was being built over Lake Pontchartrain, linking New Orleans to the North Shore. Known as the Causeway, it was a marvel of human achievement at the time. It also was a game changer. New Orleans has always been steeped in lore of pirates and Mississippi riverboats, but it had also always been far away. The bridge now gave us a direct shot to what we called the Crescent City. It allowed us North Shore kids quick and direct access to the French Quarter and as much debauchery as our conservative bobby socksin' selves would allow, which wasn't much back then. Letting our boyfriends touch our breasts (getting to "second base") was a long-time comin' and a rare occurrence at that. Regardless of sneaking to the city, my friends and I were still largely innocent, and harmless, hanging out, listening to each others' dreams. Theirs were mostly of marrying the right boy, having a family, faithful husband, nice house, stuff that somehow didn't register for me as the thing to do. Nothing wrong with it, sounded ok for them, but held little appeal to me. I didn't yet know what I wanted, or why those dreams of husbands and conventional lives weren't my dreams.

As far back as I can remember I sensed an energy, something unfamiliar in the southern air, something that seemed almost like a rhythm. Not quite audible but I could feel it. I could feel it as sure as I could feel the heat and weight of the air itself. That special brand of humidity, Louisiana style, as if the molecules themselves were pouring sweat as they worked out in an unseen gym in the atmosphere all around us. Growing up we learned it was known as the Ozone Belt and rumored to be molecularly different. At least that's what all the grown-ups talked about. Quite literally, heavier than the air in other parts of the United States. This air, a constant, damp, unwanted companion, afforded no escape, no personal space. Akin to an over-zealous Golden Retriever, hot, wet, sticky and panting, unrelenting in its need to be close.

The pancake makeup popular in those days was no match for the energy-sapping heat. The varying shades of beige and tan of the foundation, the pink and rosy hues of the rouge, stained the sleeves, collars and errant hairs of the light-colored clothing and women in the south. If it was applied too thick it would create canyons and fissures when smiling or squinting. Women did not wipe their sweat, they dabbed delicately and strategically. The intensity of the summer months was oppressive. Everything just . . . felt . . . well, *more*. Spring and fall, though, were quite pleasant—near as perfect as weather could be. Then winter, very cold, icy, and stormy, lightning hitting the ground so hard and so close you could smell the dirt cooking. Seriously.

Yes, indeed we have weathah, up close and personal.

I would learn that there are a lot of things in life a person must weather.

But I would never need to endure it alone. Through it all, no matter what, there was my mother. Scenes from our final years flashed through my mind as I wrote this book.

✺

"Mother? Mom, are you all right? No, no, don't do that. Lola has been fed already."

Mom likes to do what she calls "pickin' chicken."

Lola, the German shepherd I rescued, who was nothing but a head and a spine swimming in the floodwaters for three days after Hurricane Katrina, gets part of a rotisserie chicken every day. But in the past year, Mom stopped helping prepare Lola's meals. Her hands don't quite have the dexterity anymore.

Mom's routine is all that she can rely on, to keep her on track and moving through her days with a purpose. She still desperately wants to have a part of feeding the dog and giving her treats.

✺

If I try, I can just imagine my tiny little mother, Novell Kilpatrick, at maybe three or four years old, clinging to her sister, Flo, as their momma put them on a train from New Orleans to Alabama about a year or so after the crash of the stock market that plunged the United States into the Great Depression. My grandfather on my mother's side was a fall-down drunk, as the story goes, and her mother didn't feel it was right to have her baby girls around a drunken father. She was tired, too. She'd lost what little income she had. She couldn't take care of her children any more. She thought they'd be better cared for by their paternal grandmother. So, she sent them away. I don't know if my grandmother's hat was pulled down low on the platform of that train station that day to cover the shame she might have been feeling. I don't know if that day was sunny or cloudy. But

PEGGY'S AUNT FLO AND MOM, NOVELL
ALABAMA, 1921

when I hear my mother talk about that day, I can hear the sound of the whistle and see the smoke billowing, like some iron monster come to snatch up innocent little girls. So much hurt and anger, which Mom never forgave entirely. Nowadays, there is no way two tiny children could be sent off on a train, all by themselves. Not without a child welfare agency getting involved. I can see those small faces pressed up against the window watching their mother diminish in size as the distance increased until she was nothing. The future looming larger and closer, held entirely by a strange old lady they had never met.

The spark of hope for a warm welcome and a bit of comfort was immediately extinguished upon arrival at the train station in Alabama. "Well, there you are." A seemingly ancient woman grunted tersely as the conductor deposited the tiny tots onto the platform. "There will be no sniveling," she continued, while looking them over. Her lips pursed as her face grew more stern. She bent down and stuck her face closer to the girls. "No whinin' at all. Everybody gots to work. Even y'all. There's a Depression going on." She stood up. "I don't wanna hear you cryin' for your folks, neither. You're here and that's that." She spun around to walk away from the station. The girls looked at each other as the train's engine started to churn and chug. The whistle blew its forlorn departure song. Flo grabbed my mother's tiny hand and they ran after their grandma.

Grandma was working in the cotton mill and that's where the girls went every day, too. Soon as possible she put the both of them to work. Mom says she didn't last but a month in the field, as she was too skinny and sickly to keep going. This shared abandonment seemed to fuse the bond between my mom and her sister for the duration of their lives.

Aunt Flo was a feisty, natural red-head and got herself married to Frank Blossman at the ripe old age of 17 and thus escaped the cotton fields. My mother was a brunette with a glint of red and a stubborn Irish streak. The man who would become my father, Sam Caserta, met Novell at a dance in Abita Springs, Louisiana. Tall, dark and handsome, and twenty years my mother's senior, he fell hopelessly in love. Rock solid in reputation, the security he embodied, and his extraordinarily kind nature swayed my mother. He wooed her, she let him, and they soon were married. They settled in Covington, Louisiana and I was born about a year later.

Sam Caserta proved to be a good husband and father all the way up to his dying breath. He worked for the postal service as a letter carrier and our dog Kim, who was a big, beautiful, black and tan German Shepherd, used to ride with him on his route. If Kim somehow missed my dad heading out the door, shortly he would catch up, running the few blocks to jump into the car and wait until Dad walked out of the post office with his deliveries for that day. After work, my father used to stop off at Tugy's bar. Dad wasn't a drinker, but it was a place to socialize with the other men from town. Kim became as much a fixture there as Dad, getting a Hershey's candy bar from Tugy. He got so he'd put his big 'ol paws up on the bar on his own, asking for his Hershey's. Tugy once called Mom and said, "Novell, Kim is down here wanting a candy bar and Sam's not here." Mom said, "Go ahead and put it on Sam's tab. He'll take care of it." After a while Tugy said, "How 'bout I just give Kim his own tab?" Mom agreed. After a few weeks Tugy would call saying, "Novell, Kim's tab is up to a dollar now." Then Dad would pay it the next time he stopped in. As far as I know Kim was the only dog in Covington or maybe the whole state of Louisiana that had his own bar tab. He did live a good long life, despite what we know now about not giving chocolate to dogs.

There were a lot of kids living in close enough proximity for me to play with, as well as friends from school. Being an only child, some kids may have felt like they were missing out, not having any brothers or sisters, but it never bothered me. My parents always treated me well and we always had food on the table. We weren't rich by any means, but we were just fine.

I think the only time I ever heard my parents fight was about my father playing poker. Mom told Dad if he ever gambled again she was gonna take me and leave. Where? I don't know. It's not like there were a lot of opportunities for a young mother in those days. She must've convinced him she meant it, because as far as I know he never dared play poker again.

There were only minor tensions I suppose, but mostly I recall a pretty smooth idyllic life. Somehow, I was keenly aware that my father worked hard to keep us housed and fed. Seems like back then everybody's dad went out to work and everybody's mom stayed home and worked on the domestic front. I appreciated what my mother did, but wasn't really interested in the typical domestic arts expected from young women of my era.

※

Mackie's Pine Oil Plant employed a lot of people in Covington, Louisiana. They made turpentine out of the oil extracted from grinding the needles, branches, and bark of pine trees. Our biggest fear was that Mackie's mysterious pine oil process would blow up the town. All of us kids knew that if Mackie's blew up, it would pretty much be the end of the world. Our world. We would talk in breathless whispers, our eyes all big and darting in the direction of the plant. The scenarios we conjured in our imaginations were fierce and apocalyptic. How fragile we are as children. How very small our worlds are. To us kids in Covington, our little town was the entire United States. It was all we knew.

Mackie's finally did blow. One afternoon there was an enormous BOOM! It shook the windows in all the businesses in town. I heard that the butcher and his patrons looked at each other and all cried out, "Mackie's!" As they hurried out onto the street, the baker came out of his shop screaming, "Mackie's!" The men in the hardware store turned to one another and simultaneously yelled, "Mackie's!" All of us kids ran towards Mackie's. Our dreaded communal fears were coming true. Black billowing smoke was tumbling out of the sides and roof, flames shooting out and setting the ditch on fire. We thought it was the end of the world. Mackie's Pine Oil plant had finally, really, blown.

That ditch full of swirling flames, thick with oak and brush, seemed like the devil himself had come to Covington. We kids thought, "We're all doomed!" I don't know where we got the notion that fire was gonna rage all over Covington, that the flames were going to snatch us screaming and burn us alive. When you are small, I suppose many misunderstood things, especially in small towns, frighten you in a disproportionately big way. But this fear, for me, did not last long. I could not have moved away from the South, experienced the adventures I have in life, without losing much of the fear of childhood. Through life, people have called me strong, but we know better than anyone who we are. I don't necessarily see myself as strong as much as I see myself as not afraid. I'm just not afraid, and that's maybe because of my upbringing. My parents never instilled fear in me.

*

The other girls were dreaming of finding the right guy and settling down to domestic life, and while I had no desire towards this virtue, I did have a drive to make money, which I knew would be a means to aid in my departure. I began to think a lot about escaping the small-town confines in a manner that was sane, civil, and wouldn't twist my sweet parents into a fit.

I was fifteen when the thought of getting a job occurred to me, but in the 1950s, there were not a lot of choices for a fifteen-year-old girl in the back bayous of Louisiana. However, I liked to swim. In fact, I did it well. Maybe I could earn money as a lifeguard. Between Bayou Bogue Falaya, the Tchefuncte River and Lake Ponchartrain, all us kids spent as much time as possible in the water during the summer, as the heat was relentless. I enrolled in a course for future lifeguards and excelled, and by 16 I had been certified for lifeguarding, and got a job at the Covington Country Club making sure that no one drowned in their Olympic-sized swimming pool. No one did.

Soon after, I began teaching swimming to very young children, intermediates, and senior folks. The lifeguarding job was short on pay because it was a modest, flat rate. Swimming lessons, on the other hand, had a much greater earning potential, especially when you were acting as your own boss. At $7.50 per person per hour, with ten students per class, that equaled $75 an hour. I taught about four classes a day, five or sometimes six days a week, and the money began to stack up to an amount that seemed to be sufficient for me to try to bail, at least across Lake Pontchartrain to New Orleans.

But what would I do once I moved to the big city? That question was soon answered when I met a Delta Air Lines pilot who frequently played golf at the country club, then cooled off with a swim later. He told me about stewardesses, but informed me that I was still too young. Stewardesses had to be single, childless, between 5'2" and 5'9", weigh no more than 135 pounds and be 20 years of age. I had all the physical requirements, except the age. No problem, everyone gets older and so would I. I could kill a couple of years in college, hopefully learn something and then I'd be old enough to fly.

I didn't want to bear down on my folk's finances with the cost of sending me to a university when I knew that a diploma was not the goal. Then, along came a card in the mail, addressed to me from Alabama. It simply read, "Dear Peggy, you go ahead on to college. Anywhere you want. It's paid for. Love, Grandpa." I was stunned. I handed it to my mother.

"Hmmm. Well ain't that somethin'," Mom sighed as she studied it further, then handed the card back to me. "Might as well take it darlin'. You know he's got the money. Been selling moonshine all over Alabama for nearly 20 years."

My best friend was going to Louisiana State University but I had heard negative things about LSU not being as "accepting" of some as others—including Italians, which I was. Instead, I literally stumbled one day upon a community college north of the Mississippi Gulf Coast, kind of in the backwoods—small, charming, not at all intimidating and I loved its look and feel. At the time, I was happy to be in a place without any sorority sisters or the small minds I equated with a university that discriminated against so many groups. I got my Associates degree and headed for my career as a stewardess. My parents seemed okay with the idea of me being a stewardess, but stricken with the thought of their child actually leaving town. We had to work on that. I had saved all that money from teaching swimming, and by golly I was EXCITED! I knew it would be fun.

It wasn't fun. It wasn't long, either, before it became painfully apparent, especially to Delta Airlines, that flying wasn't for me. Flying made me airsick. Shortly after the plane left the ground, I would turn a lighter shade of pale, then a greenish hue, and would spend most of the flight in the restroom with my head in the toilet. This was not exactly what the airlines wanted out of a flight attendant (the now-correct career terminology).

In the meantime, some friends suggested being a *Playboy* Bunny, since they were holding auditions in New Orleans. I had quite an impressive bust line, so I thought it wasn't a bad idea. The *Playboy* try-outs were like a miniature Miss America contest. You answered simple-minded questions, and pranced around scantily-clad, wearing bunny ears and a fluffy tail serving drinks and being charming. It was not the alternative I was looking for, so I never took it further than the audition. I just wasn't cut out for it, so the more obvious and practical solution to my airsick dilemma was for me, and Delta, to figure out an alternative to flying. We agreed that in the near future, I would ground myself and work in operations.

In the meantime, I vomited and endured. The enduring was made easier by moving to the French Quarter, where a lot of flight personnel lived because you could run around The Quarter all night if you wanted to, which worked well with their crazy flight schedules. The clubs, some strip joints, the Frolics and the Sho-Bar, a sprinkling of gay bars, Dixie's, the Gaslight, Lafitte's, some jazz clubs, Al Hirt's, all stayed open 24 hours. Imagine that! And it wasn't unsafe.

※

By the time I had turned 20 years old, I was beginning to understand that the dream of a handsome husband seemed like a nightmare to me. But it wasn't until I was living in the French Quarter that I discovered why the expected trajectory of "get a man, get married, have babies" was just not that compelling. I ran into my college friend, Pat, who was also a stewardess. She mentored me in many ways. I first heard the word "beatnik" from her, *and* she introduced me to my first girlfriend, Linda, who turned me on to marijuana.

Getting high, smoking a joint for the first time, was a revelation. We had to go into what was thought of as a rough bar in the Quarter. I vaguely remember through the haze, that it was called La Casa de Los Marinos (House of the Mariners). It was all so secretive and alluring. I don't remember if I'd heard of "Reefer Madness," but I was fairly sure it wasn't something any of my high school friends were doing. When we got the "weed," we went back to Pat's apartment to smoke it. I was smoking cigarettes by this time, so it wasn't a great leap to inhale. But I wasn't sure what I was supposed to act like once I was high. I think I acted higher than I was because I thought smoking it was supposed to get me relaxed and less inhibited. I do remember I just felt good. Not all woozy and having to pee like alcohol made me feel. I just felt happy and relaxed. The music sounded even better, and some of the rough edges of life had been shaved off a bit. I liked it. A lot!

PEGGY'S GRADUATION PHOTO FROM DELTA FLIGHT SCHOOL

*

My first job with Delta's ground operations meant a transfer to New York City. Yep, step right out of the Deep South and into the biggest city in the country. Admittedly, that town blew my little southern mind. I was only twenty and had never been anywhere that would prepare me for New York City. My parents held on tight and had to do some preparing themselves, because they didn't want me to go any farther than New Orleans. I worked for Delta and enjoyed the Big Apple, though I was still naïve. My first impression was how the buildings went through the clouds. It was stunning to pull into that town to see how enormous it was. And it seemed as though day and night fused together, with people in motion after dark.

A lot of stewardesses lived in the East 70s in Manhattan. I rented a ground-floor patio apartment with my girlfriend, Linda, (who was a stewardess) on East 79th Street, and we settled in.

One night we heard some noise at the back door.

"Sounds like someone is trying to get in," I whispered.

Not quite knowing what to do, one of us said, "Ssshhhh!"

Next came the sound of breaking glass. Then, panicked, Linda called the police. I don't know what possessed me but I ran toward the sound. All I could see was a hand, groping through the busted frame of glass. He was trying to find the door handle and was fumbling with the knob.

I screamed, "Get out, get the FUCK out!" He grabbed a hold of the knob hard and I could hear the weight of his body slamming into the door as he tried to shove it open. Thank GAWD the deadbolt held! I grabbed a knife and began stabbing him in the arm and hand as hard and as fast as I could. He started screaming, withdrew his hand, and ran away. Linda and I breathed a sigh of relief for a few moments as we waited for the cops to show up. They never did. Neither of us slept that night.

Two days later the police came by. We said, "Thanks a lot we could have been way dead by now." They didn't bother to apologize. Instead they told us, "We want you to know we believe that we caught him." They went on to explain that a stewardess had been murdered a couple of weeks before in the same area. Apparently, this guy had it in for stewardesses.

A couple of months later, Linda and I went our separate ways. She was beautiful and from a good family but liked to play rough—way too rough. Hitting me in the head with a telephone was farther than I wanted to go, sexually, or any other way. I took to dating male Jewish lawyers for a while. Mostly, though, I just kept to myself, living alone in a new apartment I had rented right across the street from Bellevue Psychiatric Hospital.

It became more and more apparent that I was no Domestic Goddess. One night I bought a steak and was looking forward to having a nice little home-cooked meal. As I was cooking it, I thought it looked kind of funny. The oil seemed to be more sticky than greasy and the steak was a greyish color and it didn't smell like I thought it should. I flipped it over and the reddish pink turned grey as the steak sizzled in the pan. I finally decided it must be done, sprinkled some salt and pepper on it and sat down at my little table. The first bite tasted bitter and salty. I thought, "You sure are no-good at cooking. This is awful." I kept eating, because I didn't want to waste the food and finished as much as I could stomach, filing a mental note that perhaps I should stick to more simple meals. Like maybe sandwiches.

When I went to rinse off my plate I noticed a bottle of Mr. Clean on the counter next to the stove. I thought, "Humm, that's funny. I don't recall getting that out." When I went to put it away I saw the cooking oil in the cupboard, the bottle nearly identical in shape and color to Mr. Clean! No wonder the steak tasted so bad. My next thought was, "I've done gone and poisoned myself by my own cooking!" I then remembered I was just across the street from a hospital. A mental hospital sure, but still a hospital. I called.

"Bellevue Hospital, may I help you?"

"I live right across the street and I thought I'd call you because you're the closest hospital."

"Ok M'am, what can we do for you?"

"First off you need to know that I'm not crazy but I think I just cooked a steak in Mr. Clean."

"You cooked a steak in what?"

"Miss Ter Kuh Leen." I enunciated slowly and clearly, trying to sound sane.

He muffled the receiver and I heard him say in the background "Joe, we've got a live one."

"No, no, you don't understand," I reacted, my voice sounding more and more frantic as I continued. "It was a mistake! I used Mr. Clean instead of oil. I'm not a very good cook and it wasn't until I ate it all that I noticed what I had done."

"Ok miss, do you think you can make it over here? Where did you say you were at again?'

I told him that I was just across the street, gave him the address and hung up.

I paced around, wondering how bad this could be. I mean, I thought I might die. My mother is a very good cook and she would have to live with the shame of her daughter dying of her own bad cooking. Cause of Death: Culinary Failure.

I put on my coat and made my way over to Bellevue and found the entrance. As I got to the reception area and started to explain who I was and that I was not crazy, a small team showed up and said, "We've been waiting for you." They flanked me on both sides and steered me through the security doors that led down the hall into a room, where they sat me down onto a gurney. They were all very nice, and very skeptical.

"How long ago did you say you cooked this steak?"

"Have you ever felt like killing yourself?"

"Have you lost a job or a spouse recently?"

I kept telling them, "No, it was just a mistake. I'm a terrible cook. I don't like labels so I often don't read them."

By then my stomach had started making noises. Loud noises. My intestines were cramping and I started to feel like my meal wanted to come screaming out one end or the other.

"Look, can you hear this? I'm getting sick! Regardless of what y'all think, I didn't do this on purpose and I need you to help me and stop acting like I'm crazy!"

That shut them up long enough to where they heard the protests emanating from my gut. "Ok! Ok, Miss!" They began to take off in all directions, chattering directions back and forth to one another. "We're going to have you lie down and we're going to pump your stomach."

They made me drink that God-awful charcoal stuff and then began pumping my stomach. Once that was done they let me rest for a while. After several hours, they sent me home and told me I'd probably have diarrhea for a few days. I recall farting bubbles but I was glad they didn't lock me up!

Not long after the Mr. Clean incident, I was at work in Operations, where I shared the duties with a bunch of coworkers. As I walked into work one morning, one of the first people I passed said, "Did Pest Control come today?"

"I don't know," I said. "I just got here."

"It sure smells like pesticide," she said, sniffing audibly.

"Now that you mention it, it kind of does," I replied.

We got to work, and some time passed when one of the guys walked by me.

"Pest control come today?" he asked, sniffing the air.

"I don't think so, but she says," I nodded towards the woman who sat to my right, "that it smells like the pesticide and I kind of think so, too."

"Yeah, it's pretty strong. Pee-uu!"

Next thing I know the woman who sat closest to me got up, and as she walked by my desk, she stopped.

"Peggy, it's really strong right by you."

"It is?"

"Yes it is. In fact, it *is* you!" she exclaimed as she bent down, sniffing around my shoulder and hair.

"What!?"

"It's you. When I'm farther away I hardly smell it, but when you came in was when I first noticed it." She leaned in and took another big whiff. "Yep. It's you alright. What the hell did you get into?"

"I don't know. I just came to work like usual."

"Well, whatever it is it's all over you."

The comments kept coming throughout the day. I was so glad when I was finally able to clock out and go home. When I entered my apartment, I noticed I had left my ironing board out since I was in a hurry that morning. There was the iron, as I had left it and the can of spray starch. I picked up the can and went to return it down to the cupboard under the sink. I got a good look. It was a big ole can of RAID.

✳

I still hadn't found the place to soothe that restless rhythm inside of me. That Siren's call that had propelled me from the South, continued to tug at the edges of my consciousness, beckoning me forth. I began to think of other cities where I might work for Delta. San Francisco was especially alluring because I had heard of the "Beatniks." It wasn't that I understood who they were, what they were doing or trying to do, but rumor had it that they sat around in coffee houses, reading or reciting poetry and trying to make some sense of it all. I was a simple girl with base aspirations. So all that sounded good to me. The approval came through fast. God bless Delta Airlines, they really worked to try and help keep me out of the skies!

I found San Francisco to be more of a "fit" for me; I felt more comfortable, understood. Hard to explain, but I felt like the city liked me. It wasn't nearly the frenetic pace of New York.

Since I had gotten my AA degree back at Perkinston College in Mississippi, I thought perhaps I'd further my education. After all, I was in the city of Beatniks and I knew they were thinking and discussing things of great import. I enrolled in San Francisco State and took a few classes between my shifts at Delta Airlines.

The education I began picking up *outside of* work and college would come to define my future . . .

Part Three

I FIRST SAW AND SPOKE a few words to Janis Joplin one afternoon when I had gone home for lunch from my Delta job, in the days when I was still getting Mnasidika off the ground. I had opened my window and she was opening hers at the same time, just across Ashbury Street. She happened to notice me, hung her head out the window and said, "Hiya honey!" dripping with her strong southern inflection. I said, "Hiya!" back, made a minor mental note that she sounded like a Southerner and sat down to eat.

    At that time, The Haight really was still a quiet little neighborhood, filled with friendly people, who recognized our own kind. The next time I saw Janis was at the Matrix, a small club down near the water in San Francisco. There on stage was the woman I'd waved to from my kitchen window. Kimmie, who was already my lover at the time, had come into the store talking about this woman she'd heard singing, someone with an unusual gravelly voice. Kimmie was great at identifying talent, so I took her seriously when she praised someone. I rarely went out in the evening at that time, as I was so focused on making money and keeping my store going. But Kimmie was heading out, and persuaded me to put business aside and come along to the Matrix.

    What I experienced was a force of nature. Big Brother and the Holding Company, the band she was singing with, was a perfect match for Janis's electric, plugged in, a-thousand-women-at-once voice . . . and oh, the delivery! Even so, many of the club-goers that night seemed oblivious. They were talking over the music, meanwhile I was in awe, with chills running through me. Seeing and hearing

Janis that night with Big Brother was a mind-altering experience. It shattered all conception of what was possible to convey within the realm of music and vocalization. Electrical, elemental, primal and progressive, Janis, with Big Brother and the Holding Company's sound, screamed from the depths of the earth and kaleidescoped in from the far reaches of the cosmos.

I remember clearly what she sang. When she began, slowly at first in that distinctive Janis Joplin voice, singing "Bye ... bye ... bye ... baby, bye bye," I about fell out of my chair and the hair stood up on my arms. I gasped and thought, "Oh my God." I knew at that moment there was something truly unusual about this girl from across the street, which was *so* raw and *so* real. I don't want to be trite, because that's been said about her by many others before, but when I saw her she wasn't famous, yet that's what hit my mind. I thought, "My God, something's different here." Her soul was just pouring out of her mouth—so much so that I turned to the people next to me to see if they were getting what I was getting.

"Excuse me. Excuse me. Do you see anything unusual in that girl?" I asked.

"Yeah, she's good," they said politely.

Then they kept right on talking. I was stunned. How could they not be seeing this?

"Oh my God!" I exclaimed, incredulous, "C'mon, man!" I interrupted again, then again, "Can't you feel her? Feel what's going on here?" They just looked at me and shrugged.

So, I turned to the people on my other side and said, "Pardon me, pardon me," I said emphatically, "don't you notice anything? Look at the hair standing up on my arms! Look! Something is happening here!"

But nobody else in that room seemed to get it. The come-ons, the conversations, the tinkling of ice in glasses continued in the oblivious background noise that could have been any bar, anywhere. While for me, truly, there are hardly words to describe the impact of such bare, raw, sonic deliverance. How could this relatively diminutive woman fit all of that inside of her? It seemed impossible, but there it was, pouring through her in seeming endless supply. Jaw dropping, aching and beautiful. I was instantly a fan.

A few days went by and then Janis came into Mnasidika. I introduced myself and told her I had seen her and Big Brother and that I felt she was incredibly talented. She thanked me sweetly, and asked if I worked there.

"Yes, yes I do," I answered.

"Whaaall, do ya think I could put fifty cents down on these?"

She set a pair of jeans down in front of me that normally sold for $4.95. I didn't know what to say. Plenty of people low on funds had asked me to lower a price, or worse, tried to steal something. But this was a new request. I was also taken aback, because there was something about this girl with the wild long frizzy hair and the carefree manner that set her apart.

"I'll keep bringing you fifty cents and maybe even a dollar sometimes, until they're paid off if you'll hold them for me?" She asked this rather shyly. Hope, doubt, and expecting "no" played alternately across her face.

"Yes, you can . . ." I said, and her face brightened. "But how 'bout you just take 'em?" I don't know why I offered them for free. Maybe I was in awe of her talent. Perhaps I wanted to help, in some tiny way, to keep an artist like that going. Who knows?

"What? No, I can't do that," Janis said, shaking her head, visibly surprised.

"Sure you can. Go ahead, you can take 'em."

She leaned in closer. Her eyes darted from one side to another, like she was looking to see if anybody was listening. "Won't you get in trouble?"

"Nah, don't worry. It's ok, really."

She beamed, but still hesitant.

"Ya sure you're not gonna get fired?" Janis asked in a low voice, I suppose, in case "the boss" might hear.

"I'm sure. Really, take 'em." I smiled. "Just take 'em."

Rather sheepishly and excitedly, she scooped them up.

"I promise I'll pay you. I really will. Thanks."

She then gripped that pair of jeans tightly, and hugged them in close, as if worried someone might take them from her at that last moment.

Maybe a week later, Janis came striding back in, and confronted me, "Now I know why you won't get fired!"

I played coy. "Why?"

"Because you own the joint! That's why you could give me those jeans!"

"You're right," I said, laughing.

Thus, our friendship began.

Janis was a very smart woman. Yet she did have an innocence, a childlike excitability and a way of looking at the world with awe that was endearing. Both of us being from the South, we soon discovered common ground and it wasn't long before we were good friends.

JANIS AND GEORGE, LOVING IN THE HAIGHT

© HERB GREENE.

Her rise to stardom, once it began, was quick. The Haight was bustling and by then had become known worldwide. My store was successful, and I'd already branched out with a second location. Delta was a memory. Since I already knew a lot of musicians because they shopped at Mnasidika, and Janis and I and all our friends lived in The Haight, our circles easily overlapped. Janis began making substantial money, and yet was rather cautious about much of her expenditures. I wasn't making the money that Janis and the other top musicians were earning, but I was making enough to hold my own; I could afford to keep up—eat in expensive restaurants, stay in nice hotels, buy better-quality drugs. This allowed us to hang out without her footing the bill. Financial independence gave us both freedom with, and from, each other. Sadly, it became increasingly difficult for some of her other friends to keep up as her star and bank account rose. Kris Kristofferson, who wrote songs for Janis and often shared her bed, once said, "Hell, it ain't cheap hanging out with Janis! It costs a hundred dollars a day even when you're doing nothing!"

Aside from the Southern thing, she and I shared the same sense of humor, a laid-back sensibility. From the beginning, it seemed we liked each other for who we were, and it was easy to keep that respect and admiration at times when our friendship was tested. We didn't start out as lovers, but as friends, just two twenty-something young women working hard to make their unconventional dreams come true, friends who could talk about anything, laugh over everything, and try things this wild, new life offered. We were having so much fun together. So very much fun.

Meanwhile, as Janis and I became friends, I was deeply in love with Kimmie. She was someone I was attracted to in a mysterious and stubborn way; she was so unlike anyone I had ever met. Physically she was attractive in an Adonis-like masculinity, contrasted to her beauty in lithe femininity. She was otherworldly in her clarity, fun, and oftentimes brilliant perspective in her mania.

"Hey Kimmie," I called out one day as Kim strode into the store.

"What?" Kim asked, as she pulled down the hood of her sweatshirt that she wore underneath her leather jacket, and shook out her hair.

"There was a package delivered for you."

I RAN INTO SOME TROUBLE

"Where is it?" Kim asked, squinting.

"It's in the dressing room."

"Why is it in there? I don't like this, Peg." Her brow furrowed. "Someone could send me a bomb, ya know?"

"I had the boys put it in the dressing room, because it would block the aisles."

"Huh. Let's see what Jack is in the box." She shrugged, put her hood back on her head and walked towards the dressing room, looking ready to fight.

"I don't think it's gonna bite you, Kim."

She flung back the curtain and let out a shriek when she saw the shiny green and silver Triumph 500 motorcycle.

"Oh, you are so beautiful! What? Who? Peggy! Come see!"

I made my way over, grinning ear to ear.

"Do ya like it?" I asked.

"Aaaaaaye, love it!" She threw her leg over the seat, straddling the bike.

"It's yours," I said with a smile.

"You? For me?" Kim shrieked again, turned the key in the ignition, pounced onto the start lever and fired the Bonneville up.

"Yes! For you!" I yelled over the sound of the motor.

Kimmie hit the throttle a couple of times making the engine growl.

"Look out!" she yelled as she kicked the bike into gear and roared through the aisle between the jeans and jackets, out the front door, and onto Haight Street.

I wandered out onto the sidewalk just as Janis and a friend of hers walked up.

"What are you smiling so big about?" Janis queried.

Just then Kim came flying back around the corner and drove up onto the sidewalk.

"This," I said, pointing at Kim and the motorcycle.

"How would ya like to have that for competition?" Janis asked of her friend.

Her friend shook her head.

"C'mon Peg. Hop on!" Kim scooted forward on the seat and I slid behind her, waving at Janis and her friend as we rode off.

HIDING KIM'S TRIUMPH IN MNASIDIKA. PEGGY WITH BOBBY BOLES

A few days later Wes Wilson came by and asked to put up some posters for a dance, as he often did. Several dance promoters now found success selling tickets through my store, and I'd get the foot traffic.

"Go ahead, Wes. Just take down the one from last week, would ya?"

"Sure. Hey Bobby!" Wes waved over to Bobby Boles.

"Hey Wes!" Bobby waved back and resumed cutting leather.

Wes and I chatted for a while and somehow the subject of Kim's motorcycle came up.

"Wow, that's really something, Peggy! Do you ride?"

"Yeah. I've been riding it all week." Which was kind of true because Kimmie had been trying to teach me in Golden Gate Park. Neither one of us was very patient about that, but I had gained a modicum of confidence.

"It must be fun," Wes said, wistfully.

"It is," I replied, then exuberantly asked, "Hey Wes, wanna go for a ride with me?"

Wes's head jerked around. "Yea, yea, sure Peg. Why not?" he grinned.

"Ok, I'm just gonna put on my motorcycle jacket. I'll be right out."

I grabbed the keys and straddled the bike, balancing on my tippy toes. It took me a few tries to kick-start it, but on the fourth try it came to life. I motioned for Wes to climb on.

"Hang on!" I cried out, and put the bike into first gear. I applied the throttle and let out the clutch and we leapt out into traffic and through the stop sign as pedestrians scattered. Wes grabbed hold of my waist and dug his nails into my jacket. I clicked the bike into second gear and the engine wound out until I engaged the clutch and we jerked through another stop sign, and began to climb a hill. The engine screamed as I tried shifting on an incline, protesting in a high-pitched squeal as we rocketed around a corner. After climbing another couple of blocks, I turned onto a more level street and, still not having my clutch/throttle dance down, succeeded in pulling a semi-wheelie as the bike instantly engaged into third. I could feel Wes's head buried into my back, and his grip hadn't loosened for a second. I thought the wheelie was pretty cool, and felt bolstered in my skills. Then we turned downhill. I tried to downshift, but ended up hitting fourth gear instead. We were flying down the hill and zipped through a stop sign, cars honking and people running away. I tried to downshift again and found second gear, without braking. I felt Wes hit my back hard, and my face got shoved towards the gas tank; I hit the throttle and slammed us both into the upright position, then found the brakes as I brought us to a halt at a stop sign where I forgot to engage the clutch and killed the motor.

"Put your feet down!" I yelled.

Wes put his feet down.

I let go of the brake and let out the clutch. The bike came back to life.

"Put your feet up!"

Wes yanked his feet back up onto the foot pegs, as we hurtled through another intersection, did a U-turn and careened back down the hill.

We jerked and swayed and I gunned it feeling like I was getting the hang of it. After another near wheelie we rolled up to the curb in front of the store. Wes was wide-eyed and sweating. He said, "You didn't know how to ride it, did you?"

"Not really, I guess!"

"Uh, yea Peggy. That was uh, uh, an experience." Wes stammered as he walked away stiff-legged down the street. Mind you, Wes wasn't a wimpy guy by *any* means. God Bless him, it wasn't until the following week, that I realized what a death-defying feat he had endured.

That time, I had taken off on the Triumph, out of The Haight and decided to head straight up Nob Hill, which is one of the steeper inclines in San Francisco. As I made my way up the first block, foolishly I thought I needed to put the motorcycle into a higher gear. I could feel I was losing momentum as I crested the third block, so I gave the bike more gas. I leaned forward as if to will the bike on and for a brief moment felt as if I were suspended in time. Then came the sickening feeling in the pit of my stomach as I realized I was no longer climbing, but descending. Backwards. On a large, heavy motorcycle. Each dizzying second seemed to double the speed I was travelling. Out of control I careened diagonally across traffic until I jack-knifed the front wheel and dumped the bike in the intersection. I could feel the hot exhaust pipe steaming through the leathers I had borrowed from Kimmie (Thank God!). I could hear the screeching of tires and horns honking all around as I lay underneath the bike. I wriggled and cursed, trying to extricate myself from beneath the eight-hundred or so pounds of steel. I could see wheels spinning by, and feel the heat of exhaust as cars slowed, then zoomed past me. It is a most unusual perspective to be eye-level with the tires of moving vehicles. As I continued to struggle, some guy lifted the bike off me and another helped me up and I limped to the curb. They asked if I was all right to which I responded, "No." I was badly shaken, but realized I had to get myself and the motorcycle home. Against their protests, I got back on and tentatively made my way back to Mnasidika. In first gear.

I never drove the Triumph again.

*

"Sah-*man*tha" Ned began, with his signature, mischievous grin, "I have an idea."

I glanced at Stella, who merely grinned and offered a barely perceptible shrug as she handed me the joint.

Ned continued, as I took a couple of hits off of the joint, and handed it back to him.

"I was thinking, maybe the ground isn't the best way to move pot across the border." He took a long drag, holding the smoke in his lungs for several, long seconds, letting it out with a slight cough and a grin. "I was talking with a couple of the guys and apparently someone has some land just this side of the border, complete with a smuggle-tested makeshift landing strip."

"Really?" Kimmie exclaimed, pausing as she lifted the now half-

STELLA AND NED

smoked joint to her lips. "Peg, do ya hear this?"

"Yeah, Kimmie, I'm hearing this."

"There are waaaay less people to get past in the air, as opposed to the border," Ned offered.

"Think about it, Samantha," Stella piped in, "less people, less chance of getting busted."

"Does anyone know how to fly?" I asked.

"Peg! I can do it! I've always wanted to learn. I drive everything! I can surf!" Kim had jumped up, putting her arms out like wings. "I can be stealthy, too!" she said, crouching low, toning down the volume on her engine noise to a hardly audible hum.

"Hmmm," I said turning back to Ned. "Looks like you could have yourself a pilot."

Ned's eyebrows shot up, and he began laughing heartily. Stella eyed Kim with an appraising curl of her lips, and nodded.

"There's a flight school in San Rafael, you guys! Gnoss Airfield. I've gone out there lots to watch the little mosquito planes," Kim prattled enthusiastically.

Once Kim was enrolled, she studied devotedly. She really was a great driver of both motorcycles and cars. Crazy at times, but definitely good. When it came time for her first solo flight she begged me to join her.

"C'mon Peg. It'll be fun. We can fly anywhere we want to."

"I gotta work."

"It won't be that long. I need the hours. C'mon it'll be fun. We can see our house and the Golden Gate Bridge."

"Well, that might be cool. Maybe later in the day?"

Then Kimmie said, "Hey, let's take just a lick of a hit of acid, maybe the plane will disappear around us?"

I pondered that idea for a second and since I had paid for her training said, "Hmmm, ya know, it does sound like fun," and chuckled excitedly, "Wow, do ya think you could still fly it? On acid?"

"Of course, Peg! I've driven cars and motorcycles on acid. Flying should be even better. Less traffic!"

"Ha, you're right!" I was all in, now. "I'll see you out there around eleven."

Once I arrived at the airport Kim jumped into the passenger seat of my yellow Mustang. Reaching into the inside pocket of her leather bomber jacket, she pulled out a small glass vial and a pair of tweezers. Grabbing a tiny piece of paper with the tweezers she held it out and said, "Stick out your tongue, Peg."

She touched just the merest corner of it to my tongue and dropped it back into the vial.

"What about you? I thought we were doing this together?" I asked, taken aback that she hadn't indulged.

"Well," she glanced up at me intently, referring to herself in the third person as she often did, "Kimmie's not crazy, ya know. Flying is serious business!" I giggled to myself at her random act of sanity, as she slipped the ampoule back into her pocket.

We walked over to an office near a hangar and runway, where smaller non-commercial aircraft taxied around. Once Kim got her preflight paperwork in order and the keys to the Piper that we rented, we climbed up into the cockpit. Once on board, she started the craft and we set out for the runway. The take-off was without a hitch and up we rose into the sky above Marin County. We oohed and aaahed, pointing and gesturing as we came over Mount Tamalpais and saw our little house in Coon Hollow. The mild dose of LSD had kicked in for me and made the topography more defined and alive. We saw the ocean shimmering, deep and cobalt, undulating and vast out to the arc of the horizon. Next, we buzzed around the hills and valleys of Marin. Then over to check out the marina in Sausalito, where boats looked like toys lazing rhythmically against their docks. It was a nice sunny day and the visibility was good. As we turned towards the city and took in the San Francisco Bay I gasped and thought, "What a gorgeous contrast of metallic sunset-colored architecture the Golden Gate Bridge is!" The color blazing against the intermittent fog that reached in gossamer patches here and there below the arch. As we dropped in closer, we saw a psychedelic Porsche convertible streaking onto the Golden Gate from San Francisco. It was impossible to miss the vibrant coupe. Kim and I looked at each other.

"Oh wow, look Kimmie, it's Janis! She's leaving orange and blue streaks behind her on the bridge!"

"Let's dive bomb her!" Kim squealed.

"Yeah, she'll love it!" I replied exuberantly, giggling.

Kim pushed the controls to ease the nose down and throttled the little plane towards the Porsche, timing it so we made our pass where the support cables that drape along the outer structure of the bridge were lowest. We waved and yelled and Janis was looking around but not seeming to realize it was us.

"Honk the horn, Kimmie. You gotta honk the horn!"

Kim started laughing. "There is no horn! Why dontcha flash your tits, Peggy? C'mon flash your tits."

"No Kimmie, no. That's not gonna work."

"C'mon Peg, you have to this time. Flash your tits! For sure she'll know it's us!"

She nosed the plane higher, then turned back to set up for the next dive and pleaded, "You HAVE to Peg, it's the only way she'll know it's us."

"She'll never be able to see us, Kim."

"Oh yes she will." Her face was determined. "I'm getting *really* close this time. Get your tits ready."

The plane dropped fast. I pulled my top up and fished my breasts out of my bra and pushed them out the window.

Janis was whipping her head around looking up into the sky. We came in so close you could just about make out the "Mother Fucker!" coming out of her lips. We lifted away as Janis exited the bridge and we laughed hysterically, wondering if she knew it was us.

We did a little more sightseeing above the city and around Oakland then headed back to the airport. We had taken separate cars, so as Kim logged her hours I headed to the store.

When I arrived back at the shop, my boys were standing around with very stern looks on their faces. Most of them were gay and could be snippy, as only queens can be. Rick spoke first.

"Where have you been, Miss Peggy?"

"Why? Did I miss something? I don't recall having an appointment or meeting."

"We received a phone call."

"Yeah, and...?"

"Were you in an airplane?"

"Yes, as a matter of fact I was. So?"

"I answered the phone," Rick said, his tone measured, "and it was Janis. She wanted to know if you were here at the store."

I started to put it together.

"She said, 'Do you know what your motherfucking boss did?' I said, '*No*' and then she went *off*! She was really animated, even for Janis. She was shrieking and laughing and saying, 'Do you know how crazy your boss is? She is certifiably fucking crazy. *Insane!* She was in some plane, some little goddamn airplane and buzzed me while I was driving across the Golden Gate Bridge. More than once they flew over me. Over the Golden Fucking-Gate AND she hung those big 'ol tits of hers out the damn window.' And I said to her, 'Oh my, she did?' And she was laughing so hard and practically screaming in my ear 'That's right! She did that! She hung her fuckin' tits out the window of that mother fucking airplane. Your boss! You tell her she's fucking crazy. Stone fucking crazy!'"

"So, there," Rick said through pursed lips, "I've told you," and spun around and swished his prissy self back behind the counter.

✳

Kimmie had started to become violent. It began with disparaging remarks and quickly escalated into full on screaming fits and throwing stuff. First at the walls and then at me. I started throwing money (figuratively) at her to keep her happy and out of my space. Crazy, I was still in love.

Meanwhile, I would often meet up with Janis when she was recording or touring in New York or Los Angeles, and I was traveling there—sometimes by coincidence, sometimes on purpose—to attend various clothing trade shows or meet with vendors. Then, Janis and I began meeting up more often on the road, in Boston and various other cities. Janis knew about the precarious state of my relationship, and one night was expressing concern about how Kimmie was treating me. Kindly, she tread lightly around the subject. I was crying badly, and Janis offered to give me something that would make me feel better.

Heroin.

"No, Janis! Nothing is going to take this pain away. Nothing can. Not until I don't love her anymore."

"How are you gonna do that?" she asked gently.

"Fuck, I don't know. You know everybody wants the same damn thing."

"What's that?"

"To love and be loved by the person they're loving."

"Man! Ain't that the truth! I'm always loving the wrong one. Seems like whoever I'm diggin' is diggin' someone else. Too much fucking competition." She sighed. "You sure you don't want some dope?"

"Yea, yea, I'm sure. And I wish you wouldn't do that."

Janis shrugged, and went into the bathroom to "fix."

Though by then we were close friends, I had not yet witnessed Janis shooting heroin in my presence; she always slipped off into another room for that. I'm not sure if it was out of respect for the fact that I wasn't using, or simply because it was something she preferred to do alone. We had never talked about it much prior to that night, except for me to occasionally urge her to slow down her use of the drug when she was expected to show up on time and record.

But maybe I was also just conveniently ignoring how much of a role heroin was occupying in her life. Just like I was ignoring everything that was wrong between Kimmie and me.

I didn't understand what manic/depressive paranoid, schizophrenic meant in terms of how a person would behave. Kimmie had received that diagnosis during a stay in Langley-Porter Psychiatric Hospital, and I just thought she had been misunderstood. She had this way of viewing situations that were crystalline in clarity. She could distill the essence of a moment down into something that would leave me in awe. Sometimes the world through her eyes was a most wondrous place. Sometimes, I found out later, it was horrific. But the crushing depression, paranoia, and schizophrenia chipped away more and more of the delight, and I was ill-equipped to understand that this was something beyond my ability to soothe. Not love, not money, not cars, nor exotic locales could appease the cruelly insane chemistry besieging her. I could not make sense of it. Not for years and years.

I kept thinking that each time I suffered abuse at the hands of Kimmie would be the last time, because she would always be so sorry, as abusers often are. "I'm sorry, I'm sorry, I don't know why I did that. It'll never happen again." But it did. I just kept thinking that it would get better, but more and more the thought crept in that it would not. I could see that I was going to be the recipient of physical abuse forever. And when I began to pull away from Kimmie, Janis was right there to pull me in—Janis and heroin. These were to be my escape from Kimmie, my way of controlling my life again.

A few months before the night Janis offered me heroin, Janis had been performing in New York, and Kimmie and I had been vacationing in Jamaica. We swooped in and met up with Janis at the Chelsea Hotel Bar. I was trying to make a room reservation, but the desk clerk was having none of it. Janis came to see what the hang up was, and lit into the poor guy about how she was going to move her whole band and entourage out if they didn't find us a room. Instantly, he said he had overlooked a cancellation, and the key was pressed into my hand with great apologies. I thanked Janis, she grinned and hurried back to the bar.

There were always subtle cues when Kimmie was becoming agitated. Pacing, with her brow furrowed and a dark look. After a few days, Janis caught what was going on between Kim and I, and she would turn away like friends do watching a friend in pain and being helpless to do anything about it. I needed to see a couple of clothing dealers in New York, so I shoved a bunch of money at Kim and convinced her to go on back to San Francisco to check on the stores. As she had no real job at the time, I knew this would often make her feel responsible and purposeful, and she immediately booked a flight back.

At the time, I had a terrible crush on Janis's guitar player, Sam Andrew, and I'm sure he knew it. Kim and I had a basic agreement. We could fuck men as much as we wanted, and once or twice, we had a three-way, but sex with another woman was taboo. With Kim back on the West Coast, and knowing Sam was in New York along with the rest of Big Brother and the Holding Company, I called and asked if I could join him.

"In my room?" he asked without an ounce of emotion.

"Yes, Sam. In your room."

"When are you coming?"

"Tonight"

"Ok," he said flatly and hung up.

Awhile later, I made my way over to Sam's room, slung my hair back, stuck my tits out and knocked enthusiastically on his door

He opened it and looked at me rather coldly. "What are you doing here?"

"Um," I stammered, "um, you said, I uh, called, remember? To come stay with you?"

He looked at me, turned around, left the door open, walked into the bathroom and shut the door behind him. I sat on the bed and waited. And waited. And waited. He finally came out of the bathroom, turned his back to me, stripped down, got into bed, and turned his light out without a word. I stripped down, slid beneath the covers and snuggled up to him. No response. It was actually not the first time we had played this game. I spent the rest of the night smoking and staring at the ceiling, wondering what the hell was wrong with me.

The next morning around 11 a.m. Sam got up, said he had to go to the studio and for me to wait for him to return. So, I did. I waited. And waited. And waited. I made some calls to clothing manufacturers, had some food delivered, and waited some more. About 4 a.m. Sam comes in, and leaves the door open. I hear jingling and jangling and Janis is in the hallway. Her room was directly across from Sam's and she was fumbling with keys.

"I didn't know you were here!" she said excitedly then frowned. "Why didn't you call and tell me you were still here?"

"I was going to but Sam asked me to wait, and . . ." I finished, as I realized I sounded foolish.

"Well, c'mon! Why don'tcha stay in my room?"

Sam finally looked at me, as I looked longingly at him, my eyes pleading for him to ask me to stay.

"Go ahead," he said and turned away, locking himself into the bathroom again.

"Well, Honey, ya coming or what?" Janis quipped in a Mae West dialect, hand on her hip.

I stared at the bathroom door a few seconds longer, then got up and grabbed my suitcase, and dragged it across the hall to Janis's room.

Immediately she started rattling on about how it was going in the studio, how they're all fighting, what was going well and what stunk. Then she stopped and cocked her head.

"You're really hung up on him, aren't you?"
"Yea, yea I am."
"He's a mind-fucker you know."
"A what?"
"A mind-fucker," she said, a look of concern on her face.
"What does that mean?"
"It means, the only way you're gonna get fucked by Sam, Honey, is in your head. That's how he gets off. You're not the first chick to swoon over beautiful Sam."
"No, probably not."
"You got business out here?"
"Buying some clothes for the store."
"Why don'tcha meet me at the studio tomorrow?"
"Yea, that sounds good."
"Cool, Honey. Make yourself at home."
"Ok."

I undressed, climbed into bed, lit a cigarette, and pondered the meaning of "mind fucker."

Being in New York was so different from when I lived there just a few short years prior. All that we had been doing in Haight-Ashbury had spread. Greenwich Village, known as a mecca for the east coast Beatniks, spawning folk singers—who roamed, jangled and twanged. Solo players hung harmonicas around their necks and blew emphasis on songs of social commentary. Others harmonized, and inspired groups of kids to sit in a circle joined in song. The counterculture had become contagious and the youth of America were happily infected by the thousands. What began in a small, foggy neighborhood, grew into the rapture of possibility, lots of sex, and the belief we could somehow change the world.

We saw each other in more and more places. Seeing ourselves, we were emboldened. It was around this time that I got the idea to write about what was happening. To chronicle the humble beginnings of a movement we didn't know we were creating. It seemed in such stark contrast to just a few years before. The television-era family life, in black and white, portrayed in TV series such as *Father Knows Best*, *My Three Sons*, and *Leave It To Beaver*, was fading away, along with the specter of June Cleaver being what women were expected to aspire to, replete with drab tones of conformity, starched and uptight. It is a wonder anyone of that era was able to have a successful bowel movement.

"So Honey, ya wanna come down to the studio tonight?" Janis asked the next morning. She and Big Brother were recording tracks for the Cheap Thrills album.

"Sure, yeah, that would be cool. I have to meet some clothing dealers this afternoon, place some orders, then I'm free." My mind invariably tuned to the fact Sam would be there.

"Do you know where it is?" she asked, as she threw a pack of Marlboro cigarettes into her purse.

"No. Actually, I don't."

"Shit, I don't really know the address. Wait a minute." She began rifling through her purse. "Fuck, it's not in here." She sighed, exasperated. "Oh, they know at reception. Just have them call you a cab. That's what me and the boys do."

"Ok, that's what I'll do then. When should I get there?"

"You can come whenever you want. We'll be good and warmed up by about 9 or 10 tonight. But meanwhile, are ya hungry yet?" she asked as she slipped an embroidered blouse on. "We can grab something downstairs. It's actually pretty good."

"Yea. Let's go."

I grabbed my briefcase and we headed out.

After I was done with my store business, I grabbed some dinner and returned to the Chelsea Hotel to change clothes and freshen up. I had the desk clerk call a cab to take me to the studio as Janis had suggested. Once there, I was greeted warmly by Janis and ignored by Sam. Every time she got a break she'd come and ask what I thought about whatever song they were working on. I'd tell her I wasn't a musician and didn't know and she'd counter, "Well, ya know if ya like it, don'tcha Honey?" I could tell she was starting to feel her liquor.

"But I'm only hearing pieces, Janis."

"Well, do you like it?"

"Just when I start to groove, y'all stop. So no, I don't like it."

"You don't like the song?"

"I don't like that I never get to hear it all the way through."
"Well, that's how we gotta do it."
"Ok. So stop asking me," I retorted, mildly annoyed.

That night, Janis got progressively more drunk during the studio session, and when she ran out of booze, she asked me to go find her a bottle. All the liquor stores were closed and I objected to the request because I thought that her drinking more wouldn't be good for her or the music. With much pleading, I finally succumbed, and found a place open. While I was out searching all over hell and creation, someone else had shown up with some Southern Comfort and by the time I got back, Janis was sloshed. The producer asked me to get her home and I tried herding my drunken velvet-draped friend to a cab.

I was aware that a drunk Janis was an affectionate Janis. But a really, really, drunk Janis was a really, really, affectionate Janis. She kept trying to kiss me. On the lips. I kept asking her to stop, as I was feeling very uncomfortable since the taxi driver was quite interested in what was going on in the back seat. Once we arrived back at the Chelsea, she vomited as we got out of the cab. I paid the driver and from there it seemed to take forever to get her up to the room. She was swaying in the hallway outside the door, swearing as she dug through her purse looking for the key.

"Fuck, mutha fuckin' keys are in here somewhere . . . fuck!" She plopped down on the floor in the hallway and turned the purse upside down, dumping the contents out on the floor. Laughing, she said, "Oh, there you are!" as she snatched the key out of the pile of randomness, raked the rest of it back into her bag, and with a great effort, hoisted herself upright and lurched towards the door.

"Janis, here, just give me the key!" I put my hand out to grab the key, as she was having quite a time matching the key to the hole it was supposed to fit in.

"No, Peggy. No, jezz gimme a minute, fuckin' key, c'mon fucker, ah shit, ok, ok, ok, wait a minute." I could see her close one eye and try to open the other wide by cocking her head and raising her eyebrow. "Got it!" she said triumphantly, then, "Whew!" as the momentum of the door opening drew her off her already precarious balance and carried her sailing through the room to crash up against the bed.

I closed the door and went to help her up. She reeked of vomit, booze, cigarettes, and New York.

"Janis, ya gotta go take a bath." She looked at me, startled.

"A bath?" she responded meekly, looking like a little kid.

"Yeah Honey, a bath. I won't be able to sleep at all with you reeking like this." Her little face fell. I immediately felt bad.

"C'mon, I'll help you" She brightened and leaned into me as I helped her to get safely into the tub.

I checked in on her every once in a while, to make sure she didn't pass out and drown. She finally made her way out, a little sheepish, climbed into bed and passed out.

When she woke, it was with a groan. "Oh jeezus I must've had a good time last night." She smacked her lips as she got up on one elbow and squinted hard as she surveyed her surrounding, then turned to me.

"Did we fuck?"

"Uh, *no*. You were shit-faced drunk." I was taken aback. We'd never had sex before.

"It feels like it. How come we didn't fuck?"

"Like I said. You were shit-faced. You puked all over as we got out of the cab."

"Well, that never seems to stop anyone."

"Do you wanna fuck?" I said, slightly annoyed.

It was her turn to be thrown off. "Um, I just figured. Ya know, like we . . . well, I just thought we would sometime, ya know?" Now she was looking down and seemed almost shy.

My mind was reeling. This, this was opening up a whole other can of worms. I still loved Kimmie, and even though I had endured a couple of harshly physical episodes, I kept thinking things would get better. I still had a crazy attraction to Sam Andrew, and yet, I also really dug Janis. We were good friends, but I had never seriously considered sleeping with her. But compared to Kim and Sam who seemed to delight in putting me down, Janis was always so sweet to me. Really. She always seemed genuinely happy to see me. We had a lot of fun together. On one hand my thoughts were, "Ah, hell, what could it hurt?" On the other hand, I thought, "Are you out of your fucking mind? If Kim finds out, she will quite possibly kill you." I wasn't quite sure what I wanted to do. One thing for sure was that I did not want to hurt Janis's feelings.

"Hey, we probably would have, but you were barely conscious."
This seemed to satisfy and perk her up a bit.
"I think I need to eat something. You?" she asked.
"Yeah. Let's go."

That morning's breakfast with Janis consisted of her ordering a banana split and some coffee. I could hardly eat my plate of eggs seeing the sugar mountain she was indulging in with such great gusto. Minute by minute she was getting more lively, and seemed to be shaking off the previous night like a pro. Which I suppose she was by then.

"Are you coming to the studio again tonight?"

"Yeah, I could. I'm not going out to get you a bottle though. You'll have to send someone else."

"Ok, Honey. I'll stock up!" she cackled.

"Here's for my part." I handed her a ten-dollar bill. "I've got to get going."

"Ok, see ya later."

Things were different at the studio this time. I could see Janis wasn't nearly as loaded as she had been the previous night. Sam ignored me, again. I listened and tried to understand what was going on as they did different "tracks." They would play back part of a song with only the drums and bass for example, then a guitar would be added and they would listen to that a few times and decide whether or not it was what they wanted it to sound like. Sometimes they agreed. Often times not. They would discuss and argue back and forth until someone would bring up the issue of "time being wasted arguing when we should be recording" and back around it would go. It was clear there was a lot more to making a record than I had ever thought about.

Sometime, in the wee hours before dawn they decided to finish for the night. Janis and I took a cab back to the Chelsea along with Sam. We rode the elevator together, then parted ways in the alcove between the two rooms. I looked wistfully after Sam for a moment and then followed Janis into her room. There was something different in the air tonight. For one, Janis was not nearly as drunk as the night before, or near as drunk as was her custom. She even seemed a bit shy. A bit awkward. Her usual prattle was absent. She fussed about quietly, changing out of her clothes into a more casual long blouse and sat on the bed and began to read. I watched her, amused. Her somewhat coy, and decidedly subdued manner endeared her more to me and I decided I'd take up the topic from the previous morning.

"What are you doing?" I asked as I slid up next to her.
"Reading."
"What are you reading about?"
"*Billboard* magazine. Music stuff."
"How terribly interesting." I took the magazine from her.
"What are you doing?"
"What I didn't do last night."

The afternoon sun darted through a crack in the black-out shades that sought to shield the fragile eyes and pale skin of the nocturnal artisans and their lot. Janis lay asleep next to me, and my mind reeled with thoughts of Kimmie, and what this might mean. I shook off the dread, and grinned at my friend as she woke up, smiling big and sheepish as she slipped out of bed to the bathroom.

From then on we "played together" often; we never talked about loving each other. We never discussed our relationship. She knew I loved Kim, and whatever opinion she may have had about my situation, she kept to herself. While I was writing down some random notes about The Haight, she once asked me if I was going to write about us. I told her she'd have to wait to find out. She laughed and said I had better make it good.

I did start to feel myself falling in love with Janis, and I didn't want to do that. I didn't want to be invisible. And when you were with Janis, at the peak of her fame, you were invisible. I did not want to be Peggy Joplin.

Still, at this point in our lives the 20-something-year-old hormones were raging, both of our careers were exceeding anything either had imagined, and we were having so very much fun. We giggled about hot men, and confided our inspirations and ideas for our respective work like giddy school girls. If she found some really groovy man, who happened to be a great fuck, she would send him my way. On occasion, we would have a three-way. Personally, I often found these trysts to be a drag. Kimmie and I had a few and it seemed that someone was always getting too much or not enough attention. Or someone would go along with the idea to make someone else happy when it wasn't really their thing. What did seem consistent though—most guys had no problem with two women together. Just so long as they got to be in the mix.

Janis and I were both virtually on top of the world. Since I flew all over the country for business, this made it easy to catch up with her during her tours and recording, with a little bit of careful itinerary changes, a few days extra here, an extra short flight there. Janis had grown particularly fond of spending weeks at a hotel in Hollywood called the Landmark. It was less than an hour from San Francisco by plane, especially if you took the $15 late-night flight. The drive wasn't bad either. I'd hop into my Mustang GT, and then later my Shelby Mustang ragtop, and barrel down California Highway 101, enjoying the scenery. The five-hour drive never seemed that big of a deal. Top down, music blaring, I was living the dream.

※

"Peggy, phone for you," someone called out to me from the payphone in the store.

I picked up the receiver from the top of the payphone.

"Hello."

"Samantha, they've arrested Ned," my pot-smuggling friend Stella said quietly. She was always so cool under pressure, but I knew her well enough to hear the mildest twinge of concern.

"What?!" I gasped. "Oh shit, for what?"

"They got him for a few kilos of pot. Five to be exact."

"Oh shit, that's not good," my tone dropping low to avoid attention as I partially covered the receiver with my hand, attempting to muffle my voice to anyone who might overhear. Marijuana possession was a felony in any amount for any reason in the 1960s.

"I need to get him out," Stella said.

Marijuana arrests were just starting to become more commonplace, and young lawyers Michael Stepanian and Brian Rohan had recently set up shop as The Haight-Ashbury Legal Organization (HALO).

"Have you talked to Stepanian or Rohan?"

"Yeah, they can work on it. But I gotta bail Ned out first."

"How much?"

"Ten thousand dollars."

"What!?" I yelled. Stella didn't have this kind of money. But I did. And I knew that she knew it.

"That's the full amount. But I talked to a bail bondsman and I can get him out but I need collateral."

"Do you have it?"

"No."

"Can you come by?" I half whispered.

"I just left the bail bondsman, and I'm on my way home. I'll stop by."

"Just come straight back into my office."

"Ok. Bye."

"Bye."

Stella and Ned had been "importing" marijuana from Mexico for several years by now, but this was the first time they had had any run-in with the law. Unfortunately, Ned was looking at the potential for doing some serious time in a penitentiary. In other words, prison. Stella explained that she couldn't pay the bail because all she and Ned had was the kilos of pot, now in the evidence vault in the downtown San Francisco Police Department, and the questionable jalopy that was their current transportation. I offered to put up my house as the collateral. Soon, Stella and I were off to the bail bondsman together.

The office was a tiny, hole-in-the-wall affair, with huge black letters painted above the door, "Bert's Bail Bonds," and below that in slightly smaller letters, "Anytime Day or Night." There were bars on the small window next to the door and across the door as well. A small sticker was stuck above the intercom speaker next to the door that read "Press Buzzer and Wait." We did as instructed and a gruff male voice said, "Bert's" over the intercom.

Stella leaned towards the speaker. "I need to bail my husband out."

Within seconds there was a buzzing sound and a click. "Come on up."

There wasn't much to the place, just an empty space and some stairs. We walked up to the second floor and were greeted by a big, greasy, bear of a man with several gold rings on his hands and a gold tooth he flashed with a quick grin as he stood to greet us from behind his large mahogany desk.

"Ladies," he said in a welcoming tone, and gestured toward the seats opposite him. "Please, have a seat."

Stella answered Bert's questions and he began to draw up the paperwork. I became increasingly uncomfortable as Bert stared at my chest while talking to Stella.

"So—what have you got?" He glanced at my eyes for a second then fixated onto my tits again. "Besides the obvious?"

"My house. Use my house as collateral," I said as I put my briefcase up on his desk, unlatched it and pulled out the copies of my trust deed.

"Can I take you out?" Bert inquired, as he took the paperwork and placed it before him.

"I'm taken," I immediately blurted out.

He presented us with a contract, which in essence stated that if Ned did not show up for court, Bert would legally have the right to seize the collateral—and take my house. "He needs to show up on April 27th for his trial. If not, you have until 11:59 p.m. that night before you lose this." He waved the deed before us, his voice serious. Bert's earlier charm vacated and his eyes were suddenly cold as he said, "You really want him to show up."

"Yes, sir. He will," Stella responded.

"He better," I said, forcing a smile.

"Thank you, ladies." Bert rose from his chair. Stella and I got up to leave.

"Thank you," Stella and I said in unison. Hurriedly we made our way downstairs and out to the car.

Once Bert had posted the bail, Stella picked up Ned from San Francisco City jail, then stopped by the apartment. Ned thanked me, we smoked a joint and discussed the probabilities of him having to do time. This was all new to me, and frankly a little exciting seeing as how I hadn't ever really known anyone in trouble with the law before. My teenage sweetheart was a sheriff back home in Louisiana, and that was pretty much the extent of my intimate dealings with the police.

Over the ensuing weeks, and upon further consultation with the attorneys Stepanian and Rohan, things were not looking good for Ned.

A few weeks later Ned announced, "We're going to Mexico." His smiled belied the fear I could see in his eyes.

"Oh, for how long?" I asked.

"I don't know. I may not ever come back."

"Ever?"

"I don't know. I just can't do the time, Sam. At least if I'm not in the States they can't arrest me," he said, as he pulled a long drag off his filterless Camel cigarette.

I thought about what it might be like to do time, and sympathized. Then I panicked.

"But wait, Ned. If you leave, I lose my house! Oh, fuck, Ned!" I was sick at the thought of losing my house. Or ten grand.

"Whoa, whoa, Sam. Samantha!" He leaned forward. "Look at me, Sam!" he demanded, his eyes intense. Then he broke into a big smile. "I would never. Never, ever let you lose your house. Ever!"

"Ned. Ned! I can't, I just can't lose my house! Dammit! I can't afford to lose ten thousand dollars either!" I continued, exasperated.

"No, Samantha. It won't happen. I've got some stuff in the works. Stella will get the money to you. I promise!"

"God, I hope so! I mean, dammit, I don't want you locked up. But fuck!"

Ned flashed his charming smile, "I promise. Don't worry, Sam. I have a plan."

When his court date arrived, there was no word from Ned and Stella. I opened the store, worked all day, placed several calls to them. At noon, I went to the bank and got ten thousand dollars, cash, and hid it in my office when I got back to Mnasidika. I walked up the street a couple of times to see if they were home. Nothing. Nada. Nobody. About 11 p.m. I get a call. It's Stella.

"Fuck! What's going on Stella? Where are you? Where is Ned?" I start grilling her. She cuts me off.

"Sam. Sam. Samantha! Stop! Listen! I've got the money. I'm

coming by to get you."

"When?"

"Now."

"Ok, I'll be ready."

Within minutes Stella was at the door, and I burst out and ran to the car. As I jumped into the passenger seat, Stella gunned it and we tore our way across town. I watched the minute-hand on the clock inside of the rattle trap Ford she was driving, clicking the minutes by, seemingly way too fast. As she screeched to a halt at the curb, I leapt out and began frantically hitting the buzzer next to the entrance of Bert's Bail Bonds. In seconds, Stella was next to me pounding on the door with her fists.

"Bert! Bert!! Open up! We have the money! Open up!" Both Stella and I were yelling into the intercom.

"Who is this?"

"Peggy. I mean, Stella. Stella for Ned!"

The buzzer sounded and we could hear the door unlatch. "Come in."

We ran upstairs to find Bert in a smoking jacket, enjoying a fat cigar. Stella pulled the huge wad of cash from a brown paper bag in her purse, and began counting out the money.

Bert ceremoniously flicked his wrist to expose the face of his watch. "Eleven fifty-seven. My, my, my, you sure live on the edge, don't you?"

"Sixty, eighty, one hundred." Stella looked up, smiled at Bert, and her green eyes flashed. "You could say that."

Stella finished counting and handed the stacks to Bert.

"All here. Ten thousand dollars." He reached into the folder on his desk and handed me a manila envelope. I opened it and reviewed my deed.

"It's been a pleasure." Bert stood as well and relit his cigar. "If you ever need me again, you know where to find me." As the smoke poured out his mouth, he smiled broadly, and winked. I felt a tiny sense of foreboding, but shook it off as Stella and I made our way out into the night.

∗

No matter what craziness was going on in my life, or how much I was traveling, how much time I dedicated to my businesses, how strung out I was, I always kept in contact with my parents—mostly by phone and writing letters. I wasn't much interested in the goings-on of my hometown, and only rarely returned. It just seemed that everyone I had grown up with had done the predictable, expected agenda laid out in the 1950s. Everyone had married whom they were supposed to, and were busy having 2.4 children. To me, that was such a different world, and I had done my best to remove myself from its grasp. I didn't feel my parents particularly understood my life, but they always made me feel loved, supported, and that I was important to them. I noticed that I was incredibly lucky in this area, as many others in The Haight were estranged from their own parents.

Once, on the telephone, my mother brought up a contemporary subject.

"Dahlin', don't you have some friends that are Dead-Something?"

"Do you mean the Grateful Dead?"

"Uh huh, yes, I think that's them."

"Sure, they're friends. What about 'em?"

"They're fixing to come down here and play some music, I heard."

"Could be. They are playing all over the place these days."

"Well, they gonna come after them."

"Who? Who's gonna come after them?"

"The police. Everybody's talking about it. They gonna get 'em for the marijuana or somethin'. Said they was gonna set 'em up. They don't want 'em down here. Not even in New Orleans."

"You sure about this, Mom? Where are you hearing this?"

"Everybody's talking. People don't like hippies down here. They think y'all are commies, and crazies."

"Really? It's that bad?"

"Yes, it sure is. You might want to tell those boys to be careful. In fact, I wouldn't want to come down here if I was them."

"Wow, it's really that bad down there? Breaks my heart, but I'll tell 'em. Thanks for letting me know."

"Alright Hon, I'll be talking to you later. Love ya. Bye"

"Love you, too. Bye."

My mother wasn't prone to exaggeration. I don't even know how she was aware of the Grateful Dead, but I suppose I had mentioned them in my letters. Clearly, she had remembered them enough to feel the need to pass along important information. Bless her heart for paying attention! I got in touch with Rock Scully and told him what my mother had said, cautioned him to tell the boys that they were probably going to be set up. He assured me they would be fine and they would be careful. Unfortunately, the police did raid the guys' hotel room, arrested them for marijuana, harassed them, and made them feel most unwelcome. Southern (in)hospitality, late 1960s style.

*

I had a tiny office in my store, where I would retreat and be studious. I finally hired a gifted and by-the-letter-of-the-law accountant named Michael. He was incredulous as to the amount of money I was making slinging jeans, and began the process of guiding my cash flow like an actual, real-live business should. I was advised to buy a house, but to be honest, I wasn't that interested. However, on occasion Kimmie and I would take a mini vacation and stay out at Stinson Beach in cozy little seaside bungalows. They were owned by a gentleman who appeared to be in his mid-seventies named Mr. Kurtz, and he was always just the right amount of friendly. He gave you your privacy, but if you needed him he was there. After the accountant's suggestion, Kim and I booked a couple of nights out there. I asked Mr. Kurtz if I could buy one of the cabins, and I got a definitive, "No."

"But ya know, I do have a little shack up the road a piece I'd be willing to sell ya. Want to go and take a look at it? It's not much, needs some work. It's been sitting awhile."

"Sure. Why not?"

"Ok, let me get the key. You two can follow me up there." He turned and trundled off to his office. A few minutes later he pulled up in his car and gestured for us to follow.

We drove up Pacific Coast Highway a little bit and then turned onto Buena Vista, a windy mountain road. Part way up his car turned down into a driveway and disappeared. We followed and as we crested the driveway, I gasped. Nestled in a nook of a canyon, the "little shack" seemed to be part of the hillside itself. I instantly felt this was it. The view was stunning, and once we were out of the car, I could see the wind stirring the trees above and below us, but noticed that this area was sheltered. The structure itself was indeed rather plain, but overlooked the canyon with a seasonal creek. The Pacific Ocean gleamed in the distance and the eucalyptus trees hugged the home and yard in all the right places. This wasn't a house. This was a home! I couldn't wait to get back to San Francisco and tell Michael that I indeed was going to buy a house. Mr. Kurtz and I hashed out the details, agreed on a price, and within days I had the keys to this magical domicile. I was beside myself with joy. It was maybe eight hundred square feet. Not too big, not too small. Just right for lovers.

Once we'd been out there a few months I knew what I wanted. Sam Speerstra was the man to turn my ideas to reality, and impart his own artistic eye and creativity. Speerstra had wandered into Mnasidika long ago, looking for work. He wasn't interested in selling jeans, mind you—he wanted to build something. It turned out he was one of those entrepreneurial spirits and quite an artist, and more.

Sam built a lovely deck at my house in Stinson, and put a skylight in the loft bedroom that could be opened when desired. We used to go to a sauna across from the store all the time, so now we had him build our own private sauna under the bedroom—not too difficult because the cottage was cozied into a hillside slope. Our sauna was accessible by a trap door cut through the bedroom floor, and covered by a small burgundy Persian rug.

A bench was built into one wall of the cabin, creating a window seat where the huge bay windows looked out over the canyon and the sea. Stained-glass accents accompanied the clear glass and allowed the light to dance colors, the varying angle of the sun throughout the day drawing undulating patterns on the walls and floor. It was truly a cozy hippie cottage. Very few people were invited to visit. Contrasted to the Hippie Zoo that Haight-Ashbury was becoming, the little bungalow above Stinson Beach, up a canyon known as Coon Hollow, remained an exclusive and serene retreat.

A gay guy named Brian Hale lived in his own hideaway behind ours, and he happened to be very into gardening. I was talking with him one day and noticed a plant with beautiful burgundy and purple flowers. I inquired as to what it was and he told me it was a Fuchsia. I bought one from him, as its rich vivid colors reminded me of Janis and the clothes she wore. When Janis came over later that day, she squealed with delight. She already knew what it was and we set about planting it near the entrance to the driveway. I can't say either of us had much of a green thumb, but we were certainly enthusiastic. That little plant looked beautiful for about two days, then half of it just flopped down and died while the rest limped along. Brian kept encouraging me to water it a bit, but not too much, and it would come back. That poor plant struggled month after month, a couple of flowers dangling precariously off sickly limbs. Every time I entered the driveway I felt so bad about that little plant. Yet there was something courageous about the way it continued to defy the odds that gradually endeared it to me.

*

I first met Kimmie in 1965, when I was looking at an apartment for rent in Haight-Ashbury.

"What," I said turning to the landlord, "was that?" as Kim bounded past me in the stairwell, her blondish hair shaggy and unkept, neither feminine nor masculine, yet decidedly both. I was instantly intrigued.

"Oh, she's friends with the person in the room across the way."

After I signed the lease and moved in, I saw Kim a few times in the first weeks. She stopped and stared at me when I said hello as she passed by.

"What are you looking at?" she demanded.
"You."
"Well?"
"Well, what?"
"Well, hello yourself."
I was in love.

By 1966, the store was doing well and Kim was badgering me to take a vacation. We spun a globe at the house in Stinson Beach and decided that wherever my finger landed, that's where we would go. It ended up landing someplace like Madagascar, so we spun it again and my finger landed on the Yucatan peninsula, the southernmost state of Mexico. We packed up, eager to get out of the chilly San Francisco winter, and in February we flew into Merida.

We rented a convertible and struck out with the map Kim had picked up. Unbeknownst to us, it was obsolete. Our goal was to head to the other side of the peninsula, drop off the rent-a-car, and take the ferry over to Cozumel.

Kim was driving and I was reading off the directions from the map. We headed out on what we would consider in the U.S. as a quiet country-side road. Mostly dirt, partially asphalt, certainly no Pan-American highway. Suddenly, through the jungle along the side of the road, I saw a stone building of some sort. I screamed, "What is that?" immediately followed by, "Stop the car!" Kim slammed on the brakes.

Kim, always involved herself with the lore of a place, brightened and squealed, "Oh my God! That's Chichen Itza!"

"What?"

"It's Chichen Itza. It's got to be." Excitedly she continued, "It's a Mayan civilization that disappeared. The ruins are supposed to be down here somewhere. That's got to be it!" She was wide-eyed with excitement as she threw the car in park and shut off the engine. "Well, c'mon let's go check it out, Peg!"

Kimmie leapt out of the driver's seat and started tromping through the dense carpet of vines, ferns, and flora of all sorts, never dreaming or thinking about what else might be in there. Like snakes, Anafuckingcondas and big ol nasty biting insects, just to name a few. I mean it was a jungle and here we were traipsing through it like, "Tra, la, la."

We got to the base of the stone edifice and didn't even think twice about scurrying up. The stones were set like steps leading up to a pyramid. The structure was about ninety-feet tall, with tangled vines, roots and tropical vegetation growing out of it. The top was flat and there was a square building up there. On the front of that building there was a seat that had a face—it looked like a dragon crossed with a jaguar whose face had fat cheeks and bulging eyes reminiscent of a human. It was on all fours, but the legs weren't distinct and the back was where the royalty must have sat. I sat on it and from that position I could see the top of the trees. I remember feeling a surge, perhaps like what I imagine a person in the position of power or royalty would feel sitting up there getting their feathers fluffed. That seat hummed with a pulsing of power and importance. We spent much of the day laughing and hooting and playing around on that thing and even ended up having sex up there.

Since we weren't sure how much farther we had to go before the sun set, we made our way back down the pyramid, threaded through the knot-work of root, leaves and vines back to the car.

Driving cautiously to avoid the presence of potholes, rocks and tree limbs, seeing scenery that varied little, we lazily cruised by miles and miles of tangled green, lush and thick. An occasional parrot, lots of Tarzan and Jane vines. Finally, the flora began to change. There was still plenty of lush greenery, but the colors had muted and even the sounds were different. According to Kim we had now entered the Quintana Roo petrified forest. We'd never seen anything like it. Trees had outlived their lifespan but didn't disintegrate. They just stood there for moments, that turned into years, which turned into decades, and on and on until they turned to stone. We were ooohing and aaahing before we even got out of the car. We touched trees, trunks and branches. Tapping them, rubbing them, fooling with them to see if they really were petrified. They felt cool and hard, like stone in the shady parts, and hot in the areas exposed to the sunlight. The colors of the broken-off pieces were amazing. The bark and concentric circles were visible.

We smoked a joint and made silly puns about being stoned with the stone trees. We thought, while uncontrollably laughing, that perhaps if we smoked enough pot we'd get "petrified" as a new level of "stoned." As we began to descend from our momentary euphoria, we noticed the time was getting on, so we returned to the car and continued. Navigating to avoid the increasing deterioration of the road had slowed our progress down to a rhythm of slow, "uh oh," and go. We were talking and wondering about our recent discoveries, taking in the scents and sensations of the warm tropical air damp, earthy and fragrant. Suddenly there was a burst of movement and the sound of voices from the sides of the road. Out of the hills rushed a group of bandits, thrusting guns with bayonets at us. They surrounded the car, yelling and screaming in a language that didn't resemble the Spanish we were familiar with. Once we had come to a stop, we could see how rusty their bayonets were, and that they were young—very young.

We were looking at each other, and then at them and that's when Kimmie said, "Show 'em your tits Peg. Show 'em your tits and say, 'Esta bien!'"

"No! No! Then we're going to get raped Kimmie, no!"

She looked at me intently and said, "That's all we've got, Peggy."

And she was right. I couldn't argue her logic. We had nothing—not a thing but an obsolete map, our suitcases, and a whole lot of jungle. We had to do something. I was twenty-six years old and my boobs were rocket launchers in perfect form. And these were, basically, adolescents who likely could be distracted just long enough for us to escape. I took a deep breath, rose up from the passenger seat, pulled the top of my dress down, and out they bounced in all their perky triple-D glory. I yelled, "Esta bien! Esta bien!"

Those young bandits were stunned. All of them. Each one of the zit-faced, peach-fuzzed boys just stared, lowered their guns, and gaped, jaws open. Like they had never seen anything like these before. (Maybe, probably, they hadn't, except in a magazine.)

Out of the side of my mouth, I said, "Put it in gear, put it in gear." Kim did and slowly we began rolling. We could see them still gawking, as we drove far enough away for Kim to slam down the accelerator and put as much jungle road as she could between us and them.

We finally arrived at the ferry location, a guy looked at us and said "Ferry? That left a couple of days ago."

"What?!"

"Yeah, it doesn't run every day. Where'd you get your information?"

Kimmie pulled out the itinerary and showed it to him.

"Nah, that's not any good anymore. That hasn't been in effect for years. It never left every day anyway."

So, we missed the ferry to Cozumel. We were going to turn in the rental car, but when we realized that we missed the ferry and we were not going to Cozumel, we were faced with a dilemma. The problem was, the only way back was the way we came . . . and frankly I was mortified. I thought eh, the tits got us out of it coming in, but I doubted it would work on the way out.

We had no choice. We couldn't stay there forever. We had to go back. We asked the guy if there were rooms to rent anywhere nearby. He pointed to one of the palapas and started pulling out a couple of hammocks surrounded by mosquito netting. Faced with driving in the dark through the jungle or hitting the road at first light, we opted to stay. The jungle was not a quiet place at night, and the palapa had no real walls. Just when we'd start to drift off, something would jump, scurry or screech and we'd jerk awake. Finally, when dawn arrived, and with much trepidation, we set out on our way back to Merida.

We were on pins and needles the entire way. Every little movement in our peripheral vision was a potential threat. It was exhausting and we certainly did not want to stop for anything. We were so grateful when we finally got back to Merida. Usually the way back from somewhere new seems to take less time because of the familiarity. The return trip that day seemed to take for . . . ever.

There, we began asking around Merida where we might charter a plane. It sounds like a big deal, but it really wasn't. We found a couple of pilots with a Piper Comanche who agreed to fly us to Cozumel.

Four of us in this little Piper Comanche: two of us, and two of them. Once we'd taken off, it started to feel like some aeronautical double date we hadn't agreed to. We flew back over the Quintana Roo jungle, in the air, and the pilot decided he wanted to feel me up. It started with an attempt by him to grab my tits, his buddy saw that and started grabbing Kimmie. Then it turned into full-on wrestling with both of us while we were up in the sky. The plane was pitching and jerking. We were yelling and screaming. They were grabbing and groping—Jeezuz! Once again we were freaked out. I thought for sure we were going to crash, but finally, realizing they couldn't navigate and have their way with us at the same time, they gave up as we neared Cozumel. They had the nerve to want to take pictures with us when we landed. We were so undone by this time and the absurdity of the request seemed so bizarre, we just conceded and had our picture taken with them.

Cozumel in the 1960s was not the lush overbuilt resort it is today. There were no cars, only mopeds. I hated the mopeds zinging along with their high-pitched whine, and it was horribly dusty. There was nothing I found enchanting.

I was carrying a lot of cash because I thought we might have trouble with traveler's checks in certain places. My briefcase was full of $100 bills, fifties and some twenties: $16,000 in total.

From the airstrip, we got in a cab and headed into the heart of Cozumel, and once we began exploring the town, we noticed a couple of characters began to follow us. Every time we'd look up, they were there. At the Mercado, they were there. At the Carneceria, they were there. They were everywhere. Kim was really freakin' me out. "There they are again." And there they would be. I started thinking that, they had figured it out because I was always carrying a briefcase. A young American woman running around in broad daylight, in a foreign country, in the tropics with a briefcase attached to her arm. It screamed *valuable*. But I was afraid to leave it anywhere.

We finally ditched the stalkers, but by then we were afraid to go anywhere and it was no fun staying. We decided to take a plane out; we didn't know where to, nor did we care. We just wanted to get off the island. While we were busy scaring ourselves, I heard a plane coming in. We looked at each other. I jumped up and said, "C'mon, let's go!"

"But it's landing," Kim countered, disappointed.

"Yeah, it's landing. But it's gotta take off again."

"Ok, Peg. Let's go!"

We bolted out of our room and jumped into a cab, screaming at the poor driver, "Aeropuerto. Airport!" and he gunned it. Once we arrived at the airport, we ran across the tarmac to the plane—no security procedures back then. We didn't even bother to ask where it was going. We were going to take that plane no matter where it went. We ended up not in another foreign country—but flew straight to LA.

And when we landed, I still had the money.

Carrying too much cash—either on my person, or in the bank accounts for Mnasidika—was something I never quite overcame in the days when my stores were making good money. My accountant Michael constantly instructed me to buy another big-ticket item. I had already bought myself a Shelby Mustang, and the house, so since I was trying to keep Kimmie happy (an impossible task, I'd learn too late), I decided to buy her a car. On the way into town one day, I asked her to pull into the Porsche dealership.

"Why?" she asked.

"I wanna look at what they've got."

Pulling onto the lot in my new Mustang, wearing a low-cut mini dress, caught the attention of the salesmen. Kimmie cruised between the cars like a predator hunting while I spoke to the salesmen. I heard a squeal and saw Kimmie circling a Porsche 911 in a bright "Vallarta Mexico" blue. We jumped in and took it for a test ride. Kim worked the little sports car, throwing it into curves, zipping in and out of traffic, and slamming the pedal down in excess of 100 miles per hour as we threaded our way through the city and rocketed along the highway. Exhilarated, we whipped back onto the lot and brought the Porsche to a halt. Kim was yammering away in a nearly breathless staccato, "Didya feel? The gears. One, two. Brrrram, brrrram. Thureeee, Four. It's got eyes on is tire feet." I exited the passenger seat as the salesman extinguished his cigarette in the ashcan just outside the entrance to the showroom, grinning nervously as I approached him.

"Well, what does your friend think?"

"She thinks it has eyes on its tire feet," I said just to catch his reaction.

"Eyes on its um, well yes that's one way to explain the engineering phenomena that is a Porsche."

"I'll take it," I said flashing a big smile.

"For you?"

"No, for us."

"Oh, I see. Yes, well." He held the door open for me. "Have a seat there at my desk and I will fill out the paperwork."

I wrote a check for the down payment and came back out to the car grinning.

"Do you like it?" I asked Kim.

"It's great. Did you feel how she handled?"

"Yeah, it was really good." I paused then said, "It's yours."

Kim's head spun around, speechless. "Really?"

"Yeah, really."

"Yippeee!" she squealed and re-started the car, put it in gear and flew back out onto the street and disappeared.

After about ten minutes I realized she wasn't coming back, so I hopped into the Shelby and headed into work.

Michael was impressed when I told him I had just bought a Porsche. However, he became livid when I told him I had bought it for Kim. I figured he was too uptight to understand love. I didn't understand that nothing, not a car or anything else, could make *or keep* Kim happy.

✳

One day, while Sam Speerstra was installing a Dutch door at Mnasidika, he set the hammer down and called over to me.

"Peggy, you like to make money," in a way that was equal parts statement and question.

"Uh huh, I do."

"Well, I have the all-time way to do it."

"I'm listening."

"Religion"

"Religion?"

"Yeah, a new religion. We should bring Krishna to the Western hemisphere."

"Krishna . . . *we*?"

"Yeah . . . GOD," he finished.

"God no less?"

I thought it was fictitious, you know, because I'd never heard of it before. He continued, "Think about it. The Catholic Church has all the wealth in the world and the reason they do is because they're pedaling religion. We can bring Krishna to the Western Hemisphere."

I still didn't get it, so I said, "We're going to make up a God?"

"No, not exactly. We're going to import one."

"Ah, count me out on this one. No sir. Huh uh."

I was being hit up for all kinds of things at that time: finance bands, get Jimi Hendrix a job, buy Jerry Garcia an amp, the list went on. Sensing my disinterest, and not being one to take "no" for an answer, Sam said, "I'm gonna do this and I'd like for you to do it with me, but if you won't, I'm gonna do it anyway."

I said, "Ok. Best of luck."

He didn't bat an eye. The next thing he said was, "Can I borrow fifteen hundred dollars?"

I thought there it is there, ya know? He hit me up. I mean there it was, out on the table. I said, "For what?"

"I want to build a temple, a Hare Krishna temple."

We went back and forth a little bit and I agreed to loan it to him and he could work it off doing carpentry at the store and my house. I would have hired him anyway, so it worked out for both of us. This guy was no mild-mannered nail slammer. He was an artist, a true finish carpenter. He rented an old building at the base of Kezar Stadium on Stanyan and Waller and it was somethin' to behold once he had his way with the building. At his studio they soaked plywood and bent it and lacquered the veneer, which enabled them to duplicate those Taj Mahal-looking steeples, transforming Victorian into East Indian. They then painted it bright gold and deep royal purple. You couldn't miss it.

The little Krishna devotee group continued to grow as they hammered and chanted and chanted and painted. Amazingly these kids were coming forth with what little they had to help make it happen. Most of them emptied their pockets, gave up their jeans, put on a diaper-looking thing and slammed finger cymbals together chanting, "Krishna, Krishna, Hare Krishna." As this was going on, I was thinking, "My God, he's pulling this off." And then he came to me and asked for another fifteen hundred dollars. He said he wanted to bring the Swami Bhaktivedanta over. I said, "Really, and why would you do that?" I wasn't quite sure what a Swami plus five syllables was, but I assumed it was another dude who wore more important diapers.

He explained, "It's because he sits at the head of the Krishna consciousness movement in India and we need him here. We want to introduce the Western Hemisphere to the Swami." I could see that he was doing what he said. In the process, much to my surprise, he had actually become a devotee of the Swami and the principals offered in this strange, new faith.

I, and many of the regulars in The Haight, were stunned by

the increasing numbers of kids who were going into the temple Sam built. The girls would cook in their long skirts and their Krishna-looking garb, serving rice and collard greens. This was all kind of bizarre stuff to me, but just based on what he had said and that he'd already built the temple, he agreed to do the work on my house in Stinson Beach for this second round of fifteen hundred dollars. He said they were going to build a float and parade his Holiness, the Swami, down Market Street.

They built a float that resembled something between a rickshaw and a two-wheeled ox cart. It had a throne type area for the Swami to sit on, big wooden wheels, and two wooden arms out front where several Krishna devotees could grab on, lift, and pull it through the streets.

The big day came, the Swami arrived and they loaded him onto the throne and took off down Market Street. They pulled him up Market to Divisadero, then onto Divisadero, and then onto Haight Street. They turned left on Haight and here they came in full regalia. These guys had on diaper looking attire, their heads were shaved back into the traditional ponytail. The girls were in gold lame sashes, long skirts and barefooted with bells and cymbals—a true never-before-seen spectacle. They're doing it.

This was like a Mardi Gras parade without any floats except the Swami's and they're coming down Haight Street, clanging their cymbals and chanting, "Hare, Hare . . . Hare Krishna, Krishna Krishna. Hare Hare." This stuff was made in hippie heaven. People were gathered on both sides of the street and the Swami's pulled right in front of the store. Now was I proud or what? Oh mercy! They pulled him down Haight Street across Stanyan to the Park, then pulled him through Golden Gate Park. By the time they got to the two-lane road known as Highway 1 the float had had enough. They got the Swami out onto the Highway and the wheel rolled off the float and dumped him. Plop! His Holiness the Swami Bhaktivedanta was dumped right onto the Great Coast Highway.

At this point the Krishnas went nuts because His Holiness, their surrogate God, was lying in the middle of PCH and of course they're tying up traffic which attracted the attention of the cops. Sam was horrified because the Swami, his revered spiritual master, has just endured a very earthly inconvenience . . . literally. I mean this is

Bhaktivedanta. It was maybe an hour or so since the Swami and the float had gone by when I got a call from Sam at the store. He was calmly hysterical. He said, "Peggy I really need your help."

I thought, "Hey I gave. I did my part, I footed the bill to get him over here and paid for the float!" But I didn't say anything and let him continue because I could tell he was upset.

He said, "The wheel fell off the float, the Swami fell off on PCH, and the cops are here. Everybody's mad. I need you to come out and get the Swami."

"And do what with him?"

"Take him to . . ." (and he gave me the name of the hotel). It was a small upscale hotel, some place in downtown San Francisco. I think it was called the Prince Albert or King Albert. He's begging now, "Please Peggy, please come get the Swami and take him down and put him in the hotel."

"Alright, I'm gonna do this, but I'm not up for any police."

"No Peg. No. We'll have His Holiness ready for you to pick up." So he told me where they were and I went. And, oh my God—there was such chaos there because now the diaper-clad people have all culminated in the same place. These are San Francisco police—they pride themselves with having seen just about everything but they had never seen anything like this. This was the first time the Swami had been in San Francisco—way before the Hare Krishnas began hanging out in airports—and no one was familiar with any of this.

When I arrived, tight hip-hugger Levi's and tiny low-cut velvet top, Sam saw me instantly and made his way over with the Swami. I hadn't really considered what a culture shock I might be to him. Sam reverently put him in my Mustang and off we went. As I've alluded, I had over-sized breasts—gay guys had informed me they were a force to be reckoned with. Therefore, I was major cleavage all the time. So there I was, in the driver's seat, with a low-cut velvet top, my large, soft, round breasts about ready to spill out of my top—less than a foot from his eyes when he got in the car.

The Swami's nose was practically into the side of my right tit. He snapped his head away toward the windshield as we began to head downtown, and then he went deep into a trance. I don't know how he did it, because he didn't do anything. He didn't chant, he didn't do anything that I could see. He just looked straight ahead and suddenly he's not there, and I mean . . . not there. Like I honestly think I might've been able to hit him in the head without him even flinching.

Halfway to the hotel, I realized this man was completely unresponsive. When I got him to the hotel I couldn't get him out of the car. I couldn't get him to respond at all. Maybe he bumped his head when he plopped onto highway? All I knew was he seemed plenty ambulatory with Sam, and now he was frozen into the passenger seat of my Mustang. I don't even think he blinked. I was exasperated by then. I went into the hotel lobby and began frantically calling, trying to track down Sam. I finally got a hold of him and was emphatically saying, "Sam, I am done with this man!"

He got offended and snapped, "He's not a man."

"He *is* a man, and he's in some kind of a trance and I need you to come down here and get this *man* out of my *car*."

Sam didn't like that I kept calling the Swami a man, because that put him on an earthly plane.

"What am I supposed to call him? Come on, Sam. Let's get serious here. This is just a guy. He shits, he pisses; he's a guy. You can call him whatever you want. He may be extremely advanced, or enlightened, or whatever, but he's still a man and his man-ass is affixed to my passenger seat."

Sam finally arrived and proceeded to get the Swami out of the car and into the hotel. I don't know how he did it. Maybe he had some sort of magic words to un-trance him. Shortly thereafter the Swami returned to India and I never saw him again. Sometimes I wonder if it was my tits. I think it was, I really do. I did see him look over at 'em. Then I saw him look straight ahead . . . and . . . he . . . just . . . checked . . . out.

✻

I found out Kimmie had suspicions about Janis and me when we were driving back from Mnasidika one day.

"Are you sleeping with Janis?"

For the life of me I don't know why I said, "Yes."

Kim didn't say a word, just looked ahead and for a minute I thought it wasn't going to be any big deal. By this point in our relationship it had become apparent that Kimmie was enjoying my money *and* chasing after other women, so I assumed our "no other women" rule was already history. It seemed that was just the direction that things were going. We *were* part of a "sexual revolution" after all.

I was just settling into thinking all was well, when suddenly I saw a shadow of movement and felt a crashing pain as something hit my eye. I yelped but Kimmie kept hitting me. The first impact was a Coke bottle, which cut me, and I couldn't see from all the blood. The next few moments were filled with Kim cursing me, and me trying to defend myself and blocking further blows to my head and face, meanwhile still keeping the car on the road. Finally, I stopped the car at a park, I got out to use the restroom and wipe the blood off to see how bad things were. a couple stopped me and asked if I was alright. Kim began screaming at them, and was out of the car pacing and cursing. Embarrassed and afraid, I plead with her to take me to the hospital and got into the passenger seat and shut the door. Enroute, she peppered me with more punches and abuse. By the time we arrived at the emergency room, she had exhausted most of her anger and had become civil. The hospital people were not amused, as I wouldn't tell them any details about the person who had done this to me. It was a humiliating experience.

The ride home was without incident. Instead of going into the bedroom I just curled up on the couch, wrapped a blanket around myself and fell asleep.

The next time I saw Janis I couldn't tell her why Kim had beaten me. I just couldn't. She was concerned, as my injuries still looked pretty bad, but it wasn't the first time she had seen me hurting like this.

"Fuck Kim, I don't want to love her anymore. Why can't I just not love her? Why?"

"I don't know, Honey."

"This is crazy! How could I let her do this to me? Here I am, succeeding at business, I can pretty much do anything I want and yet . . . and yet . . ." I broke down sobbing again.

"Love just doesn't," she paused reflectively, "love just doesn't seem to make sense sometimes. I mean look at all the love songs, man. I mean how many are happy? Really? How many are happy?"

"Well, love does fucking hurt, that's for sure. I'm tired of hurting behind love. I'm so mother fucking tired of hurting because I'm loving."

"Wellll," she said drawing out the word and sighing. "I do have a cure for the pain."

"You do?" I brightened, then frowned when it occurred to me she was probably talking about heroin again.

"It works, Peggy, it really does. C'mon, you know I'm the Queen of Unrequited Love!" She cackled at that, then she grew serious again. "Let me do this for ya, honey."

"Alright. Yeah, fuck it. Take away my pain. Please. Make it go away."

Over time, it had become clear that Janis used heroin regularly, often with Sam. I didn't like it, and had said so on many occasions. Since my own drug use up to this point included only acid and pot, both of which I liked and used often, *but* I didn't seem to physically need either on a daily basis. At the time I didn't understand chemical and physical addiction and how it created for her the need to keep shooting dope to avoid withdrawal. This may sound naïve of me now, considering how rampant all drug use was in The Haight, but just as I was able to avoid indulging in alcohol for personal reasons, so, too, I suppose I was able to wall off my exposure to the harsher facts of drug addiction that was surely laying claim to many in my circle of friends. Yes, I knew people were occasionally overdosing, requiring an emergency trip to the hospital, and possibly a stint in jail. I knew that addicts sometimes died. None of those facts, however, were on my radar at that moment when Janis had offered to get me high that first time. I was thinking only of the allure of being put out of my emotional agony.

That evening I was initiated into the rather complex ritual involved in the injection of heroin, otherwise known as mainlining. First there were all the instruments involved. Janis's "kit" included a Sucrets throat lozenge tin wrapped inside a purple velvet "tie." Within this container was a spoon with its handle bent backwards in such a way as to keep it from tipping over when set down upon a table and also for it to fit snugly within the tin. There were a couple of cotton balls and the "works," which consisted of a glass syringe, a large fake purple grape which was hollow, and a detachable screw-on needle. Once assembled, she lay the "works" down next to the tin. The heroin was contained inside an un-inflated rubber party balloon. She worked open the knot tied at the neck of the balloon and sprinkled the requisite amount of dope into the spoon. The grape was attached to the opposite end of the syringe from the needle. By squeezing the grape before putting the sharp end of the needle in the glass of water, then releasing it, the suction would draw the liquid up into the glass tube of the syringe. Then she pressed the grape again to squirt water into the spoon for "cooking." Then she struck the engraved Zippo lighter and passed the flame beneath the spoon a few times until the concoction bubbled. She set the spoon down and extinguished the lighter by flipping its lid down and set it aside.

Janis pinched off a tiny piece of the cotton ball, rolled it between her fingers until it was a little bit larger than a pinhead and dropped it into the brownish liquid. This cotton served as a filter, as she guided the sharp point of the needle right up next to it and began to draw the heroin mixture up towards the silly little grape. She then tied my arm off about mid-bicep with the purple tie-dyed velvet scarf and began rubbing my veins, then slapping them with two fingers to make them visible and accessible. Janis's demeanor was ultra-focused during each phase of the ritual, a professional in a dark art.

Once I had given into the idea of doing the dope, the process now took on the feeling of communion. As if I was about to experience some form of Sacrament. Having grown up Catholic, ritual was a familiar thing.

"This is only gonna sting for a second. Keep your arm still for me, Baby," she advised.

I nodded and stared at the crook of my arm where she had the needle poised to enter my vein. Part of me wanted to look away, and when I got woozy, I closed my eyes.

"Ok, here we go," Janis half grunted. "Umm, hmmm."

"Ouch," I gasped, but remembered to keep my arm still.

I looked back down at my arm and became fascinated as the blood began to swirl from my vein into the syringe.

Janis grinned, licked her lips, looked me in the eye and said,

"Say goodbye to your pain."

"Goodbye."

She pushed the grape and released the elixir into my veins. Immediately, she undid the tie and withdrew the needle in what seemed like one motion. Within seconds I fell back on the bed and experienced my breath coming slow and easy. I felt a very subdued smile emerge on my face.

"Pain?" Janis asked.

"None," I murmured.

As Janis busied herself with cooking up her own hit, I reveled in my euphoria. For about three minutes. Then, suddenly, I exclaimed as I sat up, "Uh oh. Janis. Janis! I'm gonna be sick."

"Here ya go," she said, shoving a small trash can in front of me. "Puke in this."

"Oh fuck-yaaaaaaak." I began to heave into the can. I wiped my mouth with the back of my hand and asked, "Does this always happen?"

"Not everyone gets sick their first time. But most do."

I grunted as I heaved again. Then I heard myself saying, "But somehow it's not so bad. I kinda don't mind."

Usually I'd do almost anything to avoid throwing up.

"Yeah, not so bad, right?" Janis said as she shot her hit.

I felt like I was in and out of a dream. I was vaguely aware of the candles burning, and their gentle glow seemed to match the warmth and softness I felt from the dope. I didn't care about the nausea. I didn't really care about much at all. All heartache had been erased just like she said. Rather convenient, I thought. One could go from destroyed to detached in a matter of minutes. I finally understood the "why" that compelled her to indulge. I was yet to discover the "why not."

I couldn't understand Janis's affinity for heroin until this night, when I felt so ripped apart inside and desperate to ease the raw wounded feeling. At that moment, it seemed that my friend was offering me, with tenderness and kindness, the solution I needed, one she herself had been employing to ease her own pain and maybe some fears, too. She knew the drug that would cure my heartache. The drug that would bond us in yet another way. It worked. Too— Damn—Well.

For me, the heroin was not only an escape from Kimmie's abuse, but also a way to get closer to Sam, and ultimately it drew Janis and me closer, too. Over the years, I have faced wrath for allegedly being the catalyst for Janis's heroin addiction. The truth was, she introduced me to it.

This is not easy to say, since heroin ultimately leads to such pain and loss of control, but we did it because we enjoyed it. It was fun. It made us feel hip, along with soothing all the pain of life. Gone was my torn heart for Kimmie and gone, too, it seemed, were some of Janis's deeper fears. It was also a way to "come down" from the incredible adrenaline surge and palpable energy slam that hit artists performing in front of thousands of fans.

And then there was the sheer sensual, sexual thrill of doing heroin with a lover. This is a difficult thing to describe to those who have never done it. But it is very phallic. In the beginning, Janis used to "fix" me, or inject me, because I did not know how to hit my own vein. The bond formed by this type of intimacy is unique in its depth and reach.

As she went through the ritual of preparing the heroin, I would get worked up and turned on in anticipation. Once the needle penetrated me, a spasm of warmth would spread from my arm throughout my body, leaving me nearly unconscious in its wake. She would follow suit, melting into her own rush.

∗

Shooting heroin together became part of our friendship, incorporated just the way we'd done with sex. Meanwhile, life tumbled on, for both of us. Once, Janis and I were both in Hollywood, her for music, me for clothing. What I witnessed in Janis when she started her rise to fame was that it took her awhile to realize just how famous she'd become. Long past the time that she had established her importance in the rock world, she was still worrying about whether or not Big Brother was going to fire her.

She'd get upset and say, "They're gonna fire me." And I'd say, "They're not!" And she'd say, "Yes. They ARE!" And I'd say, "No. They're. NOT. They can't." And she'd say, "I, I know what you're tryin' to say . . ." And I said, "I'm tellin' you, I'm on the outside looking in and they cannot be that crazy. It's not *their* names being screamed out here, it's yours and it's past firing time." And it was. But she could not seem to get it that she was making it in the music world. The odds of that weren't in her favor. How could she understand that in less than five years, she'd gone from being voted "Ugliest Man on Campus" and all the other hateful things people had said to her, and about her, back home, to having people screaming her name with want and desire? It took her a long time to reconcile that. Other than her friends from Threadgill's Bar back in Austin, Texas, where she had once played acoustic guitar, and sang folk and blues songs, the majority of folks she had been in school with in Texas hadn't been supportive of her being herself. The more she was herself in the landscape of her childhood home, the more she was trashed and put down. And she still carried that with her, even as she was appearing on the covers of magazines and selling out concert venues.

There is a famous photograph of Janis, naked, with beads barely covering her breasts. When I look at that picture I see those breasts, and that body, as perfect.

One time, I told her how pretty she was. She looked at me, her eyes tearing up and told me that nobody had ever said that to her before. I could not imagine why. Perhaps it was because I was falling in love with her that I always saw Janis as so beautiful. I think she was developing an affection for me, too. When I would enter a room, her face would light up. So much so, that people commented on it. How could I not love somebody who appeared to like me so much?

The more she was herself in Haight-Ashbury and within the hippie community, the more she was loved.

And in 1969, at Woodstock, everybody saw her the way I did—as talented, as beautiful. A half-million strong, these were Janis's people and I was so happy to have shared the moment with her. Yet, I almost did not make it to Woodstock.

"You gotta come," Janis told me on the phone.

"I can't. I'm working," I replied.

"You can stop working," she said. "Please come."

"Janis, I've seen it on the news. I can't get through all those people." The New York State Thruway was backed up, bogged down, and impossible to navigate. Then I blurted out what I thought would be a joke. "The only way I'd go is if I were airlifted," I said.

There was silence. Just enough silence to make me wonder if Janis got the joke. Then she said, "Ok. I'll airlift you in."

"Yeah, right," I said, with the proper amount of sarcasm in my voice.

"No, I have a helicopter. All you have to do is make it to Howard Johnson's, and I'll take it from there."

I have never been religious, but somehow, I felt, somebody wants me to make it to Woodstock. So, I thought, I'd have to try. On the plane from San Francisco to New York, I did not meet God, but I did travel with Country Joe McDonald, also headed to Woodstock, where he would make history with his anti-Vietnam War chant. We landed and parted company, and I rented a Ford Fairlane from Hertz. It was the last rental car available in New York City, they told me.

Logic says I should not have made it to that Howard Johnson's.

Off I drove, but I immediately got bogged down in the worst traffic jam I had ever seen. But, Janis wanted me at Woodstock, and I was determined to get there. I drove off the shoulder into a gully, then into a ditch, then I drove along the ditch for a while, and back up on the shoulder and onto the turnpike. I'd make it a bit farther, then repeat my dance from road to gully to ditch, never knowing if I was going to get bogged down. I drove around broken-down cars, cars that were out of gas, and one woman who was having a baby. It was like the biblical Exodus in vision and scope. Hours later, in the distance, I saw the Promised Land—a blue neon sign that said "Howard Johnson's."

Once there, I knocked on Janis's door. I heard voices and suddenly the door opened and Vince Mitchell, looking disheveled and perplexed, pushed past me. Janis handed him his shoes and hurriedly thanked him for a good time, as she welcomed me, all in what seemed like one breath.

Janis's manager insisted that she left early the next day to the heliport, to setup and soundcheck with the other musicians. She promised to send a chopper for me. After a few hours she called and said, "Go outside, there should be a car for you." At this point the Howard Johnson's was a hub of insanity. Most of the bands and their employees were staying there, waiting for their rides into the festival.

I RAN INTO SOME TROUBLE

Peggy's description: "I wish I could tell you what I was whispering!"
Woodstock, 1969

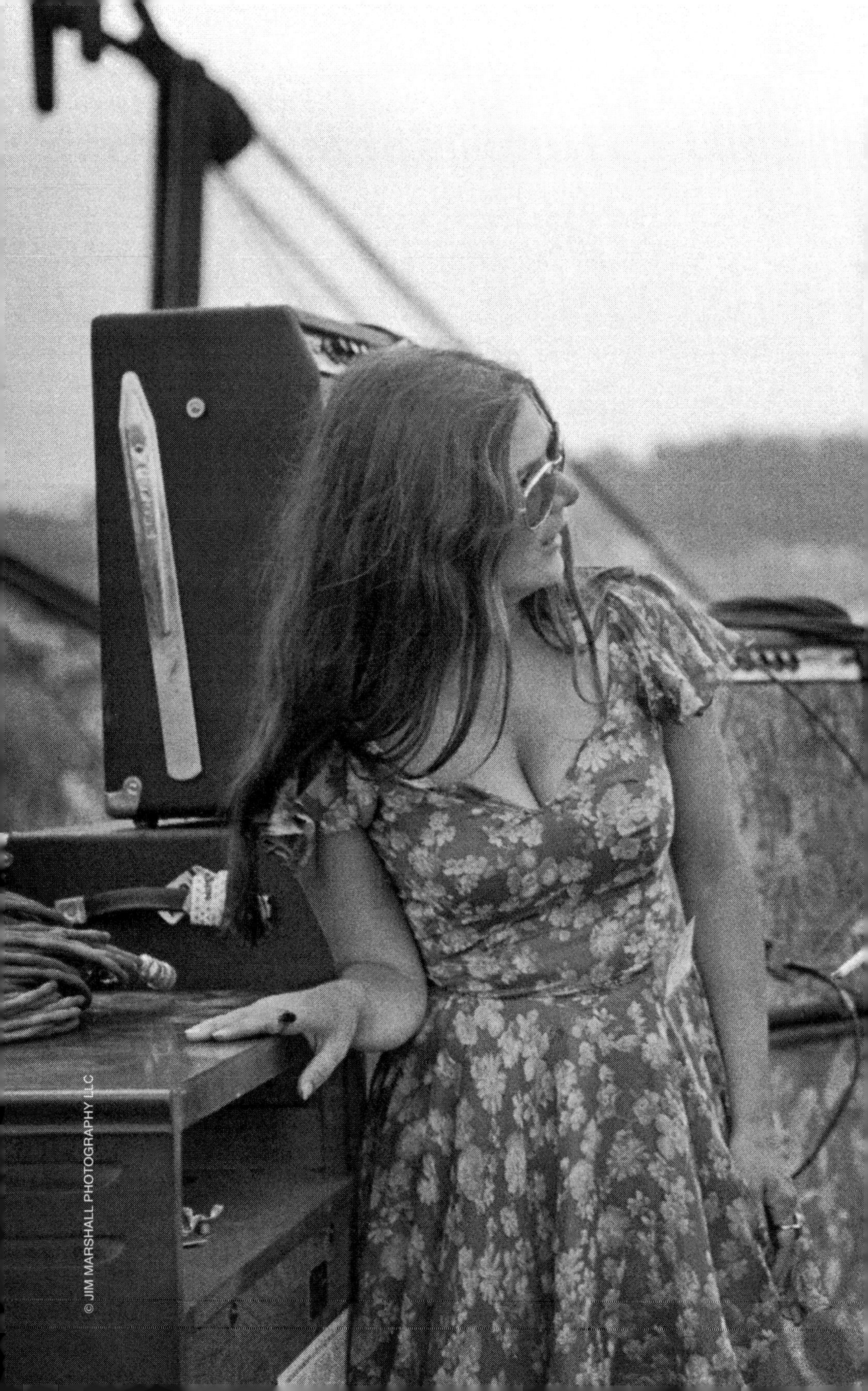

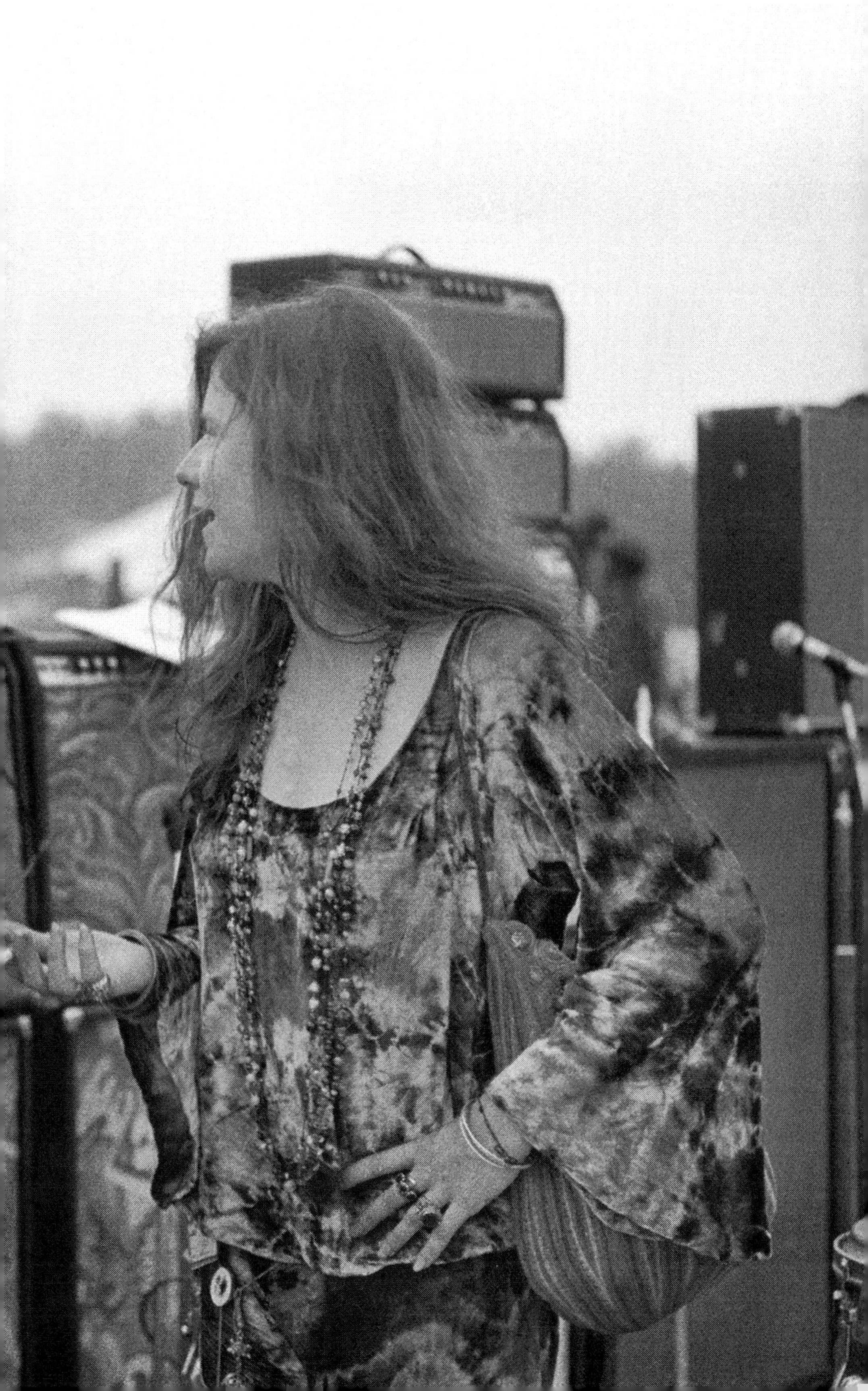

I made my way downstairs and out to the curb. And, as if on cue, a limousine was there for me. The driver looked me up and down a couple of times and said, "Are you Peggy?" I swear, Janis must have told the driver to look for a woman with enormous breasts (I get them from my mother's side of the family). I answered that I was Peggy. "This is your limo, Hon. Jump in."

At the heliport, the pilot walked up to me, and he, too, checked me over up and down. I was wearing a low-cut chiffon dress, so again it was likely my breasts that gave me away. "Are you Peggy?" the pilot asked.

As I was about to tell him that I was, I heard familiar voices yelling behind me to hold the helicopter. It was the Grateful Dead. All of them. And they were running toward the aircraft. At the time, the band was beginning to have a following, but they were not yet famous. At least, not as famous as Janis. The pilot halted the Dead in their tracks with one hand.

"Stop!" he said. "Unless your names are Peggy, you're not getting on this bird."

We all knew each other from the Haight, so the band members looked at me in stunned silence. I looked at them, shrugged my shoulders, and hopped onto the helicopter.

And that is how I arrived at Woodstock. Today, if you Google my name, the few photographs you'll find of me during this time is of Janis and me at Woodstock, me in that low-cut dress, and both of us grinning, delighted to see each other and happy to experience this moment of history together.

When Janis and I looked out over the vast gathering at the music festival, I noticed she seemed both nervous and at the same time reflective. We were blown away by the turnout, as most folks were, and to Janis the large crowd and outpouring of communal love signaled something. She turned to me and said, "Do you know what this means?"

I was thinking to myself, "Ehh yeah. It means money," because I was calculating all the records she would sell after her performance there, but I kept that thought to myself, and answered, "No, what?"

Janis continued, "Just think Peggy, this can't be all of us. There's got to be hundreds of thousands of others who couldn't make it here. Think what that means! There're more of us out there." She gestured toward the crowd and beyond, then broke into a big grin. I loved it when she smiled because it was generally followed by an infectious laugh. "It means, that united we could quite possibly throw a vote. We might could even put in our own president!"

I was moved by her broader scope that she was thinking, way beyond record sales. Stunned, I thought to myself, what insight she has.

We had left by the time that Jimi Hendrix played *The Star-Spangled Banner*, making his guitar sound as though bombs were bursting in air. Indeed, much of the crowd had left by then, but those remaining said what he delivered was spell-binding. After Woodstock, thousands of us might not have been sure about what we didn't want, but one thing I can say for pretty certain, at that time in our history, we were sure about what we did want. We wanted peace.

While Janis could see how our generation could effect change in the world, it took her longer to understand the changes in the way the world saw her. It wasn't just her insecurity over her beauty or the ridiculous idea that Big Brother and the Holding Company was getting ready to fire her, but she was slow to understand that with popularity and fame came more choices.

Once, we were at the Landmark Hotel in Los Angeles and she was still awake in the wee hours of the night. Of course. That was her gig. She worked at night and slept in the day. This night, she said, "I'm hungry, are you?"

"Yes!" I said.

"Call Greenblatt's," she said, referring to a famous deli in Hollywood.

"First off," I said, "you call Greenblatt's. And, secondly I don't think Greenblatt's will care because I don't think they're going to deliver anyway."

Then Janis said something that really surprised me. She said, "They deliver to the stars."

I thought, "Would ya listen to that. Janis knows she's a star."

Then, what happened next, surprised me even more because while she knows she's famous, she still thinks like a poor country girl.

Greenblatt's wasn't going to deliver at 3 in the morning, not even to a star, so I suggested instead we go down on Highland to Hughes Market, which is open all night. So, off we went in the middle of the night to the market together. But when we arrived, we went our separate ways down the aisles, shopping as if we were both still poor. It is what we were used to.

I found Janis holding two jars of grape jelly in her hand. At the time, Springfield jelly was the cheap one, and Welch's was more expensive. I stood back for a moment, amused, as she weighed the two in each hand, unable to decide which one to buy. I'm thinking, "Oh my God . . . she doesn't know . . . she really doesn't know".

"You're price comparing, aren't you?" I said, smiling.

"Yes," Janis replied. "This one's 30 cents more than this one." She held one, then the other up toward me.

I paused for a moment, wondering to myself if she was even aware of what she was doing. Didn't she know who she was? Finally, I couldn't stand it anymore. I walked up to her and placed my hand on Janis's shoulder.

"It's over," I said.

"What?" Janis replied.

"The days of you having to worry about whether you can afford the Welch's grape jelly are over," I said. "Get the Welch's! You can afford it! We can afford it." Janis stared at me, blankly. I said it again, with an emphasis on the first word. "Youuuuu . . . can . . . afford . . . it."

And, she looked at me, so innocently, and said with that wonderful grin of hers, "I can, can't I?"

"Yes, you can."

Janis put down the Springfield jelly and got the Welch's.

We couldn't find anything really good to go with it. I don't know why we didn't buy bread and peanut butter, but she bought crackers. That night we ate crackers with expensive Welch's grape jelly!

Eventually, Janis did understand her rise in popularity, and she grabbed hold of her fame, in ways that weren't always in her best interest. She could send someone out for anything she wanted, at any hour, and it would materialize. The "Diva-ness" Janis had begun to exhibit began taking a stronger hold, though it seemed she would grasp it and wield it for only brief periods of time before returning to her carefree, casual self. The first full-blown, fit-throwing incident

I remember occurred when Janis and I had gone to stay at the ultra-luxurious Chateau Marmont in Hollywood for a few days, both of us having business to attend to in Los Angeles. We ended up in one of the most elaborate suites, nearly the size of an apartment.

"What the fuck do we need all this room for? Two full room suites? We don't need to spend this kind of money," I protested.

"Well Honey it's nice, like a Presidential Suite or somethin.' And besides, we're already here."

"That's not good enough, Janis. I mean, a fucking conference room? What the hell are we gonna use it for? C'mon, let's get a different room."

"Honey, it's nice. Real nice, and we deserve it," she said.

"Did you just say we deserve it?"

When, oh when, did she decide she *deserved* something akin to a Presidential Suite, anywhere? It appeared that it was finally starting to sink into her Southern mind that she was somebody—a star—not just another hippie chick dragging her bottle and beads around The Haight, but, someone who was deserving of the most posh suite, at the Chateau.

She continued trying to convince me. "Ya, well why not? Either one of us can afford it now."

"Just because I can afford it now does not mean I *need* it now. I don't need a Presidential suite and I don't want a Presidential suite. I don't work my ass off for money to throw away on . . ."

Janis interrupted, "On a brand new Porsche for your girlfriend Kim who leaves you standing in the dust when you hand her the keys?"

Ouch! But she'd spoken the truth. After the initial gush of thanks, Kimmie treated her new Porsche like a cheap plastic toy, instead of something that represented months of my hard work. Still, I didn't like when Janis brought up Kim, even when she was right about my staying in an abusive relationship for reasons neither she nor I could understand.

"That was fucking low," I shot back. "It's not the same."

"Ok Hun, you're right, that was low, but I needed to make a point." Janis switched to her most syrupy tone. "C'mon Sugah. Let's just have a good time. We're here, right? Let's live it up." She started rustling through her things and pulled out her kit.

"You still gotta take back what you said about Kim and the Porsche."

"Alright," she said, patting the place next to her on the bed. "Come sit over here and Momma will show you how sorry she is."

I sat next to her. She tied off my arm, looked me in the eye just after the needle hit the vein. She gave me a sweet smile and said, "Sorry, Baby," as she kissed me, pushed the plunger in and untied the tie as I fell back on the bed, nearly out cold.

Janis was never stingy when it came to sharing anything, especially heroin with the people she liked. She had a high tolerance and quite an appetite for most all things debauch. The more she liked someone, the more likely she was going to give them a hit of dope that might—you never know—wash them right up to death's door. She tended to be a bit foolhardy, especially when she was good and drunk. Her estimate of how much to put into the spoon always erred on the side of a whole fucking lot of generous. There was no way to argue with her—at least I couldn't. She'd always throw me the line, "Who got you high for the first time, mother fucker?" or "You think you know more than me about shooting dope?" There was just no winning on some things with her.

At the Chateau, it seemed like we spent most of the day and night very, very loaded. Or maybe it was just me—I know I was loaded the majority of the time. Every now and then I'd come to, barely able to open my eyes, a half smile on my face and lapse back into the warm, fuzzy peace of heroin's embrace.

"Peggy! Peggy!" Janis shook me, once. "C'mon, wake up! You gotta see this."

"Whaaa . . . ?" I struggled to open my eyes and peered out of slits.

"Mutha Fuckers, fucking mutha fuckers. They're doing me. ME!" She said as she got more animated by the second.

"What the . . . ?" I mustered some semblance of alertness while trying to will my body to sit up.

"Look at this. Look. At. This. It's me, but it's not me. I mean they're doing me. They can't do me and not pay me. Fuck! Mutha fuckers! You need to call somebody. They can't do this!" She was really wound up now. She strode towards the TV again, hands on hips, spun around then gestured back towards the TV screen, where someone was performing and clearly emulating her style. I was hardly able to register what I was looking at, but forced myself to focus.

"Damn. It does look like you," I said as I leaned forward and squinted into the glare of the television.

"Yeah. You have to call somebody, Peg."

I shook my head to knock the cobwebs loose, so that I could be more coherent.

"*I* need to call somebody? Why the fuck should *I* call somebody? I can't do anything. YOU call somebody."

"I'm calling the TV station!" She picked up the phone, and dialed the front desk (as you had to in those days to access phone numbers outside of the hotel), and asked to be connected to the station. Of course the phone rang and rang since it was the middle of the night. She finally slammed down the phone.

"Fuck! Fucking mutha fuckers! Somebody's gonna hear about this!" She was off the bed, pacing and cursing, pausing to put her hands on her hips, growling "harrumph," then continuing to pace.

"Try Clive. He's in LA."

"Yeah, you're right, he is!" She riffled through her purse and found Clive Davis's phone number. Clive was her producer at Columbia records. She got back on the phone, and gave his number to the hotel operator. Then she waited, alternately glaring at the TV screen and tapping her little foot. "Fucker's not answering," she said as she slammed down the phone again.

"Janis, for God's sakes, it's like one or two in the morning."

"So fucking what? They make money off of me, they need to answer the fucking phone! I'm calling Albert." She frantically tore through her address book again for the number of her manager, Albert Grossman.

At this point I was still loaded but sobering up, what with all the swirling frenetic energy Janis was emitting. It was kinda like watching a movie. My little hippie chick badass singer friend who had so recently become known the world over, was shifting into a Diva before my very eyes.

"Aha, got it!" she said and dialed the desk again. This time she was standing up and twisting the phone cord around the opposite hand that's holding the receiver.

"Hello," she said. "This is Janis, Janis Joplin. I'd like to speak to Albert." There was a pause. "Yes, it's important." Another pause and

Janis glanced at me with a triumphant look.

"Albert, Albert it's Janis. Some fucker is playing me. ME. They're on TV right now. You have to turn on the TV right now and see them. They can't do that without paying can they? Can they? You gotta tune in. They are on . . ." she paused and listened. "Yeah. Um yeah, I guess not. Sure, sure I'll call your office tomorrow." She hung up.

"Well?"

"His wife answered and then he got on the phone."

"Yeah, I kinda figured. What did he say?"

"He said yeah I should get paid, but there was nothing he could do in the middle of the night and would check into it tomorrow."

"Anything else?"

"Yeah, he said this wasn't an emergency and to save middle of the night calls for life and death issues."

"Well, he did take your call, didn't he?"

"Yeah, he did. Didn't he?" she said with a satisfied grin.

Though I could see she was enjoying playing the Diva at times, Janis was never the kind to treat waiters, waitresses, or pretty much anyone, for that matter, like they were less than. She never, ever acted too good for her fans. She would, however, whip out her fame and put it to good use, like when she was buying some lingerie at the famed Frederick's of Hollywood and they wouldn't take her check without identification. Here again I was so loaded that I was waiting for her in the parking lot of what is now the L.A. Gay and Lesbian Community Services Center. Back then it was the Federal Building about a half block from Hollywood Boulevard and Frederick's. That day I was face down, stretched out in the back seat of a rented Ford Fairlane, hanging my head out of one of the back doors, puking. My feet stuck out the other back door. Janis came screaming back saying she needed me to come bring a check so she could pay.

"Honey, Honey ya gotta come back with me. You gotta bring a check."

"What?" I looked up at her for a second, and then pitched my head back down to heave a little more. "Why won't they take your check?"

"I forgot my ID. I think I left it in San Francisco."

"Oh God help us, you've been driving us around with no fucking license? Like we need to be any more illegal than we are! Shit, Janis! No lingerie is *that* good." I turned my head back to the curb and started heaving again.

"But it is that fucking good *and* it's from Frederick's! It's all picked out and everything. C'mon Peg! Just, let's just bring your checkbook and ID. C'mon."

"Oh God, are you fucking joking?" I heaved again, seemingly to prove my point. Then it dawned on me. It just so happened she was on the cover of *Newsweek* magazine that very week. "Janis, go up the street. There's a newsstand. Can you see it from here?"

She put her hand on one hip and craned her neck. "Yeah, yeah I see it, but so what?"

"Go buy a fucking copy of *Newsweek*. You're on the cover. Use that for picture I.D. That oughta at least get you your lingerie."

She just stared at me and then broke into a huge smile. "Peggy, that's why you're such a successful business woman!"

She took off down the sidewalk, bracelets and necklaces jangling in a velvety tie-dyed hurry to the newsstand, bought a copy of the magazine, and marched back into Frederick's.

"Will this do for picture I.D.?" she asked as she slapped it down on the counter, smug as can be. Without a blink, the salesperson flipped her check over, wrote "Newsweek cover" and the date. She got her lingerie.

Fame had its perks, there was no denying it. For the most part Janis seemed to enjoy all the best of what it had to offer. Yet, to my eye, she was never inauthentic. I never saw her be anything even close to untrue to herself. She was human, with superhuman talent. I, for one, adored her for both. I would venture to say most of her fans did, too.

To her fans, Janis was never a snob. She loved her fans in a very sweet, trusting way. When Janis was getting ready to do a concert at the Hollywood Bowl, she called and asked me to come down and hang out with her at the Landmark Hotel, just a few blocks from the Bowl. She said it was going to be a blast. By then, Janis had left Big Brother and the Holding Company, and had a new band. Why she invited Sam, her former guitar player, too, I don't know. I think maybe she'd heard that he was writing songs for Tina Turner and that maybe he could write her a new song.

Sam was also in San Francisco, and called me while I was over on Polk Street at a big store I had recently opened named "To Kingdom Come." "Janis has invited me to come to LA, and I know she asked you, too, so why don't we fly down together? When are you going?"

"I'm planning on hopping the Red Eye at 3 o'clock this morning," I answered.

"Ok. I'll grab the same flight."

We met at the airport, flew to Hollywood, and then things got kind of funny—not as in humorous. There was a strange dynamic between the three of us that never dissipated even as time went by and circumstances changed. I didn't know until much later that Sam was in love with Janis, or maybe I just didn't see it because I didn't want to see it. I still had some type of unexplainable attraction—or at least a form of lust—for him, so the three of us were the perfect mixed-up love triangle. As it turned out, I stayed with Janis and Sam got a room a couple doors down. Albert Grossman had arranged for a limousine to pick us all up to take us to the Hollywood Bowl. The driver was from the Ukraine and barely spoke English, didn't know who he was picking up, and apparently didn't care.

We got to the Hollywood Bowl a little bit late and a security guard stopped us and wouldn't let us in. Janis threw one of her famed fits, which by then she had gotten quite good at. "Do you know who I am, you mother fucker? Do you know who I am?" She was all decked out with her burgundy plumes and a purple feather boa in her hair. The guy said, "I don't care if you are Janis Joplin herself." Sam put down the back window, stuck his head out and said, "That is just exactly who she is! You're stopping Janis Joplin. Let us in!" The marquee above his head read: "Janis Joplin in Concert."

Eventually, we were allowed in and we separated backstage. Sam and I went out and sat in the audience, which I suppose was a strange place for him to be, having been fired from her previous band Kozmic Blues. Early in the show, John Till, the guitar player who had replaced Sam, played the lead riff to "Summertime." It was a fabulous guitar lead and John played it beautifully. However, with the first note, Sam came flying up out of his seat screeching, "That's my lead! That's my lead!" Never mind that it was originally Bach's riff, and that Sam had borrowed it, Sam was screaming bloody murder. The Hollywood Bowl was not your average rock concert venue, but a slightly more upscale outdoor theater with assigned seating and an air of decorum.

The more noise Sam made, jumping up, blocking the view of those behind him, screaming profanities at the stage, the more I worried. In short order, the security cops ran over and grabbed him. They grabbed me, too.

"Come on. You two are out of here!"

Sam was still squawking about it being his lead and trying to pull his arm free as he was flanked by two cops, and a third was at my side.

"Let's go. Keep moving or I'm putting you in cuffs," the exasperated officer said while jerking Sam forward.

"Ok, ok . . . fuck, just let me go!" Sam howled.

"Hey wait a minute. Wait a minute. I'm not causing any problems," I said. "Why do I have to leave? I'm here with Janis."

"Yeah? We all are sweetheart. I'm sure she won't miss you." The cop smirked and kept a firm grip on my arm as he led me out the main entrance and released me next to Sam.

We headed toward the backstage area, Sam still smoldering. I was trying to figure out what had gone wrong. Sure, he could scream all he wanted to about it, but that particular riff was in the public domain. We found the limousine and told the driver, "Landmark." He took us back, and, we'd later learn, simply went home. He figured he'd picked up a few people at the Landmark, and then brought us back to the Landmark, so therefore he was done. We, on the other hand, simply assumed he would go back and wait for Janis, though we never told him that he needed to do that.

Back at the hotel we made the best of a bad evening by shooting up some heroin. Sam had to drown his sorrows about being fired and then having to watch another guitarist perform with Janis. I reminded him that if he hadn't assumed Janis wouldn't miss her dope, he might well have still been her lead guitarist tonight. While it was entirely likely that there were other circumstances that played into his demise as her lead guitarist, Janis had told me she'd gotten sick and tired of her dope disappearing.

Back at the Hollywood Bowl, Janis was finished and waiting to leave. She was looking around and asking everyone, "Where are Peggy and Sam? Where is my limo?" No one knew, and everyone else in her band and crew headed out. The equipment was loaded up. Finally, Janis decided the only thing to do was walk back because The Landmark Hotel wasn't far from the Bowl, just a few blocks down Highland to Franklin. When she exited the backstage area and began walking away, so did a few hundred young fans, following behind her. So, there she went, the feathered Pied Piper of Rock, leading a parade of hippies through Hollywood at midnight. Apparently two guys in the crowd appointed themselves as impromptu security and flanked her on either side to keep the crowd at bay.

The crowds dispersed once Janis got back to the hotel. When she came to the room, found Sam and me loaded, she figured out that we had taken *her* limousine home and left her without transportation either on purpose or because we were too distracted. She was furious.

I said, "Never in a million years would we take your limousine. Who knew that the asshole driver wouldn't go back and get you?" Fortunately, she believed me and directed all of her anger at Sam.

John Cooke had been hired by Albert to be Janis's road manager. Janis said, "I don't want him. He's not one of us and he doesn't even live in The Haight!" John, a sometime bluegrass musician, photographer, and writer, lived up in the San Francisco Knob Hill district which we called "Snob Hill." We regarded him as a tattletale. Which, to be fair, was part of his job description—to keep an eye on Janis and her band, making sure they didn't get into any kind of trouble he couldn't easily manage.

John certainly had no love for me. It was too bad, really. I wasn't influencing Janis's drinking, that's for sure, because I didn't indulge. She never could understand my aversion to drinking, but it eventually became a novelty to her. There was a lot that Janis and I had in common and a lot that was different. She grew up in Port Arthur, Texas, me in Covington, Louisiana. We were both intelligent and innovative, and worked hard at our jobs. However, while I was busy being Homecoming Queen in high school, she was busy working against racist policies, which automatically cast her out of the mainstream. She started drinking early, while I abstained early. She used to introduce me as, "This is my friend, Peggy. She doesn't drink. Can you believe that?" It never seemed to be as big a deal to others as it did to her. After awhile I asked her why she felt she needed to say that.

"Well, Honey, it is unusual."

"It's not that unusual, Janis."

"C'mon," she'd say and put her hands on her hips. "Don'tcha notice whenever you're out somewhere EVERYBODY is drinking except you?"

"So what? I have a good time, I don't get sloppy. And I don't like it. I can't stand the way it tastes or the way it makes me feel. Plus, then I would have to pee too Goddamn much."

"I just don't get you, Man. You've got the personality of a boozer, but you don't drink. It's kinda fascinating."

"Well, good. Be fascinated. No one else is."

"Awww, don't get mad, Honey. I just think it's a trip, that's all."

Until Janis turned me on to heroin, I wasn't doing that either. Still, John saw me as a terrible influence. I will admit that once I did get strung out, and became a regular heroin user, shooting up did become a central part of my existence. At various times, Janis kicked her heroin habit—never for too long—and I stayed away when she was clean.

She had tried to get me to go to Brazil with her to kick heroin and clean up. She had been prescribed some Adolphine, a precursor to Methadone. She had said she could get enough for me and we could both kick. I wished her well, but was not even close to being in the state of mind to stop using heroin. It was hard to admit even then, but I most definitely thought I could just keep right on using and continue being successful in business, too.

On an unusually warm day in late spring of 1970, not too long before Janis went off to Brazil, I got a call from her at Mnasidika.

"Peg, it's a beautiful day. Why don'tcha take the day off and let's go to the beach?"

"What? Janis I'm working. I got stuff to do and . . ."

She cut me off, "You own the place, Peg. C'mon it's really a beautiful today. You can take off a couple of hours. I mean really, what do ya work for, huh? C'mon man, meet me out at Muir Beach. It'll be fun. We'll have a great time. It's so warm. It's really fucking beautiful, man." She was doing her endearing, enthusiastic, mile-a-minute chatter that I always had a hard time saying "no" to.

"Ok Janis, I'll go. Let me do a couple things and I'll meet you in about an hour?"

"Aaaah Right!" she squealed. "I'll see you out there."

I finished whatever I was doing and headed back over the bridge to Marin County, over Mount Tamalpais, and down to the beach. When I pulled in the parking lot I saw her wildly painted car and parked next to it.

There was always a bit of a chill at the beach in spring, though that particular day was warmer than I remember it ever being. It really *was* beautiful. Janis pulled some kind of Madras bedspread or tapestry and her big ol' purse from her car. There was an ever-present feather boa stuck in her hair. With all her beads and plumes, she was a psychedelic contrast to the multi-tones of greys, blues and tans that made up the seascape.

"Hiya Honey! Glad ya made it!" She gave me a big hug.

"Yeah, me too. It really is gorgeous today. Really beautiful."

"God, isn't it though?" she said, with a sense of wonder. "It's unbelievable, man."

She tossed the bedspread over her arm, slipped off her heels and started to walk toward the ocean. I, too, slipped off my little heels and followed her to a nice spot in the sand where the breeze seemed to be blocked. She spread out her version of a beach blanket, then jangled around in her purse, grabbed a cigarette, lit it, and then pulled out a bottle of whiskey. She had the biggest grin on her face. I sat facing her, enjoying the scene as she lit my cigarette. The sound of the waves crashing nearby, accompanied by the cries of seagulls, and some other sea birds, the sun on my face, all made me relax a bit. She was right. It was a good idea to take a little time off.

Janis started chatting about this and that and then there were some quiet moments where we were both taking it all in. All of a sudden I felt her grow introspective, quiet, and almost shy. I was puzzled but let the silence be.

All of a sudden she said, "So . . . you don't like penises, do you?"

"*What*?"

"You don't like penises, do you?" she repeated herself, looking at me quizzically, then grinning.

"Not really. I mean, some of them I like . . ." I stammered because I was taken off guard.

"Like why? Why do you like the ones you do?" She wasn't kidding. She seemed to really want to know.

"Well . . . it depends on what it's attached to."

"What do you mean 'attached to'? Like a strap-on?"

"No. Like Kris or Coyote. Their dicks are attached to something, to somebody special," I said, smiling. "Those guys know how to make a woman feel special. Not just when they're fucking you, but all around. You oughtta know, you fucked them both."

"Yeah, yeah I know. So you *do* like some penises?"

"Well of course . . . only some of them," I said. "But there is something I like for sure."

"What's that?" she asked, innocently.

"You!" I said, and she jumped up and ran squealing.

I chased her around like we were in grammar school. Running in the deep sand was a lot like a cartoon. There was a whole lot of movement, without a lot of forward progress. We were both stumbling and laughing so hard. I finally lunged and grabbed her around the waist with both arms from behind. I held on tight and we both fell down and lay there giggling. When we finally caught our breath, I helped her up and we walked back to the blanket.

Janis gazed out toward the ocean, lost in thought. She briefly closed her eyes, tilted her face towards the sun and took in a deep breath. "Man, I really love this place," she said. "I just really love this place. It's home. It really feels like home to me, man." She sighed and looked around, and then she asked, "You ever think about dyin'?"

"No," I said. "Not really. I'm too busy thinking about trying to make a decent living . . . and living."

"When I die, I want my ashes spread here. Right here, so I can always be a part of this." She swept her arms in a big arc, with her little hands wide open. "All of this." Then she turned to me and asked, "Are you gonna be cremated or buried? I'm gonna be cremated."

"I hadn't really thought about it, Janis. Cremated I suppose. Seems better than taking up space in the ground."

"I just get the feeling I'm gonna die young, sometimes."

"Don't say that. We're too young to think like that. Don't talk like that Janis. It's a drag."

"I just get a feeling sometimes, that's all. But it's ok. It's really ok. I'm having a good time." The sun was just right on her face and she had a smile of contentment that radiated.

"Well, I hope you're wrong," I said. "About dying young."

"Yeah. We'll see." We were quiet for a little while longer. Then we started jabbering about some trivialities as we gathered our shoes and headed back towards our cars.

"Thanks for talking me into coming out here. It was great," I said and gave her a hug.

"Yeah, I knew you'd like it. See ya Honey," she said as she got into her car and drove off.

I sat there for awhile, thinking about the day. I hadn't expected Janis's mood to get so heavy. I brushed it off, thinking maybe the fact that we were at the ocean made things seem more dramatic. I didn't really think too much about the conversation until later.

She knew. Some part of her knew.

Part Four

JANIS JOPLIN DEAD OF SUSPECTED OVERDOSE.

It was just unfathomable that she was dead. I knew she had begun using heroin again, after a period of being clean. Although we were close friends, there were periods of time when we might not see one another for a few months—sometimes because of the demands of both of our careers, other times because she was clean and I was still using and so I stayed away. We were just two women making our mark in our respective worlds. We understood this dynamic and it didn't bother us. We always knew we'd connect again sometime. We were friends who sometimes had sex, not devoted lovers who pined for one another. Summer of 1970 had been one of those times when our paths just didn't cross that often.

But Janis had gotten in touch sometime that summer, before Jimi Hendrix's untimely death. It was really hot and Janis wanted to know if she could go lay out on the deck at my house in Coon Hollow out at Stinson Beach. She wanted an "all over tan" and the deck was protected on all sides from prying eyes, yet still had an unbelievable view out to the sea, down through the canyon. She pleaded with me to come and meet her, and as usual I protested, citing work. Finally, she wore me down, and after getting some things in order, I drove north across the Golden Gate and over Mount Tamalpais to my house. When I arrived I didn't see Janis's Porsche and figured I had beat her there. My neighbor Brian swished down the drive between my property and his to inform me Janis had approached him with a big ol' "Hiya Honey! Where can a gal get a drink in this town?"

He told her about the Sand Dollar bar down in Stinson on the

Pacific Coast Highway. With that information, she had thanked him and roared off. I jumped back into my Shelby and headed to the bar. There she was, draped in plumes, a shot in her hand, holding court. She raised her drink high and yelled, "Drinks are on Pearl!" (the nickname she liked to use sometimes). The small crowd hooted and toasted her enthusiastically. I stopped at the door and surveyed the scene for a moment and then approached Janis, who was flanked on all sides by the happy male patrons.

"Oh Honey, ya found me!" She grinned and grabbed me close, then released me and leaned in. "Well, ya know, a girl has to have a drink and I knew Miss Teetotaller didn't have any booze at her place!" She grinned and cackled at her inside joke. She turned away and yelled, "Another round!" which was met with more raucous approval.

"Ok, Missy. I'm heading back home. You dragged me out here. You coming or what?"

Her little face crumpled for a moment like an errant schoolgirl, then she burst into a wide grin.

"Enjoy the party!" she yelled as she threw a fistful of money at the bartender. "Pearl's gotta go!" The crowd groaned, "No! Stay! C'mon Janis! Puuuuurrrrlll!"

She swung her purse over her shoulder, grabbed my sleeve and followed me outside.

"See you there?" I asked.

"Of course. I'm right behind ya, Baby!" she said, and trundled off towards her car.

We wound up the road, through the canyon, back to my house. Once there we stripped down and made our way out onto the deck. We took turns rubbing oil onto each other's back and chatted for a while before we both fell asleep in the warm afternoon sun. It was certainly a moment out of time for both of us. We were both always so busy, always working. This day was just so light and so relaxed. We didn't make love, I don't think we even kissed. But I remember it as the most relaxed, unencumbered day I'd had in a very long time. The sun dropped lower and it began to cool. Janis got up, dressed and headed back over the hill to her house in Larkspur. I went in and showered. As I was getting dressed, I noticed Janis's little blue heart ring had been left on the table. I smiled as I remembered the day she had gotten it.

It was in the very early days of her career, and Janis was notorious for wearing cheap, gaudy jewelry. She and I had been walking past a jewelry store in North Beach and stopped to look in the window. She pointed to a ring she liked, and I asked her, "Why don't you get yourself a piece of real jewelry, Janis?"

"What'd ya mean 'real'?" she asked, slightly offended.

"Janis, your cheap rings stain your fingers. It doesn't look good. You're making money now. You can afford it. Get yourself something that's not going to turn your hands green."

She looked at me, harrumphed, and walked into the store. Then she spied this adorable little blue heart ring.

The heart itself was not stone, but some type of man-made material cut like a gem in such a way that made it appear to have a lot of depth. The ring was 10k gold, which was a step up from the faux silver, nickel, and God-knows-what materials she usually wore. She squealed when she saw it, and asked the proprietor to let her try it on. She cooed and ooed, extending her hand out, playing regal and fanciful. I nodded my approval and she left with that little ring displayed proudly on her finger.

On the afternoon of October 2, Janis and I got our heroin from the same source. She was working in the studio and I had been staying with her at the Landmark Hotel in Hollywood. Before we had a chance to shoot up together, she informed me her "fiancée," Seth Morgan, was due to come down for the weekend. One part of Janis had always longed to be married, and she'd clearly found what she wanted in Seth. I was okay with finding another place to stay since I had some business to finish up in LA. Except . . . she wanted us to have a three-way once Seth got to town.

Who knew this would be the last subject we were to ever discuss in person?

"No, Janis. I'm just not into him," I told her.

"But he's into you. He's all excited about it."

"Well, I'm not. I honestly don't know what you see in him."

"He's a great fuck, I mean that guy knows how to ball. C'mon Peg. It'll be so much fun."

"Nah, count me out. I'm gonna get a room somewhere else. You two can go at it."

"But Peggy . . . c'mon . . . you won't regret it. He's so worth it. You'll see."

For once, I didn't relent and give in to Janis's wishes, as I'd done so many times, for things large and small—a day at the beach, a trip to New York, shooting dope for the first time. I gathered up my bag and headed out. We left each other open-ended as always. Just as friends do. No promises other than the assumption of seeing each other again when we could.

I checked into the Chateau Marmont after partying with some friends at a local gay bar. My friend Mudgie Rose was there, and I brought her up to my room. It wasn't romance. It was the heroin. She was beautiful and straight, and not my type, nor was I hers. But I always enjoyed her company.

We had finished the last of one batch of dope I had when Janis called.

"Peggy, have you tried the new shit from George?"

"Nah, just finished up the last batch. Haven't gotten into it yet."

"Man, you're gonna love it! It's so good"

"Really? That good , eh?"

"Yea, seems real clean. Listen, things are going real good in the studio, man. These cats are really good. I mean, you should hear the shit they're laying down. They're so tight. You gotta come down."

"I'm glad it's going so well. But . . ." I said, letting it hang in the air a minute to play with her.

"But, what? What Peg? Are you fucking with me? C'mon!"

"But maybe I'll just wait and buy the album," I teased.

"Fuck you mother fucker, I won't let you!" she cackled, then her voice dropped low. "You want to get on this dope. It's good. Let me know what you think."

"Yea, yea I will. See ya later."

"Yea, see ya Honey."

Mudgie and I started on the batch of the new dope. Janis was right. It was good, but this connection had always been good, so I wasn't surprised. I called Janis on the night of Oct 3, but the desk clerk said she wasn't taking any calls. I fussed at him awhile, but he just kept repeating he had strict orders from Miss Joplin that she was not to be disturbed. I tried again a while later and got the same message.

I figured Seth had come in and they were busy getting it on.

I proceeded to shoot some more dope.

Mudgie and I were nodding out when the phone rang in the middle of the night. I almost didn't answer. I could think of only a handful of people who would call me at that hour, and fewer who knew precisely where I was. Then I thought it might be Janis, as she did know where to reach me, so I pulled up and lurched over to the phone.

"Hello," I said, groggy-voiced.

"Peggy?" a male voice said. "Peggy?"

"Yes." I recognized the voice.

"Janis is dead."

"No she isn't . . . Seth?"

"Yes, she is," he said.

"No, she isn't, Seth. She can't be . . . I just talked to her."

"Peggy . . ."

"No, she can't be. She isn't!"

"Peggy, I'm here with the police. She's dead."

"Whaaaa . . .?" I felt my knees buckle and everything swirled as my mind attempted to absorb the word—dead.

"Janis is dead. The police are here and want to speak to you."

"This. Can't. Be. Are you sure? Where the fuck . . . Seth?" I still wasn't getting it.

"Peggy you have to come down here. They'll hunt you down if you don't. Cooke found her."

"Where were *you*?" I demanded.

"I didn't make the plane. Janis was alone."

Janis was alone.

Jeezus. Most of us close to her thought she could easily have had some sort of accident. Like nodding out or passing out drunk with one of her candles burning and catching something on fire. Most of the hotel rooms Janis so often found herself in shared an indistinct requisite monotony and rarely offered anything resembling a personality. Enter Janis, and the drab room would become instant hippie-cozy with candles, fabric, scarves, feather boas and other flammables in purples, burgundy and red, draped, hung, and strewn about. Some of the redecorating was intentional, some was just Janis being herself. All those bracelets, clanking and jingling, beads swaying and clicking, the world was in motion wherever Janis landed. She was sound and color and energy, a convergence of harmonic dissonance so intense it couldn't be contained inside of her. A cosmic force seeking release and she was the conduit.

And it was easy to think, or maybe to hope, that such careless exuberance might be what fucking killed her.

I don't remember getting into my car. The drive wasn't far from the Chateau to The Landmark. I was nearly convulsing. My legs were shaking so badly. My whole body was trembling.

Janis.

Gone.

Janis.

Gone.

My mind kept saying those words while another part of my mind imagined me getting to The Landmark and her being there, alive. It would be her grand attempt to coerce me to get it on with her and Seth. Some sick fucking joke, but she would be alive and we'd have a great laugh. Her laugh—that wild, infectious, gut-level laugh.

I somehow kept driving as the terror, disbelief, and denial made me tremble. The next thing I knew I was in the hallway of The Landmark. The door to her room was open. I headed toward it. I saw her foot sticking out from between the beds. Her little foot, all twisted. She was wearing a slip-on shoe with the hourglass heel that was popular then, a style we were both so fond of. God-awful lifeless little foot.

Thomas Noguchi, the LA county coroner, turned to me as we were standing just at the door to her room. "What do you know about this?"

"What?" I answered flatly. The air conditioner roared oblivious in the background.

"Her nose appears broken," he said and gestured toward her.

"I don't know anything about that." I hardly dared to glance over. I didn't want to see.

"You weren't here?"

"No. No I wasn't." Suddenly, I became conscious of a policeman as he took my arm and guided me away.

I RAN INTO SOME TROUBLE

In the lobby, I saw Kris Kristofferson, his handsome face drawn, pitiful, and dark.

"Did we do this?" he asked. His eyes pleaded with me to say it wasn't so. He knew, of course, that we *had not* done it, but I think he was referring to the lifestyle so many of us led, although Kris himself wasn't a drug user.

I said, "No, we didn't, Kris."

The whole scene was surreal. The police questioned me, I answered their questions. It didn't sound as if they had found her dope, or so I thought. I naïvely assumed that Janis's team would have seen to it that it had disappeared before the police came on the scene. I accounted for my whereabouts, and then they were done with me.

Seth answered some questions from the police. We couldn't have been there but a few ten, fifteen minutes.

And then Seth came to me and said he wanted to fuck. "She wanted us to. You know. We should do it for her," he said.

To his unknowing credit, Seth snapped me out of the numb denial. Suddenly, I felt a wave of righteous anger.

"She's not even cold yet, you asshole," I hissed at him and pulled my arm from his grasp.

"Oh c'mon Peggy. It's what she wanted. Come to New York with me. I'll pay for everything. I need you."

This guy, some kind of nerve. "You're out of your fucking mind, Seth. The only reason I wasn't here was because you were coming. You were supposed to be here yesterday. *Where the fuck were you?*"

"I missed my plane," he said quietly.

"How the fuck? . . . oh never mind."

I don't remember much after that. Mudgie, and a couple of the Full Tilt Boogie boys had arrived and joined Seth and me and then, knowing only that none of us wanted to be alone, we all jumped into my car and we went to the Bacchanal 70. Mudgie sat on Seth's lap in the front seat. Once there, they all began to drink. I began to get nauseated.

"Come on boys, I'm leaving . . . I don't feel well," I told them, and drove them all back to The Landmark. We parted, silently.

The horrible reality was finally forcing its way into us, though we all had tried so hard not to let it in. We were defeated. Janis's room was taped off. The Medical Examiner's van was gone. The world would know in the morning. For now, only a few people knew. For now, the pain and loss was private to her family and to her friends. Those brief hours, before we had to share what happened with the entire world, were God-awful.

She was truly gone. The reality was incomprehensible.

✶

"Janis Joplin Found Dead in Hollywood Hotel" was how some papers reported the news of her death. Noguchi, who had investigated the deaths of Marilyn Monroe and other celebrities, was examining Janis's untimely death as well. When the Certificate of Death was finally issued, under CAUSE OF DEATH, it was determined on line A: "acute heroin—morphine intoxication" and line B "injection of overdose."

That fits in nicely with the narrative the public had come to expect, and with what was to become known as the "27 Club"—tragic rock star legends who all died from drug overdoses at age 27. A heroin overdose fit the Joplin mythos; it made sense that the Queen of Sex, Drugs, Rock-n-Roll died that way. She ODd, no surprise, and if nothing else, any Joplin records that might be released after her death would sell brilliantly.

For me though, all the pieces didn't quite fit.

And I wondered why no one else questioned it.

I am in no way implying that Clive Davis or Albert Grossman were that cold. It was apparent they cared about Janis as a person, as well as her career. But for the LA County Coroner's Office, it was a pretty open and shut case. Heroin in the system: she overdosed. But why weren't they considering that the ability to tolerate a substance exponentially increases over the time one uses it? That the need for more to achieve the same effect might have meant she could tolerate more in her system without overdosing?

Eventually, I wasn't the only one who had doubts but I wasn't buying into the controversial conspiracy theories that scores of fans, feeling cheated by the Grim Reaper, have spawned. None of them make any sense if the facts are examined carefully. Yes, Janis, Jimi Hendrix, and Jim Morrison were powerful celebrities who held sway with the youth in America and around the world. Perhaps they *were* being monitored by the FBI, but I never for a moment thought their deaths were caused by others.

A few years later though, when I was clean and thinking clearly, there was a nagging sensation, a tug at the corner of my mind that wouldn't go away. I couldn't stop thinking about her having an unopened pack of cigarettes in one hand and some coins in the other when she was discovered. The desk clerk at The Landmark said Janis had come down and asked to change a five-dollar bill so she'd have coins for the cigarette machine. He reported that she went over to the machine, got her cigarettes, and that was the last anyone saw of her.

Janis and I had copped the heroin from the same connection two days before. I knew the dope she had wasn't exceptionally more pure than it had been. I remembered how she'd called me and told me how great this batch was. And later that evening, I did shoot the same dope, from the same connection, from the same batch. It was good, but no more so than usual. It is a ridiculous assumption that she'd gotten bad dope. She was aware of how potent or not it was, because she had been shooting it a couple of days already. Though there is no gold standard for the strength of street junk, that particular connection we'd bought from always had cleaner dope, since it wasn't cut six ways to Sunday with a bunch of crap. From what I experienced, the heroin that week in Hollywood was no more special than any other. So, the theory she had exceptionally pure smack, was bullshit. So was the idea that she shot too much. Janis was an expert at measuring, cooking, and shooting. To her it was an art form, something almost reverent.

And here's the other thing that doesn't make any sense whatsoever. Janis and I shot a lot of dope together. In fact, I had ODd on several occasions when I was with her and many times in the years after losing her. I wasn't nearly as careful about the art of shooting. But when you overdose on heroin, it's instantaneous. Bam! You are lucky if you can even get the needle out of your arm before it's lights out, Baby. A lot of junkies are found dead with the needle still in their arm.

Not Janis. No. We were being asked to accept that she shot an overdose and then went to the front desk, asked calmly for change, operated the cigarette machine with no trouble, and walked steadily back to her room? Where she then fell down, as a result of the overdose? No.

The theory is that she "muscled it"—that is, injected the heroin straight into a muscle, so the effect would have been delayed. Not her. She knew how to find just the right vein. Anything else would be a waste of a rush and good dope. If she didn't muscle it, then the other scenario is that she returned from the cigarette machine, shot an overdose, removed the needle from her arm, set it down, and then, for some unknown reason, gathered up her unopened cigarette pack and the change? *Then* what? She fell over? Slamming her nose and cutting her lip on the nightstand, somehow extending her legs out? *Really?*

In 2017, the television series "Autopsy: The Final Hours of Janis Joplin" corroborated my theory of Janis not being a cut-and-dried overdose case.

From firsthand experience, I can attest that when you OD shooting dope, you crumple or fall over right then, still facing the syringe, in the same position as you were when you injected it. Or you fall back when the rush hits, and the syringe is still in your hand. But Janis's foot, her little foot, twisted. Those little hourglass heels. The Landmark Hotel. Shag carpet. Big loop shag carpet. Janis loaded on heroin and alcohol, nothing new. Except, she must've tripped. She must've tripped as she rounded the corner near the bed, coming back from the cigarette machine. Those damn hourglass heels we loved so much, one of them snagging on one of the loops of that shag carpet, sending her flying forward and striking the nightstand with enough force to split her lip and crack her nose. Too loaded to come to enough to keep the blood from asphyxiating her. No. To my mind, she didn't OD. She couldn't have. It's simply not the way it happens. She fucking tripped. The unbelievably talented force of nature, known as Janis Joplin, brought to a halt. Stopped. Dead. By a pair of cheap shoes with an hourglass heel and a misplaced step on a loop of shag carpet.

For years, many people held me responsible for Janis's death. Despite the fact that it was Janis who introduced me to heroin and not the other way around. But the deeper problem was with a peculiar blindness among the hippies. They were a very heterosexual movement. It was unusual to be the only known lesbian in that entire mix of people. Some in Janis's entourage did not like me for that, did not like me for my friendship with her, and they did everything they could to get her away from me. It took me years to get over their blame, but I know that I was never the catalyst for her death. No one, and I mean, no one, could persuade Janis to do or not do anything she chose.

A memorial was held for Janis at the Lion's Share in San Anselmo, and her ashes were scattered over Muir Beach. Sam and I got loaded together, our way of "toasting" our lost friend. We were quite certain it was what she would have wanted. Janis's sister Laura was there, bless her heart, and many of the old neighborhood people of The Haight. God, she was most certainly loved by so very many.

I hadn't been home to my house in what seemed like weeks. I think I was still in a state of shock. After the memorial, I wound over Mount Tamalpais to go home and just breathe. As I came upon my house and started to turn into the driveway, I gasped and slammed on the brakes. In front of me, that feeble little Fuchsia Janis and I had planted months ago was strong and full. Its many purple and pink flowers danced like her laughter on the ocean breeze.

※

On Christmas Eve 1971, I was strung out and needing an end-of-the-year boost in capital. Janis had been dead for 15 months. The Haight was no longer an innocent parade of flower children. I began to wonder if San Francisco had always been this grey. Gone were the tie-dyed and wide-eyed. All the color of psychedelia had somehow bled out and left in its wake pale corpses haunting the streets, strung out, broke, sick, and dirty. The "Peace, Love and Brotherhood" ethos that encapsulated the feeling in those early years of the Post-Beatnik era of our accidental tribe had devolved by late 1969 under the weight of popularity. The majority of this later wave of young people were here purely to take. They came with no ambition, no creativity, no money, and no sense of responsibility. Add in the resurgence of methamphetamine, basement pseudo-chemist concoctions, severe untreated mental illness, and our little Utopia turned ugly, fast.

At the To Kingdom Come store, the men's-only clothing store I'd opened on Polk Street, we were visited that Christmas Eve, not long before closing, by two guys who were later known as the "Salt and Pepper" bandits. They came in armed, fucked with all of our minds and fucked one of my employee's with the barrel of a loaded pistol. One of them tried to rape me, but he couldn't get it up. I kept insulting him. I was so pissed off. At one point, I thought I'd better shut up before he shot me. And the kicker was, part of me almost didn't care. They did, however, take all the leather jackets and all the cash. All I could do after the shock wore off was to shoot more dope. To Kingdom Come had opened its doors for the final time, and the last petal to be plucked from the flower of the Peace Movement was Love-Me-Not.

*

Ned and Stella were never ok with my heroin habit, never. After I lost my businesses and, more or less, myself somewhere around 1972, they had had just about enough of me being strung out, and, longing to have their ole friend back, they set out to find me. I was lying around a funky apartment in what was known as the Villa Elaine on Vine Street in Hollywood, waiting to be called to help edit the book that I *thought* I had written. I had been journaling my experiences and observances of the very colorful scenes playing out all around me. My own role seemed inconsequential to the "whole." I sensed that what we were involved with, or swept up in, may possibly have historic import. The breadth of the movement was truly staggering, as I had witnessed the streets filled with youth from all over the world to participate in *our* experiment.

Kimmie had a friend who mentioned that I should contact a publisher in New York about the manuscript I had started. He said it would be a good idea to mention my friendship with Janis to get them to listen. Still numb from her death, yet still maintaining some measure of business responsibilities, I picked up the phone and called the publishing company. A receptionist answered and was rather cool. Remembering what Bill said, I mentioned Janis as she was ushering me off the phone. I was put on hold and then the publisher came on the line. He listened and offered to send me a ticket to fly to New York and bring them the manuscript I had. I was elated! So elated in fact, that I shot some extra dope in jubilation. When I was due to fly out, I became concerned about staying loaded enough to make the trip and still have enough heroin once I got there. My habit was monstrous by now. I overestimated my dose and missed my plane. A couple hours later I recovered enough to call and say that I had missed my flight and that I would come the next day. Well, I thought I had it figured out, but I overdid it. Again. Finally, they threatened me that if I didn't show up they were not going to read my material. Somehow, I made it on a plane and arrived in New York, my briefcase stuffed with several lined legal pads of cursive handwriting, offering complicit witness to The Haight-Ashbury's inner scene.

I fixed before leaving the airport, and arrived at the publisher's office feeling just right. I was truly excited about the prospect of penning a complete book. I could hardly contain myself as I watched him thumb through the first few pages, trying to gauge his response. He finally looked at me as he set the pad down and with a flicker of something a hair kinder than contempt said, "This is—*pedestrian*."

"Oh," I said, not sure whether that was good or bad.

"But, I'll tell you what. My daughter's fiancée can work with you and make a book out of this."

"Really?" I brightened, thinking this was probably a good thing.

"Yes." He smiled, cooly. "We will draw up the paperwork for the contract. You can work with my guy in Los Angeles. Is that agreeable?"

"Yes. That should be fine. Yes, thank you," I said, happy to have this go seemingly so well.

The next day I had a publishing contract in hand, and was feeling good about what I had accomplished as I flew back to California. Kimmie and I were giving each other a lot of space those days. I would venture out to the house at Stinson Beach on occasion, but for the most part we had gone our separate ways. No fanfare, no decisive break, just hundreds of cracks to the structure of who we were as a "we." Her staying angry. Me staying strung out. The social movement, innocence, and our tender dreams lay buried beneath our resentments, the dope, and bitter tears.

While working on the book I was always loaded. Very, very loaded. Not just "well." Not just "fixed," but seriously, deeply stoned. I would appear on the designated days, but not necessarily at the designated times. One time, while working with a writer in a hotel room, I used the bathroom, only to overdose behind the locked door. Apparently after a normal "potty break" time had elapsed, someone came looking for me and had to break down the damn door. Not too long after that I took a cab to the store for cigarettes. However, I needed to get some dope first. I had the cab driver take me to get it. Then I had him bring me to a service station, and it was there I overdosed. The cab driver thought I was trying to avoid payment, and alerted the management. There were other people waiting to get in so it was high drama when the door had to be jiggered and jammed to save my sorry, junkie ass. I was absolutely, out of control. Whereas before, my pursuit of money had been for a lifestyle, it now outwardly appeared to be a death wish.

At some point along the route of pre-publication, the businesswoman in me began to sell "interest" in the book like stock options. I set it up through an attorney to insure people got paid. I, of course, thought people would make money on their investments above and beyond their initial outlay. In the meantime, I had some money for dope. When the royalties began to come in, they went straight to the attorney. He then distributed to those investors before I ever saw it. In the end, after everyone was paid, I believe I ended up with about $2000. This quickly, and completely, disappeared into my arm.

About a year later, a badly written memoir with my name on it, full of errors and exploitative of Janis, appeared in bookstores. The "collaborator" who had pumped me for dozens of hours of interviews, filled in what he didn't know, and the editors bypassed showing me the final text. Or, at least that's how I remembered it. Perhaps I had signed away that right in my drugged haze.

Nevertheless, that book, the lurid and graphic sexual content and raw drug scenes depicted, hurt everyone, including my poor parents, so badly. I cannot blame anyone for me being strung out on heroin. My instincts were dulled at best. I naïvely believed all would be well, as I had been assured. I received my first copy of the book while in Mazatlan. I remember looking out at the ocean and reading the first paragraph. Instantly, I got a sinking feeling in my stomach and my hands started shaking. I thought, "Oh my God, they didn't." I couldn't read anymore. I just fell apart. What could I do about it? It was already in print. I only remember going off the rails, Ned and Stella being fed up with me, shooting dope, and then returning to California.

※

Mom's distraught.

"Dahlin', remember that man who called Dad and I about that book?"

"Yes, Mother. Unfortunately, I will remember him for the rest of my life."

"He seemed so nice. We were so happy for you. He told us we were gonna be so proud of you and that book. All the while knowing that they had done the opposite?"

"Yes, Mom. I don't think he's a very nice person at all."

"Why would someone be so mean? Why bother calling us at all when he's just gonna lie?"

※

Ned and Stella had somehow found me there in Hollywood. Following Janis's death, everything in San Francisco had seemed too close and I couldn't quite get far enough away, though to be honest, I didn't have to move to get away. That's one of the things junkies love about heroin, at least this junkie did: it takes you away from your life. It made me not care that I didn't care. And if I started to care, then I'd just shoot some more dope and that feeling would go away until the next fix. This is also the thing that tears up the friends and family of people with addictions.

As heroin made its way through the middle class, no one was ready for young addicts. It wrought a lot of havoc, broke a lot of hearts and ended a lot of promising lives. David Dalton, a founder of *Rolling Stone* magazine, said to me recently in conversation, "You were wildly successful back in the day. How did you spend all that money?"

I said, "First off, David, I wasn't *wildly* successful. I was just successful. Blue Beard's was what I would consider to be wildly successful." (Blue Beard started out as Mnasidika North, which I opened on a whim in Seattle, then later sold to my accountant. Seattle was too cold and I hated having to fly up so often to monitor it, though it proved to be a hit, right from the start.)

David then asked, "Can you honestly spend that much money on heroin?"

"Did I spend as much money as I made just on heroin? No . . . that's not what happens. What happens is, probably like an alcoholic, once you're immersed in the drug and the usage and what comes with it, you stop taking care of business."

That was it in a nutshell—I had stopped taking care of business. That's what happened with me. I didn't spend all the money I had made. I had stopped making money because I wasn't paying attention to business anymore. I was too busy being a junkie.

*

At the Villa Elaine, I still had access to a little money. I still had my Shelby Mustang GT 350 and I still had my house in Stinson Beach. But Ned and Stella corralled me and I agreed to go with them to northern California where they had a secluded cabin. They were also planning a trip to Mexico, and wanted me to go along. Apparently, their plan included having me get clean first (kick, cold turkey), and then execute *the plan*—and what a plan it was.

Still, I absolutely refused to consider heading north until I got "fixed" first, so I wouldn't be kicking, vomiting and chilling on the near 600-mile drive. But Stella, in her beautiful, relentless, Jewish mother way pleaded, cajoled, begged, and threatened me to get cleaned up and come with them. The evening dragged on with Stella and me arguing about whether or not I could make the trip without drugs in my bloodstream. I definitely was not going to do it, unless I had a jump on the onset of withdrawals.

They eventually relented because they could see I was NOT going anywhere without my dope. So, I scored, cooked up, drew up, tied up, registered, and shot it. In my twisted way of thinking, I was shooting up to ward off the coming hell of kicking heroin after to the long car trip to Healdsburg. They rode in the cab of the truck, and I was in bed in the camper, already freaking out over the monstrous kick that was sure to come. And come it did. Withdrawals are not fun, but some are way worse than others. This was gonna be a doozey.

When we arrived in Healdsburg, it had begun in earnest. I was already pissed off, having bounced around the camper, when the withdrawal symptoms began—bone chilling shakes, the runny nose and the bad attitude. I was green with nausea from swaying back and forth like a palm tree in the back of the pick-up truck and the activation of my bowels from their narcotic slumber. My teeth were chattering and the involuntary shivers were coming in more frequent waves. Already horribly miserable, fear gripped me as the terrifying truth of going through with complete withdrawal suddenly became very, very real. Stella locked me in a room and took a righteous amount of verbal abuse as I howled and cursed and writhed pathetically. God bless her. She bathed me, soothed me and took my insults over the ensuing days.

Not that she wasn't capable of shooting a few barbs back herself. Stella was heavy and I don't mean physically. Back in those days it was an energy, a kind of presence that one could virtually throw around. She could give a look and add a few choice words that could devastate many so-called tough guys. Yet as hard as she could throw a vibe, she could throw her love; God help you either way. She was going to love me into getting clean, and by God, she did. This time.

In four or five days, the heroin would be out of my system and I would be clean, but it took me at least seven or eight days to be able to take a shower and get my strength back. If I showered too soon, the shower spray would feel like I was being pelted with little shards of glass. I remember hearing The Jimmy Cliff song "I Can See Clearly Now" as the withdrawals subsided. To this day, whenever I hear that song, I think of Stella, her love, and of getting (but sadly, not staying) clean.

※

After I kicked in Healdsburg and Stella was certain I was clean, we went to Mazatlan, Mexico, where Ned and Stella had a quarter ton of pot that had been cooked down into grass oil. The still that was used to cook down the weed was up in the hills with the harvested pot. Our plan was to rent a small mansion in Mazatlan so we would have a safe place to pack the oil into the drive shafts of several old jalopies, and then drive them across the border. Once across, the cars would be dismantled, the oil emptied and packed into bottles, then distributed. Previous schemes were packing weed into icons of the Mother Mary or the Lady of Guadalupe. No Catholic Federale was going to take the chance of going to hell for busting up a statue of the Sacred Mother. Another one was a line of cosmetics. Appealing, professional labels were affixed onto cosmetic jars full of pot oil, and carried into the U.S. It may not have tightened sagging skin, but it probably induced a happy glow!

One of the cars they had used previously in this smuggling scheme was driven by a guy who called himself Otis. He did a couple of runs across the border, and then when driving the last car across, he disappeared into the U.S. and was never seen again. Stella decided she didn't want to hide oil in the shafts of cars, and instead was going to drive a Pepsi Cola truck full of pot across the border herself to make up for the loss. The truck was packed floor to ceiling with the best pot the hills of Mexico had to offer. The only thing separating the pot from the eyes of the border guards would be a single row of soda bottles, floor to ceiling, just behind the roll up door. As she got ready to pull out and head to the United States border, she looked at me and said, "Are ya comin?"

"No! Hell no!"

"Really?" Her green eyes flashed as she raised her eyebrows.

I begin to squirm.

"What's a matter, Samantha?" she continued. "Are ya scared?"

I was more afraid of being thought of as not ballsy enough to hang with her, than whatever might happen to me getting caught at the border.

"No. No I'm not scared." I cleared my throat several times. "Um, yeah, I'm coming."

This is only one of several examples of Stella challenging my courage. She never wanted to miss out on anything heavy that might turn out to be a rush, and she cajoled or coerced me readily via head tilt or raised eyebrow into action, too. This round, Stella won. While

I was hooked on heroin, Stella it seemed was hooked on adrenaline . . . and getting over on the authorities.

After the soda truck run, we headed back to Mexico where our nearest neighbor in Mazatlan was the El Commandante, the Chief of Police, the Commander. His guard stood in front of his gate in the morning and followed the shade over to stand in front of our place in the afternoon. Ned had this theory: if you're gonna do something illegal, do it in plain sight. We ended up splitting the cost of the guard with the Commandante. We loved it.

*

"You want me to *what now* exactly?" I exclaimed.

"Do a jailbreak with us, Samantha" Ned said, smiling.

"That's what I thought you said. Would you tell me what you mean by this?"

"Well, Ted, who I know you don't care for, and his brother, and three other guys got busted on a sailboat down here. This has put a real dent in us financially because there was a lot of pot they got caught with, and it was mine." What Ned meant, was, people had given him money to get the pot back up to the States. "We gotta get them out of there."

"Ned, you know I love ya, but there is not a chance in hell that I'm gonna do this. So, know it now and don't ask me again. I'm not doing it. I'm *not* helping you break somebody out of prison. Not!"

He dropped the subject.

A day went by and the next night Stella was cooking for us and the boys who were running the pot across the border. Ned motioned to me and said, "Come on, Sam. Let's go for a ride." I thought that we were going into Mazatlan on a grocery run. Instead, we headed outside of town where there were no streetlights. In 1972, Mazatlan was a primitive-like town in a third world country. I remember there being only two public telephones in the whole town and we would have had to camp out and wait our turn in a very long line if we wanted to use one of them. The mansion had a private phone.

After a few minutes, I asked, "Where are we going?"

"You'll see," he said as we bumped along a dirt road, through potholes and ruts, until we came to this primitive, prehistoric wall that looked like decaying stucco.

"What is that?"

"It's Mazatlan Federal Prison," he said, laughing.

Normally I would have asked what we were doing here, but I was so stunned by the appearance of this dilapidated obstacle.

"No, Sam. Really, that's Mazatlan Federal Prison. That's where my boys are. Paul, Mike, Mace and Frank. Along with your not-so-favorite guy."

"You're kidding me," I laughed. "We could push that down with a backhoe."

Ned had a twinkle in his eyes, and I knew what he was doing by bringing me out there.

I matched his look with a sparkle of my own, smiling widely and chuckled, "I'm in." And that was it. The deal was sealed. Later we would work out the details.

We turned around and went back to the mansion. Stella didn't say a word. She knew that he had gotten to me . . . and they both knew me well enough to know that just below the surface of this formerly responsible business woman, there beat the heart of a reckless adventuress.

After a few days of prep, I understood my role. In the Mexican prison system at the time, prisoners were permitted to have outsider visits not just for a few minutes or a few hours, but for days, weeks, even months. While the factors that went into the officials' convoluted decision about which prisoners could have long-term, conjugal visitors remained a mystery to me, it boiled down to this: I had to work my way into their graces so that I would be approved as a long-term visitor. Unbelievably this meant I lived, on and off, for periods of a few days to several weeks at a time, in the same cell (really a small hut) with Ned and Stella's imprisoned drug runners: Paulie, Mike, Mace, Frank, and Ted.

I walked into what was the reception area for Mazatlan Federal Prison. Driving up to Mazatlan Federal Prison the first morning that I was to meet the guys, sent me into shock. What had appeared to be a crumbling institute by the shadowy hue of parking lights, in the light of day was transformed. This was a fortress whose exterior had jagged, broken, glass bottles at violent angles imbedded in the adobe walls. Topping the looming edifice were cyclones of razor wire and more glass, whose points glistened sharply as they caught the sun. The Mexican earthiness a contrast to the dull cold steel and concrete of American prisons. It was a visual I'll never forget. Once I walked into the reception area, I was then surprised by the lack of modern, bureaucratic props. It was simply a room with just a table. No machines, no phones, no photograph, no identification, no paperwork, nothing. Just me, them, and a table from which they passed me on through to another vacant room with an officer of some kind. When they figured out I was American, the guard spoke English.

"What are you coming in for?" he asked.

"To visit a friend," I replied.

"Ok. You carry anything? No?" He waved me on. "Ok, go in."

They didn't ask for my ID, or fingerprints, *nada*.

My primary duty was to distract the guards and I had no problem doing that. We talked, played and I learned some Spanish. It was a Tuesday when I went in as a guest to Mazatlan Federal Prison, and if you didn't come back out that day, you were in until the following Tuesday. Or the one after that. Or a month later. I was doing my job, distracting the guards so the guys could dig a tunnel from their hut to the outside, a process that took months. But I was also learning, as most prisoners know, that drugs are easy to come by behind the wall.

Once I missed the next week Stella got suspicious. She said, "Uh oh."

Ned said, "What?"

"Think about it Ned, something is going on in there. Sam hasn't been out in two weeks."

Yeah, there was something going on alright. All I had to do was wake up in the morning, walk across the dirt courtyard to the connection, score, get high and distract the guards. I was well qualified for this assignment.

Inside there was a big courtyard—a square with a guard tower in each corner. It was quite like a movie, at times, a comedy. The queens, the Mexican Queens, were called "Tortillas" because they're the *same*, so to speak, on both sides. They wore ruffled blouses and skirts. They made their job sweeping the dirt and keeping the courtyard clean. They kept it clean. They would do people's laundry, make little hors d'oeuvres from what they could get off the Tobaccoria/Canteen. The prison food consisted of tortillas and beans, and for a beverage, Kool-Aid. There were women who would come in with chickens, kill them and cook them right there. If a wife had a husband in there and she wanted to go in and live with him, she was free to do so. I didn't see anybody being tortured, abused, beaten, or threatened. In fact, the guards would likely sell you a fucking gun if you had enough money. One of the guards was bringing the heroin in to a prisoner who was my connection. This guy was doing seven years for selling heroin on the outside. He sold a lot of it in prison, too. I knew just how to have a jolly good time. It was great weather, too, nearly every day.

Unbelievably, the men were free to build their own huts, a *caraca*, by using slats of wood for the framework and draping the burlap on the sides and the front. Around the inner perimeter wall there was a roof which everyone utilized for the ceiling. To get the slats someone on the outside could bring them in, or deals could be made to procure them.

Early on Stella would bring us food and stuff, so it was not unusual to have things delivered. Soon, though, neither Ned nor Stella came around as they wanted to remain unmemorable.

On several occasions, I stayed for weeks because I got busy hanging out and being charmed by Michael Cooke, and he asked me to stay, telling guards I was his wife, and the fun began. I had heroin on the inside, and a man to play with. For about fifteen pesos, which was equivalent of a dollar and a quarter, I could get the dope I had to pay fifty to a hundred dollars for stateside. Like I'm gonna leave that? Plus, Mike was handsome, and clever.

"Todos bien a la hora de siete," (All is well at the hour of seven) the guards called out as they made their way from one tower to the next. The guard in the North tower would proceed to the East tower. The guard in the East tower proceeded to the South tower and on they would rotate every half an hour. *"Todos bien, a la hora de siete y media."*

There were inmates that were doing short time called *Quince-ados*. These guys were simply drunks sentenced to fifteen days. One day a Quince-ado guy sobered up, wanted a drink, took a running start across the courtyard. He jumped up and caught the edge of the roof that was around the wall, and pulled himself up onto it. Then he ran across the roof and lunged several feet between the first inner wall and the second outer wall. Miraculously he made it, but he stumbled. This immediately captured the attention of all the guards. The guard in the north tower shot at him but missed. Everyone froze as the Quince-ado disappeared over the second wall. For a split second it was quiet, then mayhem as everyone realized one of the guards in the other tower took the bullet intended for the Quince-ado. His head and arms slumped over the partial wall of his tower, followed by legs and feet as he tumbled out of the tower. Plop. He landed in the courtyard. As far as I know he was dead. Most of us retreated as far away from the scene as we could when the authorities came rushing in and dragged him out.

That was the only violence I saw there. Everybody seemed pretty content. The Mexican inmates had been in before and knew how to do their time. They have their *mammacitas* coming in to fuck 'em at night and bring something to cook and eat. It wasn't a bad life. It just wasn't a free one.

As for drugs, everybody seemed to be dealing. The foxes were guarding the henhouse, metaphorically. The other side of the prison was called the Grande. Someone had dug an escape tunnel over there. Unfortunately for them, they had just dug it out underneath the street and a truck drove over it and the tunnel caved in. *Trying* to escape wasn't nearly as big a crime in Mexico from what I understood, as it would have been in the U.S. They figured it was natural for someone to try to escape and the consequence was comparatively minimal, by way of the Napoleonic Code, left over from the laws of the French Invasion. However, *helping* someone to escape was a very serious crime. Being shot and/or incarcerated was a definite possibility for any accomplice, something that no other friend of those boys was willing to risk.

Five guys running and attempting to scale the walls to the outside was clearly not going to happen. Our boys needed to do something far less dramatic: more tunneling. The distance appeared possible, and the risk seemed reasonable considering it was likely they'd spend decades locked up when facing sentencing. After a few days of discussion, the groundbreaking ceremony occurred quietly in the dark of night beneath a cot. Chipping methodically with a butterknife for days, they finally broke through the concrete floor.

Anyone who's seen "The Shawshank Redemption" knows that when digging an escape tunnel, the biggest problem is where to hide the dirt. We packed the dirt up under our cots, poured it down the pipes in the bathrooms next to our caraca, under crates—everywhere we could. That's all we could do. We packed it under our cots and under our crates—everywhere we could. We kept thinking that sooner or later they were going to call an inspection.

Those boys dug that tunnel for seven months. Seven months on their bellies with coffee cups, soup spoons, and the butter knife, in a passage just big enough to crawl through. Once, I tried to go down into the tunnel but it was too hot and claustrophobic.

One day I came back in the *caraca* and I could tell something was wrong by the dark look on Mike's face.

"What's wrong?" I said, puzzled.

"We hit a sewer pipe. Paul fucking hit the sewer pipe," he said.

Chipping away with the butter knife, their primary digging tool, he had gouged a roughly one-inch wide by three-inch long hole into the side of the pipe.

"You what? Oh fuck . . ." my voice trailed off.

"Yeah, fuck," he lamented.

The boys had to repair the pipe or else the tunnel would be discovered. Not only that, but all the piss and shit in that prison had filled the entire ten feet of tunnel and gurgled inches below the floor in our *caraca*. Thankfully the pipe was well-below grade so it didn't overflow up and over, and there was a gap of a few inches above the muck line and the roof of the tunnel. The smell though, was not subtle, and was already starting to make my eyes burn. Of course, no one wanted to crawl through that putrid, reeking muck on their back with their mouth, nose, and eyes mere inches from frijole-laden turds and gallons of urine. To his credit Paulie had tried, but discovered our guys were just too big to successfully maneuver in those conditions.

Someone suggested we get little Benito to try to repair the pipe in exchange for some dope and the chance to escape. Benny was a small, young junkie who could never seem to stay out of prison. He was serving a pretty hefty sentence so we figured it would be worth the risk.

Someone sent for him and when he arrived, everyone was on their feet, grinning, "Hey Benito!"

Benny smiled and looked around a bit nervously. He was getting a much bigger welcome than he was normally accustomed to.

"Hey, *amigos*," he said as they all exchanged back slaps and handshakes.

"So . . . Benito . . . we have a proposition for you," Mike said.

"Yeah, I figured. What's up?"

"You want to get some dope right?"

"Yeah, fuck yeah, uh huh," he said, his eyes darted around, as he rubbed his runny nose, typical early withdrawal style.

"We will get you fixed twice if you do us this little favor. *And* you can escape with us."

Then someone explained.

Benito leaned over the hole and started to gag. "No fucking way, man," he said as he shook his head and backed away from the hole.

"C'mon man. You're junk sick right now. We will get you fixed. We've been working for months. You just gotta do this one thing," someone said.

"Nah, no fucking way man. That . . . that shit is nasty," he said as he shook his head. "And it *is* shit. Real fucking shit."

"We'll get you some dope and get you fixed when you get out."

"You'll get me fixed?"

"Yeah man. You do this, you got it coming."

"You'll keep me fixed? For how long?"

"Don't get greedy, man. We will get you well now, and high when you're done."

Benito glanced at the hole again. "Ah, what the hell . . . ok, you got it."

What a junkie won't do for a fix!

We decided to execute the repair in the middle of the night, scored Bennie's dope and waited.

"*Doce in la noche. Todos al bien.*" Shortly after the guard in the fourth tower confirmed that "all was well," the shadow of Bennie appeared at the entrance to our *caraca*.

In the meantime, we had a small piece of window screen and a coffee cup full of cement that we were hanging onto for "as yet" unknown reasons. Mace cut a patch from the window screen and premixed the cement after removing the rocks and smeared it onto both sides of the screen (like a pancake). The guys then slid it into a Yuban coffee tin along with a couple of strips of a torn shirt to clean the pipe a bit, and also to secure the patch into place. They snapped the lid into place to keep the materials clean and dry.

Benny then carefully began to ease into the opening. He had to enter head first, and on his back. Benito gagged and cursed as his face was mere inches from the roof of the tunnel and a fraction of an inch from the foul, slimy soup which gurgled and lapped over most of his body. We cringed and chuckled nervously as we heard him choke in earnest, apparently getting a mouthful of the putrid mess. "Fuck! Ffffff uck!" he sputtered, as he continued his way to the breach in the pipe. We could hear him grunt and slosh as he plugged the hole with the cement "bandage" that the guys had fashioned.

He skimmed some of the "floaters" off the top of the waterline with the coffee can for good measure, and the guys helped him out to avoid his face sinking below the mess.

"Get this shit off me!" he sputtered once he was clear of the hole. "It's done! Where's my dope?"

We had been waiting with buckets of fresh water, which we poured over him a little at a time, then wiped him down, so as not to call attention to the literal "shit show" going on in our *caraca*. One of the guys had already paid the connection for Benny's dope. As soon as he had his face rinsed off, he was off.

The sewer incident set progress back weeks. We couldn't risk trying to hide all that wet smelly muck. We had to bide our time. We all made the best of it, at least Mike and I did, with plenty of sex to distract us. Heroin was good, cheap and plentiful, so I wasn't in any hurry to go anywhere. What more could a girl want?

Finally, just before New Year's Eve, there was the last scrape of the spoon and the light fell into the tunnel, along with the smallest rush of air. The thirty-seven-foot tunnel was complete. The gravity and reality of what we were about to attempt was quite literally breathtaking. I made my way out past the reception area and hoped my legs would carry me out the door for the last time. Ned and Stella were waiting for me and we went back to the mansion to prepare.

Within a few days Ned told me, "We have a problem. You have

to go back in. They miscalculated."

They'd dug too far in an arc, and were still on the inside of the second wall. Back in I went. The palpable, yet silent frustration of thousands of thoughts blaming each other, blaming themselves hung in the air pervasive as the Mexican clay dust that permeated everything. One night, after yet more hours of pacing, Mike exclaimed, "I've got a flute!" He leapt all wide-eyed over to the crate where his meager belongings were housed and rummaged through his stuff. I was thinking he had really lost it and that he'd finally snapped and was going to start playing the flute in a maniacal bout of madness. He located the flute and held it up triumphantly for a moment.

"Yes!" he said emphatically and dove into his bag and rummaged some more. He pulled out a small square mirror, threw it to the ground and stepped on it, breaking it into fragments. We're all watching him, thinking, "What the fuck is going on? Did he just ensure us seven years of bad luck?" He got a strip of cloth and someone had the presence of mind to ask him, "What are you doing?"

"A periscope. I'm making a periscope!" he said, and by God he did. Genius. He got down in the tunnel and carefully stuck the end of the flute up through the ground in what we'd come to call "No Man's Land"—the space between the two walls. He realized in what direction they had to dig next—just a few more feet to the outer wall. Maybe a week or so more to go.

Unfortunately, the little hole in the top crust of the earth to accommodate the periscope compromised the integrity of the tunnel. After months of nothing but arid, dusty, semi-inland, Mexican weather, it rained. No, it poured, a deluge, and that little hole widened by the hour. Down into the tunnel Mace and Mike went. And when they emerged, their faces muddy and stained, the guys were grimly optimistic. Little by little the rain abated and the tunnel held up, muddy but intact. They decided to wait until things dried up. Each day that went by made it more likely that the search we always feared would happen was becoming increasingly imminent. There hadn't been a full prison search since the guys had been brought to Mazatlan Federal Prison. It was merely a matter of time.

Each day one of the guys would go down and check the status of the tunnel, and day by day, a long face would emerge, head shaking.

"No. Not ready." Then it happened: a search was called. On the other side of the prison there was chaos. Everyone on our side hung around their *caracas*, fidgety and restless, trying to act casual. We were all smoking cigarettes and talking in hushed tones, trying to act cool. Everybody was likely hiding something, guilty of one thing or another. As the Federales got closer, the possibility of defeat began to weigh heavier. Suddenly there was a commotion and the guards took away one of the guys just a couple of *caracas* away from us. Apparently satisfied with what they found, they stopped. All we could do was exhale.

A few days after the search, a grinning face emerged from the tunnel. "It's dry, we're good to go."

Tentatively, the digging began and then went non-stop. Mike would dig until he couldn't any more, and then Mace would take his place. The guys rigged up a relay system to remove the dirt: a string was tied to the handle of a bucket and it was pulled topside when it was full. The person on bucket duty would pull it up, distribute the dirt and then send it back down until the next tug.

Finally, it was time. Ned was in one rental car, and I was in the other. We could just make out the guards in each of the four towers. My heart was pounding so hard I honestly thought it was gonna beat out of my chest. My knees shook. I don't think we really believed until we were gone that it was gonna come off without a hitch. We waited and waited and waited. Nothing. By 4 a.m., we headed back to the mansion.

We went back the next night. We waited. Each of us, in our cars, smoking cigarettes, playing the radio low, hardly daring to blink in case we missed something. Hours went by. Nobody showed up. We slowly pulled away and slid back to the mansion to make another attempt the next night.

But shortly after we drove away, there was slight movement, and then the first little head popped up out of that hole. All that time digging, sweating, planning, waiting was about this moment. First, there was the shadowy image of a head. Next hands and arms appeared and pushed up to reveal a torso and upper thighs. One knee caught the rim of the hole, then the other. Slowly each guy got to his feet and upwards to stand while remaining pressed tightly against the wall. Then shuffle, shuffle, shuffle sideways to make room for the next guy. Each repeated the process, flat as possible against that old wall. After the last head popped up, stood up, pressed against the stone edifice, and side-stepped over, they all stepped out from the wall, and urgently, but with great constraint, they walked across the street, out of sight of the towers. By then it was almost daylight.

I heard Ned's voice in my sleep.

"You're where? Fuck. Yeah, yeah. Ok. We're on our way."

There was the sound of a phone being put back on the receiver in a room nearby, then I heard Stella's voice and felt the bed shaking, "Samantha, Samantha? They're out! They're out!" I was in that weird twilight place between asleep and awake.

"Who's out? Wha . . . ? Oh shit!" I bolted up and sprang out of bed.

"I guess we just missed 'em, Sam. We gotta get to 'em. Shit!" Ned cursed, and threw me a set of keys. I had fallen asleep fully clothed, so I shot out the door behind him.

We pulled up to the prearranged meeting place when we saw the guys. They seemed to head towards us. It was hard to tell in the low light. Then they disappeared around the corner in the opposite direction. The tail lights of Ned's car lit up and started to pull away, making a slow U-turn heading away from the guys, heading in the opposite direction. Confused, I followed in my car, creeping along and saw the guys, way at the other end of the street, but now coming towards us moving briskly, their feet kicking up little puffs of dust. Ned pulled over into the shadows, out of the glare of the prison lights, and I followed. The guys shoved their hands in their pockets and attempted to appear casual, though their stride increased with every step. Silently they got into the cars. No one dared say a word. Our hearts were pounding as we drove away. There was no screeching of tires, just a steady acceleration as we left Mazatlan Federal Prison farther and farther behind.

Once we had gotten up into the mountains we stopped, all piled out and started screaming. Everybody was hysterically happy. Everyone but me. I had heroin, a syringe, a lighter, and a spoon in my pocket. All I needed was water. Apparently, it had rained enough up here to leave a few puddles. I only needed a little water, and that one puddle would do. I now had it all. I disappeared from all the jubilant chaos, pulled water out of the mud puddle with my syringe, put it in the spoon, cooked it up, pulled it up into the syringe and shot up quick. I got back into the car and I was loaded *and* happy. I had planned this little celebratory fix way in advance. But I didn't have anything to hold the water in. When I saw that mud puddle, I thought that the Zippo would kill whatever germs were floatin' in it. I really did. It seems absurd, totally absurd, now. Pull water out of a mud puddle in the mountains and shoot it? Straight into a vein? I did. I don't know what got into me, how I got that crazy to begin with. In my fantasies, I was still just a normal girl from the South.

✳

We drove through the Sierra Madre mountains to Durango where Kris Kristofferson, Bob Dylan, and others were filming *Pat Garrett and Billy the Kid*. They were all at the Durango Hotel when we checked in. I remember writing Kris a note and leaving it at the front desk: "Hi Kris, I know you're making a movie. I'm here on other business." And I drew a smiley face. "Love to see you." But the next day we left, so I never got to see him. He told me later he had gotten my note after I had already left. Ned put the guys, complete with false papers, on a train through El Paso. Then we went back to the mansion in Mazatlan.

I started acting up not long afterwards, meaning using heroin almost constantly. One day at the beach, I looked up, and here comes a really attractive girl in a bikini, along with a guy who looked a little like Dylan, though I knew it wasn't him. Still, as soon as I saw them, I knew they were stoned on heroin. Ninety percent of the time I could spot a junkie. I struck up a conversation.

"I see you guys are loaded."

They laughed and said, "Yeah, why? Do you use?"

"Yes. I most certainly do."

Originally, coming down to Mazatlan, I was supposed to be staying clean. That ended in the prison. Soon, I was hanging out with this new couple, and went over to their place. We had bought some dope and I was in the bathroom shooting up. I remember feeling my brain start to sizzle.

"Oh shee . . . it!" I knew. I'd been there before: once with Janis, and one other time in the filthy restroom of a Chevron service station in the Fillmore District of San Francisco all by myself on a Christmas Eve. ...this is it! I blew it! Then I saw the floor came up and hit me in the face, but of course that was just me passing out. That's the last thing I remember until I woke up staring at the sky.

It must have been around dawn when I came to, since the sky was starting to turn that purple color, when there are no clouds and you know the day will be lit with blue skies. As I opened my eyes, I saw nothing but stars and purple. It looked like the sky of another world. I could feel wind, like I was flying through this purple, starry haze.

Oh God, I'm dead. I overdosed. Oh. My. God. I did it, I overdosed. My poor parents!

I'm flying through the sky. But before the fact of my death sunk in, my first thought, my first feeling, was of my parents, my sweet loving parents. They would soon know that their only child died of an overdose, died a junkie, and her body thrown unceremoniously into a cow pasture in Mexico.

My solo ascent into the great unknown was suddenly interrupted by four or five kindly, brown-skinned male faces framed in white ruffles, holding musical instruments in their hands, peering down at me. *Angels?* These are Angels! Holy Shit, you die in Mexico you go to Mexican Heaven? *And* you have to listen to Mariachi music for eternity? I thought, "Oh, no, no, no, noooo, this is awful . . . I'll never be all right in heaven without hearing the Rolling Stones!"

One by one the faces turned away and I began trying to make sense of this new reality. A blade of grass waved in the breeze, touched my cheek, and I absently slapped my face. Immediately, I thought "Hey, I felt that!" I began feeling my face, touching my face. *So, I'm not dead! This is my face!* I sat up and I could see the musicians walking across the field way in the distance. I looked around. I was in the middle of a cow pasture. The way I figured it, I had overdosed around eleven o'clock at night. When I came to it must have been about five in the morning because dawn was breaking.

In the far, far distance I saw lights that I was sure were the beach hotels. Apparently, I had overdosed and had all the signs of being dead: blue lips, pale, no discernible pulse. I got here, in a field, because those folks weren't going to take the beef for my being dead or overdosed, especially in a foreign country. And I can't say I blamed them. I reasoned that they threw me in a cow pasture because they did believe I was dead. Imagine their surprise when I saw them later, on the beach.

"It's alright. It's alright. I'm not pissed and I'm obviously not dead. Really. I understand."

"We thought you *were* dead!"

"I know, I thought I was, too. I woke up dead."

Meanwhile, Kim showed up in Mexico because she'd heard I was doing Yoga, and clean. She arrived while I was missing in action and knew that meant I was off doing heroin. Kimmie tracked down Susan, the female part of the junkie ensemble, and threatened her, trying to find out where I was. Thankfully she didn't know. Hell, I don't even know where I'd gone off to. I mean I wasn't proud of my behavior. It was another junkie mess I made. Here it was supposed to be a happy reunion with Ned and Stella and Kim and me, and everybody was gonna be joyful. Well . . . I didn't do what everybody wanted and expected . . . and I didn't do what *I* wanted and expected.

The incomprehensible nature of addiction. The inability to live the way everybody wants you to. Even yourself. So, it was ugly when I finally did reappear. Kim had flown back home angry. Ned and Stella were mad at me and together they decided to send me back home. I was an increasing liability. I had just gone off and nearly died in a cow pasture, so I agreed to leave. I amended my plane ticket and flew into Aspen instead of directly home, and partied. I don't know why I did that. I don't ski. I was simply out of my mind. After being there a few days I flew on to San Francisco and promptly got completely and utterly strung out again.

✺

Mom and I fought today. She refuses to use her hearing aid. I asked her if she was ready for lunch. She went into a panic.

"What do you mean we're not having lunch? Why aren't we having lunch today?"

I calmly try to tell her, but she can't hear me clearly, plus she's nearly hysterical. So, I start raising my voice. Then she gets upset.

"Why are you yelling at me?"
"Mom, I wasn't. You don't hear me."
"Yes, I do."
"No, you don't."

I get furious because I get no sleep—maybe two hours straight at any given time. "You refuse to wear your hearing aids, Mother! If you keep on like this I'm gonna have to just stick them in your ears myself!"

A while later I see her sitting on the edge of her bed. She's arranging her pills, books, magazines, tissues—all the little things she keeps on her nightstand. She's quietly putting them in order, and at that moment, she's just so precious. So very precious. I feel so bad for being upset with her. So awful that this last stretch of her life, however long it will be, is fraught with us arguing. I'm so tired. She is such a trooper. Every day she gets up and arranges her ensemble of clothing that she's gonna wear. She fixes her hair and then sprays it into place. She puts on her lipstick and greets the day just like she's going somewhere, even if most days we go nowhere. She wants to look good wherever that might be. My heart goes out to her.

※

For most of 1973, I continued flopping around San Francisco, sleeping here and there. Sometimes I stayed in the back of a truck with a camper shell which was parked outside of the lesbian bar Maud's. Other times I stayed in a hotel when I scraped up enough money to afford that and my precious dope, too. I hocked, sold, or traded my jewelry. I even traded a ring Janis had given me, for a bag of dope. I once sold a pair of socks to a weirdo who picked me up when I was hitch-hiking across the Golden Gate. He asked me how long I had been wearing them. When I told him about a week, he offered me ten dollars. I held out, he became more desperate. I finally let him have them for twenty. It was a good trade.

By now I stayed away from The Haight as much as possible. Truthfully, I tried to stay away from most everyone. I couldn't stand what I had become but I also couldn't stand to be any other way. Bobby Boles was still flourishing. He used to plead with me, begging me to stop using. I could hardly take it. I really loved Bobby. We "got" each other, and it was torture to see his face as he grabbed me, his voice choking, tears in his eyes as he looked deep into mine, searching, I think, for a "me" that had gone dormant.

"Peggy, please, please don't do this. You've got to stop. You can stop. I know you can. I'll do anything. We can still make tons of money. There are still good times to be had. Please, please believe me. C'mon Peg, you've forgotten who you are."

That last line, *You've forgotten who you are,* hurt the most because he was right. Seems I could now only remember to be the junkie Peggy and all that went with it. I didn't want to be reminded of what had been. It was just too much.

Rarely would I head out to my house in Stinson Beach. Kim was living there and I didn't want to risk a beating for showing up to my own house loaded. Nor did I want to feel the reality of my situation. I couldn't face officially ending it with Kim, though by then there wasn't much of a relationship left.

Meanwhile, I had met a gorgeous dyke named Dee and her girlfriend Lana. Dee was an intelligent person, but also a junkie who once had a decent position at Dean Whittier until heroin led her out of the corporate world and into the High Low Life. She was very attractive and thoroughly butch with dark curly hair and sea green eyes. I found her stunning. Yet, the real catalyst for our eventual coming together was that we were the same kind of junkie—all or nothing.

I was about to go into my *nothing* phase.

I wanted to be in LA. For some reason, I felt that if I were there, I could make an honest attempt to stop using heroin. Also, by then I wanted to get away from the backlash from that awful book which carried my name and purported to tell "the truth" about my friendship with Janis. The salacious, sexually gratuitous focus of that book had embarrassed my parents mercilessly and destroyed the friendship I had with Sam Andrew. I was so ashamed for allowing that to happen to the story, not just Janis, but the story of The Haight, and all of us who were there in the beginning. I couldn't face anyone in San Francisco anymore. When I was being honest with myself, I understood that I had signed away all my rights for what at the time just seemed like a big publisher's check, not my soul. I used every cent for dope money. I never dreamed of the repercussions, and each hit of dope I shot kept that reality just far enough away to get me through another day.

*

Dr. Rita Scharff was a big Janis fan who had read the book, and wrote me a letter that arrived at my Stinson Beach post office box where I occasionally still checked my mail. I didn't know precisely what her agenda was, except that she was now offering to help me get clean, help me get off heroin. To do this, she explained that she was connected with a man who was in charge of Suicide Prevention Center of Los Angeles, which also housed a Methadone clinic.

"There's a waiting list, but I can move you right through to the top of the list and get you into this clinic for treatment. If you'll come down here, you can stay with me."

Dr. Scharff didn't know me, and I wondered why some doctor out of the blue would track me down. It had to do with the book. I convinced myself to accept her invitation. I left everything and went to LA. Dr. Scharff, true to her word, provided me a place to stay and I began the process of getting off of heroin and switching over to Methadone.

In the meantime, Dee was also getting clean. "I'm down here cleaning up, I don't want to see you unless you're clean, too," I told her.

She assured me that she was, so I said, "Well, come on down. You can stay here if I tell the doctor that I need you with me to help me stay clean."

Big mistake.

Once Dee arrived, she and I found our way to some dope and I don't even recall having the thought of *not* using it. Here we were both clean and suddenly, we used. It's the oddest trait of addicts. All logic or reason disappeared—one moment we were drug-free and sober, and the next we picked up again like we'd never skipped a beat. From an outsider's perspective, it makes no sense, but at that moment it seemed like a perfectly natural thing to do. It was as if we'd never been clean. There we were wandering around LA one day, clean, and the next, we were at the doctor's house shooting up. The worst part is that we both ODd there. The good news was the doctor had the antidote to an overdose. I was out cold and it was Dee who somehow managed to shoot us with the medicine. When Dr. Scharff found us, and learned that the antidote had been used, she made us leave. I don't blame her. If we had died, likely she would have lost her license.

From there somehow, Dee and I got back to San Francisco and all hell broke loose. Between Lana, Kim, that book, and the dope, I couldn't take the pressure. It felt impossible to stay. I had to get out of San Francisco again. And somehow, some way, I had to get away from drugs. Now anybody would laugh and well they should, that my decision to get away from drugs was to move, once again, back to Los Angeles. Hollywood, no less! Brilliant, huh? I believe that in those twelve step programs, they call that kind of moving logic a "geographic." Usually you "pull a geographic" to go somewhere where you believe the dope *isn't*. Not me.

On one of my phone calls home, Mom suspected something.

"Peggy? Peggy, you sound like you got that shit in your mouth again."

"No mom. I'm just tired."

"I've heard you tired all my life. This ain't tired."

"Yes. It. Is. Mo-ther!" I took care to enunciate each syllable.

"I don't believe you, Peggy."

"Believe what you want Mother. I don't want to talk to you if you're going to be like this."

"You're doing it again, aren't you? Oh God, I can't take it!" She hung up the phone.

I impassively hung up mine, and sat on the edge of the bed for a moment. Sighing, I fished out my syringe. Next thing I knew, oblivion.

I RAN INTO SOME TROUBLE

❋

"I never go anywhere. I want to go outside!" Mom says.

"You can't. It's 107 degrees with 97 percent humidity."

"Just for a little while, darlin', can't I just go out for a little while?"

"Mother, the news reports say to keep the elderly, children, and pets indoors."

"I've been in the south all my life. I can handle it."

"No, you can't. I'm not letting you. The last time it was this hot was a hundred years ago. Three years before you were born. You are not going out!"

Mom pouts.

Three days later, she asks, "Peggy, please just let me set outside awhile. Just a little while?"

"Mother, it's not safe, and I'm NOT sitting out there with you."

"Just let me set a bit. Can't be that hot out."

"Alright mother. Go ahead. You'll see."

She has her walker, two cans of Busch Lite, her sunglasses and an attitude. She's ready to go. I open the door for her and she makes her way out and sits in her chair, takes a sip of beer and looks quite content. I walk away from the door.

Minutes later I hear, "Peggy? Peggy?! Peggeee!!??"

"What, Mother?"

"It's awful hot out here."

"I know, Mother."

"I want to come in!"

This goes on for three more days. She goes out in the sweltering inferno and in minutes she's done.

It's exhausting. It's my life, now. A labor of love, sprinkled with me getting hysterical.

❋

Part Five

NOT LONG AFTER "the book" I was staying at a place on Geary Street, which borders the Fillmore District. This area, though famous for the concerts that Bill Graham produced, was also famous for not being safe. It was known for drugs, pimps, hookers, gangs and crime. Thus, it's attraction to a desperate junkie like me.

It was raining when I was standing on the corner somewhere near Geary, my thumb out, hitching a ride to look for a connection named Mop. My nose was running and withdrawals crawled out of my bones and up my throat. I saw a Porsche coming down the street, headlights on . . . damn if it didn't look like my Porsche. Sure enough, it was the Porsche I had bought for Kimmie—Surfboard Blue I called it. There wasn't another like it in San Francisco. I know she saw me because I just couldn't be missed. I was the only thing happening on that corner. The car slowed down for a moment, then sped up to become just another set of taillights fading into the mist.

"Fuck . . . ing bitch," I muttered. "Ain't that somethin'?"

I was still managing to make the payments on that Porsche, strung out as I was. My Shelby was in the shop waiting for me to pay for its repairs. But I chose to spend my money on the dope rather than fixing the car. I was so indignant that Kim had the nerve to leave me standing in the rain, while under her ass was the vehicle I was still paying on. But that was Kim. I know she was angry about me using dope, but after she had beat me repeatedly, all that love I used to have for her had turned to disdain. The dope had been what made the pain bearable. Still, on this evening I had enough feeling left for some self-righteous anger. A lot of good it did me.

I finally got a ride deep into the Fillmore, to an area I thought I had once copped some decent dope, when out of an alley came a gang of young thugs, probably between twelve and fourteen years old, the oldest might have been about fifteen or sixteen. The one who appeared to be the oldest asked me what I was doing there. I said, "None of your business." I was being cocky and sarcastic.

He said, "Yeah it is. It's my business in my neighborhood."

Next thing I knew these kids surrounded me and pulled me into the alley out back of an old building. I had sixteen or so hands on me—some had my hair, some had tits, some had ass, some had arms. I was cussing up a storm. "You motherfuckers! Let me go! What the fuck are you doing?"

The smell of piss and cigarettes was thick, and it had rained just enough to get everything wet but not enough to wash things clean. They pushed, shoved, and eventually dragged me up a stairway. I screamed bloody murder, but they just laughed. "No one is gonna hear you that cares, you honky bitch."

I figured that was probably true so I hurled insults at them the best I could. "Fuck you, you little shits. What the fuck do you think you can do? Does your mother know where you are? Isn't it time for your nap, you fucking babies?" That got me a few slaps to the face, a sock to the gut, and rougher handling until they got me to what turned out to be the roof.

"Shut the fuck up," said one of the older ones.

"Fuck you," I said.

They pushed me toward the edge.

"Hold her down," said one of them as he pulled out a knife.

I squirmed and kicked and flailed my arms.

"Hold her!" he yelled. They finally got me down and ripped at my clothes. The oldest one tore off my jacket and rummaged through the pockets. He came up with a syringe and the money I had for a fix. He stuffed the money in his pocket and tossed the syringe.

"You're not gonna say anything are you now? You junkie fucking bitch."

"Fuck you!" I yelled. "Fuck. YOU!"

"We're gonna fuck you, we're all gonna fuck you." And they pulled my pants down. The younger ones went first. A few pumps and it was all over, then the next one, same thing. Thank God I couldn't feel them—physically anyway. This went on for I don't know how long. The oldest finally had his turn, and he definitely hurt me. Once he finished, he turned to the others and said, "Now what are we gonna do with her?"

My spunk came back for a minute and I shouted, "What more can you do, you fuckers? Just leave me the fuck alone and let me get out of here."

"Nah, I don't think so."

"What if she tells?" asked one of the younger ones. I noticed he spoke like a kid, for whom "telling" was a big deal.

"Just fucking let me go!" I said in a voice low with anger, fear, and desperation. I snatched my jacket up from the littered tar roof and spun on my heel.

At this the oldest shouted. "Grab her!"

Suddenly, all these hands were all over me. Again. He began shoving me towards the edge of the roof.

"Fuck, *you*!" I screamed. The next thing I knew I was bent over the edge from my waist, my head hanging down, facing the street below. I thought for sure this was it. The end would come about in an unlovely heap of splattered junkie somewhere in The Fillmore. They were arguing about whether to push me off or not. On one level, I wasn't sure if I really cared if they did. Then the spunk kicked in that got me into trouble just as often as it helped me to succeed.

"Go ahead and push me, fuckers. Drop me!" I squawked. "You— you're the oldest. Who do you think is gonna do time for this? Not those little punks for sure. Nah, you're gonna take the rap for ALL of it." I was getting fired up now. "You think those little twits won't rat you out? You could offer them a cookie and they'd sell you out. Am I really worth you doing that much time?" He caught my eye on that last one. In an instant I felt I had him. The little ones had gone quiet.

"Bitch. Fucking bitch," he said under his breath. Then he reached over and grabbed the front of my shirt and pushed me toward the edge.

I heard, "Grab her, stupid. Grab her!" I felt a bunch of spidery fingers pull on my arms and yank me back forward. I was panting by then, slightly bent over trying to hold it together.

"Get the fuck out of here before I kill you," the eldest one said.

Some of the others chimed in, "Yeah, get the fuck out of here," trying to act tough. A couple of the younger ones stayed quiet and avoided my eyes. Looking at the ground, at their friends, at the sky, anywhere but at me. I took a few steps backwards toward the door to the staircase that stuck out like a monolith rising out of the roof. I grabbed the knob and hardly remember getting down the stairs. I made my way out of that neighborhood and out to Fillmore Street and stuck out my thumb. The trauma was setting in as well as me being dope sick. Both hit me full force as I stood on the corner, desperate.

After about fifteen minutes a car pulled over. "You look bad," said the guy in the passenger seat.

I said, "I've been raped."

They said, "C'mon we'll drive you out."

When I went to get in the back seat, the guy in the front passenger seat jumped out and had me get in the front, then he got back in beside me. Now these two guys have me wedged between them. We took off out of the Fillmore and when I said, "That's my street," they kept going. I knew I was in trouble. When they pulled onto the freeway I realized it was going to be worse than I thought. They ended up taking me to Hunter's Point, a shipyard area universally acknowledged as the most dangerous area of the city. Once they parked the driver said, "This is it. Take off your clothes."

"No!" I yelled.

"Oh, you're gonna take 'em off," he growled.

Hunter's Point is a long way from anywhere civil or civic, miles from San Francisco proper. Aside from game days at Candlestick Park, everything was empty and desolate. The Naval Radiological Defense Laboratory, where they decontaminated ships exposed to atomic weapons testing was located here, along the waterfront in addition to the power plants that supplied electricity to the City.

They stopped the car around the corner from one of the power plants that hummed sinisterly from behind the chain link fence and the "Danger Do Not Enter High Voltage" sign. They knew I didn't have a prayer of anyone coming by and stopping them. I could smell the diesel and grease of the shipyards. The proximity to the water added a chill that seeped into the marrow of my bones as the driver opened his door. "Get out" he barked as he exited and made his way over to the passenger side of the vehicle. I slid over to the door and stood up as they grabbed my arms. They pulled off my jacket and noticed the track marks. "Ah, a junkie, too." They said, "We can rape you and dump you out here and nobody will ever find you. Or even care if they did."

At that moment, I was overcome not with fear but with sadness. Not because I felt I was fixin' to die, but that I had come that far down, and let my folks down that badly. Getting raped twice in one night was simply un-fucking-believable, and I didn't want them to find out that such a thing had happened to their little girl on the last night of her life, while out trying to score some dope.

I refused to cooperate and the driver pushed me down and pinned me across the back seat and started choking me. He was proving to be the worst of the two. Still, I wouldn't give in. When I knew that I was about to die, when I could feel my consciousness slipping, I held my hand up in a gesture of surrender. Enough. He finally let go of my throat and they each raped me.

Afterwards, believe it or not, they drove me back to San Francisco and as we neared the city limits, asked, "Where do you want to go?"

I said, "Divisadero." That was a straight line from where they'd originally found me, but on the other side of Fillmore. I had been raped I don't know how many times, and all I could think of was, "I'm dope sick and hurt. I just want some dope to kill all pain."

At Divisadero Street, they let me out. The guy that was always the passenger stepped out for me to exit since I was sitting between them as before, and incredulously, asked, "Can I call you sometime?"

I thought, "Are you out of your mind? You just RAPED me and now you want to date me?" But I was afraid and I said, "Yeah, alright." What else could I do? There are some guys who honestly believe that women like it. There are men who think rape is no big deal—you got raped, you liked it. No! I didn't like it! It HURT, you bastard! So I made up a phone number because I knew the prefix around Divisadero. I gave him the made-up number and he wrote it down. I knew he would never find me because I was rarely seen in that area.

I found my way to my dealer's house and rang his apartment from the call box. He came on the intercom.

"Who is it?"

"It's Peggy, I'm sick."

Joe buzzed me in. As soon as I got in the door, I started crying. "Look, I don't have any money. I've been raped. I'm junk sick and I need to get fixed."

He could tell it wasn't some junkie sob story, so he gave me enough dope to get well, and a little extra to get high, which was a very welcome bonus. Once I had shot the dope I asked him, "How in the hell do men justify raping a woman, then asking her out?"

"Hell, Peggy. I don't know," Joe said, pausing reflectively. "Ya know, I hear guys talk shit sometimes and wonder what the hell they're thinking. Like somehow these women aren't somebody's mom, or sister, or girlfriend. It's crazy." He crushed his cigarette out in the ashtray.

"That, to me," I hesitated, "is almost as bad as being raped—that there is no consequence. Like underneath it all, we somehow ask for it." I lit one of my Pall Mall cigarettes, exhaling slowly and deeply.

"Yeah, you're right. It's like some extra bit of mind fuck." He shook his head. "No one deserves that. Seriously fucked up shit, man."

After I had become sufficiently numb, I left. I certainly didn't want to wear out my welcome with a decent connection. Had I been on this side of town initially, I would have gone to him. He tended to be more expensive, so I was trying to save some money by going to the Fillmore. After leaving his place, I don't remember where I went. It seems I wandered up Haight Street looking for a place to stay. It was horror, absolute horror. I had no wheels, no friends, no place to stay—and Haight Street had once been mine.

At some point that night I went to a phone booth and called home.

"Mom, now don't get upset," I began.

She said, "What Peggy?"

"I've been raped."

Mom started crying. "Oh my baby, my poor baby!"

"Mom, I need to get off the street. I just need to get off the street and to a doctor."

She said, "Ok. What do you need?"

I said, "Five hundred dollars. I need to get off the street and to a doctor."

"Where are you?" she asked.

"Van Ness. Send it to the Van Ness Western Union address," I instructed her.

"Ok, baby. We'll get it out right away."

I hung up and walked from that phone booth to Western Union and waited. It wasn't long until the money came. Once I got the cash, I got a room in some motel.

The next morning I went to a doctor. "What brings you in today?" he asked.

"I've been raped."

"Well, when?"

"Last night."

"Well, you know it's too early to tell if you're pregnant."

"Yes, I know."

"The best I can do is give you a shot of penicillin in case you get gonorrhea."

He gave me the shot and sent me on my way. Shortly after that I went back to Geary Street where I knew some other junkies, including a guy named Bobby who I adored, a gay guy who was strung out. A few other junkies and I were sitting at his kitchen table and I said, "I'm going to get out of this somehow, someway. I'm gonna get out of this."

I meant it.

But first, I needed to get fixed.

I copped some dope and fixed in the dirty bathroom at the Chevron Service Station in the Fillmore District on Christmas Eve. After locking the door from the inside, I pulled out my works, balancing the little bottle cap I carried on the edge of the sink. My hand shook as I poured the heroin in. I stirred a little water in with the bottom of the plunger of the syringe. I flicked my Zippo lighter open and lit the flame, passing it under the cap until it was heated just right. Flicked the cover of the lighter closed and dropped a tiny piece of cotton into the cap. Putting the end of the needle to where it was just touching the little wad of cotton, I drew up the hit, filtering out any large particles through the cotton sieve. I tied off my arm with a scarf, holding one end in my teeth. Raising the syringe, I flicked it a few times to encourage any air bubbles to the top. Satisfied that there were no bubbles, I stuck myself a few times in a vein trying to get a register. There was blood on my arm with each stab, but none in the needle. I cursed through my bared teeth, while the blood oozed down my arm. I found another vein and missed again while the blood beaded up over the needle. I stabbed again and finally saw the welcome register of blood flowing into the syringe proving I had found "home." I shoved the plunger all the way down. Within a second I knew it was too much. Down I went onto the filthy tile floor.

Lights out.

Merry fucking Christmas.

When I finally came to, apparently I had been on that nasty, wet, bathroom floor for a day and a half. The station had been closed for the holiday, and the pounding on the door had finally aroused me. Lying there, on a gas station bathroom floor in a rundown neighborhood, out of my mind, passed out, I knew that my using was now repeatedly putting myself into terribly dangerous situations.

Yet, I could not stop.

※

I get home from the grocery store, it's a muggy summer afternoon and Mom is hysterical. She's worried she's had an accident in her pants. She's all aflutter and her hair is disheveled, which is so unlike her, and she's pointing to the bathroom. I head toward the bathroom to check out this accident. Mom starts crying.

"Please, don't go in there Peggy, it's bad. It's so bad. I feel so bad!"

But I have to see what had happened. And you know what? Nothin'. There was no accident. But I see that Mom has succeeded in completely changing her clothes, thus the disheveled hair.

"Mom, it's really nothing. You're all right."

She looks at me and says, "Do you know how many tissues I have left in the Kleenex box?"

※

Circa 1975-ish, once I got out of San Francisco for good, one of the more unpleasant changes that accompanied my move to the Los Angeles area was the fact that I began to get arrested.

One of the first times I got busted in LA for being under the influence and in possession of a controlled substance I went into withdrawals. How could being in a holding cell be so hellishly cold, I wondered? The chill bumps as I started kicking were horrendous. It felt like ice had infiltrated my bones and veins. There was nothing but me, a toilet and toilet paper in my cell. I screamed myself hoarse, begging for a blanket. Finally, a guard stopped in front of my cell, her face impassive.

"Please, I'm fucking freezing. Please, I just want a blanket," I said, sniffling from the tell-tale runny nose that warns of opiate reserves gone below "E." Any flicker of hope was stamped out when she told me to shut the hell up, smirked, and leisurely walked away. I yelled a string of expletives after her, long after she was out of earshot. That made me feel a little better, so I cursed and I stomped my feet, crossing my arms tightly across my chest and rubbing them frantically. It didn't take long for me to run out of steam. Involuntary chills came in waves. I huddled in a corner, on the cold cement floor, curled up in the fetal position, but I just couldn't get warm. The roll of toilet paper was about a foot away and I stared at it as I rocked back and forth, groaning. Suddenly I got an idea. I scooted over and took off my jumpsuit, grabbed the end of the toilet paper with my left hand and began wrapping my right arm, beginning at one my wrist. I kept wrapping and wrapping, over my shoulder, down the other arm and back. Then I criss-crossed the paper like a *bandito*, over my shoulder and around my torso, doubling up over that. I continued my wrap job around my hips and down each of my legs. I put my jumpsuit back on, feeling almost warm and quite happy with myself.

About an hour later, I heard the guard call from down the hall.

"Caserta, you're up next."

I was standing at the door by the time she was within sight.

"Oh my God!" she said abruptly, as her mouth hung open.

I stared back, my eyes blinking defiantly from slits between strips of toilet paper.

"Thanks for the blanket" I said.

"You need to take that off," she barked.

"No!" I crossed my arms in front of my chest.

"C'mon, Caserta," she said, almost laughing this time. "Really? C'mon."

"No!"

"Caserta, you can't do this. You're going before the judge."

"Yes, I can. I'm fucking freezing and I'm going like this."

"Suit yourself," she said and held the door open for me.

I had wrapped the paper so tightly around my joints that it was difficult to bend my knees or arms, but I held my chin up and walked stiff-legged, arms rigid. I had the inhuman gait of an early Frankenstein monster or mummy as the cop escorted me to stand in front of the judge. I heard muffled snickering when I entered the courtroom.

"Peggy Louise Caserta, is that your name?"

"Yes, yes, it is."

"Why have you come into my courtroom dressed like a mummy? I don't think it's Halloween, is it?"

I hear more snickering.

"No, it isn't Halloween," I began and then realized that this was my chance to end the suffering of every junkie who ever had to endure the torture of bone rattling chills in a holding cell without a blanket. "I was freezing, Your Honor. They don't give us blankets in the holding cells. I might as well have been in the Arctic Tundra, it was so cold. This is inhumane."

"Miss Cah Ser Tah," the judge said, emphasizing each syllable. "You will stop talking. Now!"

"But you asked me," I shot back.

"Miss Cah Ser Tah," he began again. "You are being charged for possession of heroin and being under the influence of a controlled substance. That is why you are here. You are not here for your enjoyment. Nor are you here to waste the court's time with your activism. Do you understand?"

"Yes, Your Honor, but it is really, really cold. I'm not kidding. You should . . ." I just can't help myself sometimes.

"Enough!" he yelled. "Enough! Miss Caserta, you can take up any issues you may have with the County another time. As for now, on the charge of possession of three grams of heroin, how do you plead?"

"Not guilty!"

"The defendant has entered the plea of not guilty."

My moment of glory was gone. The sick was taking over again. The judge asked my plea for each of the charges. I went on autopilot. Not guilty. Not guilty. Not guilty. Back in my cell, it was still freezing, but I had to pee, which meant I had to unwrap myself. When they came to get me to take me back to Sybil Brand only my upper body was still wrapped.

"Let's go, Caserta," a different guard said, swinging the door open. "Or should I say, the mummy of Cleopatra?"

"You're really fucking funny," I muttered as I walked out, arms stiff as a tin soldier's, sniffling and shivering as I boarded the Sheriff's bus back to my County-sponsored abode.

After I did whatever time I got for those particular charges, I ended up having spates of extended stays as a guest of the County of Los Angeles. The more I went to jail, the more times I got to go to jail, and the more time I spent there on each return visit.

Once Dee knew I was out, she followed me down to Hollywood and we started scamming and flipping from pad to pad, motel to motel, rippin' and runnin'. Quite by accident we stumbled upon a drug previously unknown to us. We were very junk sick and somebody said, "I don't have any heroin but I have Dilaudid. It's an opiate-based pill."

"Nah, I'm no pill head. I don't want a pill. I want some real dope."

But it was injectable, so Dee said, "Well, *I* wanna get well," and she shot it. In a minute or less she said, "Huh . . . I'm well. Peggy, I'm well!"

Although one could obtain ready-to-inject Dilaudid, we came to prefer the oral Dilaudid because the rush was better when we crushed it up, watered it down, cooked it up and shot it. By then, it was virtually the same as heroin. A bonus was that there's no cut. It takes away the possibility of overdosing because the dose is the same every time, controlled by the dosage of the pill. Pills were never mixed with God-knows-what. Theoretically, you *could* overdose on it, but you would have to set out to purposely kill yourself, and say, "This is it. I'm gonna shoot twenty of these fuckers." All the junkies I knew were chasing the high and trying to keep the withdrawals from even starting. Dilaudid took away the specter of Russian Roulette that always came with heroin. You had to trust your source, and sometimes you'd get burned.

Still, heroin doesn't loosen its hold on a junkie that easily.

Nights fell hard in LA, especially on days I couldn't find any heroin. When some of the usual petty pushers aren't holding, panic sets in. Users start calling each other to see if, by chance, someone else's connection is holding. When none of the known suppliers have product, anxiety spreads and junkies are freaking out. Pretty soon everyone, in their heightened paranoia, begins to think the CIA has plotted to create the shortage! I was always more focused on the immediate problem: how was I going to stay well—get just enough to forestall withdrawal symptoms. If I got high in the process, great, but getting fixed enough that getting sick is no longer looming? That is gold. The usual drawback for a street addict is not having the money to get the drug, but the absolute pits is having the money and not being able to find the drug. Either situation doesn't leave the user with keen decision-making skills.

This was one of those occasions, Dee and I had $120 between us, enough for two $50 bags and $20 left for gas. Since we always fixed together, we were on the same clock for withdrawing—double panic.

"Gotta a plan? Anything?" I asked her.

"I'm planned out! Why don't you come up with something? You got a plan?"

Our nerves were shot and our voices were getting edgy.

"Actually, I might. As a last-ditch effort, we might could try Oxnard."

"Oxnard! Who do you know there?"

"No one," I said. "But there's the Colonia. It's known for heroin. I've heard it over and over. Maybe, of all places, someone there might still be holding. It's about an hour away. We have gas money and, short of a miracle, I don't see any other choices, do you?"

She thought for only a second and said, "Let's go."

We took the 101 freeway, making nervous talk when we realized that neither of us knew exactly where the Colonia area was. But we drove on, figuring we'd find it somehow. And the first person we asked gave us directions. On the way, we were discussing just how we were going to score since we had never been there before and neither of us knew anyone. We'd just have to ask the first person we saw who appeared to be a likely candidate to know such things. We pulled in front of one of the central project locations, turned off the lights, and sat for a minute or two. We were the only white girls in a sea of brown people, near midnight, looking pitiful, wide-eyed, and desperate. Boy, we were obvious.

Dee and I looked at each other. "Let's do it!"

I was on the passenger side and didn't want to get out of the car. I rolled down the window and motioned to a passer-by. "Hey, you live here?"

"*Si, porque?*"

Knowing that *porque* means "Why?" I thought fast, remembering the word I'd used in Mexico. "We'd like to buy some shiva."

He spoke next in English. "Yes, I can do that. I know people who have it. *Quantos?*"

"We only want $100 worth, maybe two 50's, ten 10's, however it comes."

Knowing it wasn't the wisest move, but with the beginnings of "the sick" coming on, and no other options, I handed him a one hundred dollar bill and said, "How long?"

"*Diez* minutes."

Is there anyone that believes we ever saw him again?

Before admitting that we had been burned, we waited. We and other junkies have been known to wait hours, in this type of desperate situations.

I looked around, then told Dee, "We're so obvious sitting here. We might as well be a neon light . . . blinking at that. If anybody drives by, they're gonna know, straight out, that we're here trying to score. Suppose the cops drive by? They're gonna shake us down for sure. I can't take kicking in jail tonight."

"Peg, stop. You're freaking me out. Besides, is this against the law? We're just sitting here in a car, doing nothing. We're not in possession, not even of money now . . ."

I interrupted, "Oh, we only have foot-long blood-red needle tracks down both arms and even though, to us, we're not under the influence, to a cop, guaranteed we will be."

I no sooner said that when, in the background, there was a faint glow of lights, and as a car turned the corner, then full-on headlights. I got a chill. Oh no, please God, say it isn't so, please don't let this be the cops. I'd asked God too late, I guess. It was the police but, to our utmost surprise, they didn't stop, and crept by slowly. They definitely fixed on us, though. Though Dee and I both were Italian, with dark hair, we clearly weren't from this barrio in Oxnard. As they drove on by I breathed and said, "They'll be back. What are we gonna do? If we drive away now, they'll know something's up for sure and stop us, don't ya think?"

"Yes," she said. "Let's hide in that dumpster over there and hope they don't put it together."

"I can't get in that thing."

"Would you rather kick in jail?"

The dumpster was about half full of trash and half full of garbage. At that moment, I learned there was a difference. Being nighttime, it was very dark in it and the smell was rank. We were squatted down on trash, trying to quickly assess whether we really needed to be in a dumpster, when we heard a car coming. I reached over to touch her, but what I grabbed definitely wasn't Dee. Oh God!

We got very quiet, trying to barely breathe for fear of being heard. Was it them? My heart was pounding so hard, I thought it might be audible. I heard two doors slam. I was trembling with the horror of being found. I peeked through a rusty crack and could only see solid clothing; the cops were right in front of the dumpster. By now, something was seeping through the seat of my jeans—damp *garbage*. I wasn't sitting on it but we were knee deep in it and squatting. Suddenly I was overcome with a huge sadness and remorse. Not so much for the fact that I had garbage seeping through my clothes, but about how I got here. A sadness again, for my parents. How did I get so far down? The smell and the symbolism were coming up to choke me. Me—a junkie, hiding from the cops in a dumpster! How could this be? I was Homecoming Queen. The rancid smell overtook me and I felt the urge to gag. But they would surely hear that and so I fought it with all my might.

I heard one cop say, "Where'd they go?"

"They went in to score, where else? They knew we saw 'em. They knew we'd be back, so naturally they bailed. Time to go home. I have dinner and a wife and baby daughter waiting for me. We'll get 'em another day. Sooner or later they'll get caught . . . or worse. They're just hypes."

"You're right. I'm all for calling it a day."

And just like that, they left. We were stunned. We had to really believe that they had actually gone—that they weren't just trying to flush us out. So we sat there in the garbage for a few minutes, me still trying not to vomit.

Next thing I knew, Dee and I were turning onto the 101 Southbound, back to LA. What a dismal ride back. Ripped off, dope sick, waiting for the surefire horror of withdrawals. Despair was enveloping me when I turned to Dee. "Why do we keep doing this to ourselves? I can't . . . I just can't keep doing this. We have to, somehow, get a grip and stop this madness."

She was feeling as bad as I was physically, but maybe not mentally yet. "Peg, please, I can't listen to this right now. How are we going to get fixed? We're gonna' get real sick you know."

"Dee, don't you think I know that! I can't take it anymore; I really can't. Somehow, someway, we have to figure a way out of this. God help us! I don't even think I enjoy it anymore. It's just a constant struggle. I'm so exhausted. We have to sacrifice everything to stay loaded—everything, literally everything, including self-respect . . . I can't . . . I just can't . . ."

"Stop!" she yelled. "I can't listen. I can't listen to you go on and on. I know the same thing you know, but I'm also aware that we're not going to be able to make any life-changing decisions until we're at least fixed long enough to have some form of rational thoughts about us and are able to pick up and walk. And, at least for right now, I'm focusing on how we're going to be able to get well after midnight with no drugs and no money . . . so please, please, will you lighten up!"

Silence fell over the car for a few miles. Then, going over the 101 grade somewhere on the other side of Camarillo, I just couldn't leave it alone and broke the silence. "Dee, did you know that there's a hospital somewhere around here with a detox ward?"

"Yes, I've heard that, too. It might be Camarillo State Mental Hospital."

"I honestly don't care what they call it as long as they can bring us off of this stuff without withdrawals. You know we're considered mental anyway. Junkies! We're the lowest according to society—the dregs. Folks think that people like us are mental. I want to go!"

"Now? Don't get stupid on me, Peg. We can't go now and you know it. It's after midnight."

I knew Dee was right but I was dreading what was waiting for us in LA. Actually "it" wasn't waiting at all; the withdrawals had started to creep on us.

Back at our apartment, we parked on Laurel Street, and trudged inside, dreading another episode of withdrawals. It was a truly grueling sensation—my body was freezing and my head felt like it was in an oven. I began shaking and complaining. The night wore on. It felt like a hundred nights while I slowly agonized until daybreak. Dee was under the covers, continually kicking her feet in an attempt to stay warm. I was in the bathroom retching when the phone rang around 7:00 a.m. I wiped my face with a towel and stumbled into the living room, hoping so much that the call might give some hope.

"Hello?"

The voice on the phone was a close friend of ours, Damian, fellow junkie. "Hi Peg, did you guys find anything?"

"No, we didn't. We're sick. Did you?"

Pause. "Yeah, I did . . . got any money?"

That she even asked while we were in such bad shape made me furious. "Damian, Don't! Really, I mean it! As many times as Dee and I straightened you out when you didn't have a dime! Don't do this. We're so sick, we can barely stand up. Come over and at least get us straight. How far away are you?"

She was too slow in her answer, so I threatened her. "You might not think it now but, eventually, you'll find out that by not coming to this rescue, you're making a mistake. You know this will eventually turn around and it will be us holding and you sick. Don't dare call us and ask for us to straighten you out if you leave us like this. Seriously, think about it!"

She finally said, "Relax Peggy. I'm about 15 minutes away and, of course, I'm gonna help you guys out, but I can't promise you I can get you high. I can only spare enough to get you guys well."

Desperate, I interrupted, "That's fine . . . well is good enough for right now." And it was. Just to get the chills, bone aches, crawlies, and the nausea gone—great.

"Dee, show your face." She was completely under the covers, hiding from the boogie man. Problem was, there's no hiding from withdrawals; the boogie man is within. "Dee, Damian is coming over to get us straight."

That perked her up. "When?"

"She said about 15 minutes." She slumped back under the covers.

"Dee, once we're well, I want to head out for the detox place. Seriously, it'll only be a matter of a few hours and we're going to be sick again. Maybe we can get admitted before that happens."

"Peg, fuck, how can you be so practical at a time like this?"

"I'm scared and tired. We need help. Come on, say you'll go."

It seemed like an hour or more before Damian came through the door and within a matter of a few short minutes, we both had fixed the small amount of heroin she gave us. Only enough to take the sick away, not enough to get high. That was all right with me because I was hell bent on getting to the detox hospital, truly scared of the pending withdrawals. I had been using heroin for so long, uninterrupted, I knew withdrawing was going to be a bitch. But something kept me hopeful that we could do it.

"Come on Dee, we've gotta go. Start pulling it together. Put some things in a bag," I coaxed her. "By the time we get it together and drive back up there, we might be in time to get dosed before we start coming down. Come on."

"Peg, you're dreaming."

I was getting irritated, but I was willing to tough it out long enough to get some relief with methadone. "Come on," I pleaded. "Think of the alternatives—not good. We're going to get sicker and sicker. Please, Dee, use some reasoning!"

Somehow, I convinced her and we begin to throw some things in a flight bag. It was still morning as we made our way over Laurel Canyon to the 101 freeway. We didn't talk much. Catching my reflection in the vanity mirror, snippets of my life made brief stops as they passed through my mind. A scene at San Francisco airport where I picked up the first box of clothing my mother made for the store. Lazy day fishing with my dad on Bayou Bogue Falaya when I was about 10 years old. Meeting up with Stella and Ned in New York and thinking how the green madras dress she wore made her eyes gleam like emeralds. The salesman handing me the keys to the Shelby. The blood from my vein filling the first syringe Janis stuck in my arm. The sound of heartache fracturing my mother's words as she asked, "Why? What has happened to you? Don't you love us anymore?" The crusty scabs on my arm this morning as I pierced, stabbed and jabbed looking to register a successful hit. My gaze settled back on the pale, thin ghost that trembled inside the oblong mirror. I could find little empathy for her as the San Fernando Valley whizzed by in the background. I lit a cigarette, blew smoke at the image and locked my gaze on the bumper of the car ahead.

Once we had arrived in the parking lot and Dee had turned off the ignition, I started thinking that maybe I didn't really need to go. Even though it was inevitable that I had to in order to get *clean*, I didn't want to give up getting *high*. If I didn't love it so much, it's not likely that I'd have sacrificed so much to keep shooting up. I felt like I was climbing the stairs to hell. At the entrance, I opened the door and was astounded by the exuberance with which we were met at the door.

The staff opened their arms to us with a real desire to help. I was happy about that, but I dreaded the long admitting process. We learned that we would have to participate in a group session before getting our first dose of methadone. God help us. Both of us began to feel the effects of Damian's gracious get-well hit slowly waning, and the last thing we wanted to endure was listening to a bunch of addicts talking about how they got there, how they had trashed their lives doing it, how they had disappointed everyone on their way down, blah, blah, blah. Gads, it was so depressing. It made me want to leave and get high. I knew, however, that a dose of methadone would come quicker than we could find a hit of heroin back in LA so we stayed and listened.

As group finally ended, we noticed some of the residents milling around a glassed-in box—likely the dispensary, so we started milling around the same area. From a distance, I saw a woman and a small man coming down the hall, and as they drew closer, I could see that the woman had a snarl, unlike what we witnessed when we entered the hospital.

I turned to Dee. "Oh my god, its Nurse Ratchet! And we're in her Cuckoo Nest!"

Dee knew I was a little on the mouthy side and short on tolerance. She begged, "Peggy, please, please don't mouth off with her. Just keep your mouth shut."

"Ok, ok, as long as she doesn't give me any trouble."

Dee knew me well enough to know that was not a definitive, "No."

The bitch walked straight up to me and said, "I know your kind."

"I beg your pardon. Just exactly what is that suppose to mean?"

"Oh, I know your kind," she repeated. "You think you're better than everybody else. Well let me tell you something, Honey. I've been doing this for a while and you're not!"

"No, I don't think I'm better than anyone else. No, I don't . . ."

"Well, we'll see," she interrupted. "Get in line if you think you're going to get your methadone. The end of the line!"

We didn't last very long at Camarillo State Mental Hospital's Detox Unit. Only desperation to avoid a brutal withdrawal kept me from walking out the first night. The minute we were cleaned up enough, we bolted. This pattern repeated at numerous detox facilities. The idea of detox would be bright and hold promise. The idea of not using would seem so attainable. But then, someone would pick us up, or we'd have a car and head back to wherever home was or had been or was going to be and within hours, inexplicably, we were loaded again.

✽

There was a horror of what the evening was sure to bring . . . withdrawals. For some reason, it always seemed harder in LA. Maybe it was because you just knew that drugs . . . *the* drug was all around you, but of course, unattainable without money. There I was, out of money, broke again and out of game. I had run about all of them. For whom the bells toll . . . they felt like they were tolling for me . . . more in the sound of a death march, when I knew I had nothing left but to call my parents, and ask for money. Oh God . . . it hurt so bad and most of all, knowing how it was going to hurt them . . . again. Mom knew; she was very hard to fool or lie to, but Dad, bless his heart, always so ready to believe the best of me. This was nearly debilitating ... reason, rationale and the power to refrain from asking is choked out by the grip of the drug. I always seemed to go into a mode of slow motion, trying to stop myself, but knowing, for sure, that I wasn't going to be able to not ask. Every step I took toward the pay phone hurt—like a dagger in my heart. Stop, stop, I would be thinking as I kept advancing toward the phone. My hands were trembling as I deposited the coins and waited.

"Hello."

"Hi Mom."

"Sam, it's Peggy." Dad picks up the extension phone. "Hey Darling, how are you?"

"Ok Daddy ... but not real good."

"Why? What's wrong sweetheart?"

"I'll bet she wants money, Sam," Mom said.

"Mom, don't say that."

"Well you do, don't you? You never call us unless you want something."

"That's not true. It hurts so bad for you to say that."

"Really! It hurts *you?* Really? And just how do you think it makes us feel for you to be in this shape? It's killing us, Peggy! Why? Why do you hate yourself so much? And us, too? What did we do to you, Peggy? We've always loved you."

"Mom, STOP please. You didn't do this! You did nothing: this is all my stuff ... and I can't answer *why*. I don't know; I really don't. I want so badly for things to be different."

Dad breaks in, "You two stop. What's going on here?"

"Oh Sam, I know it's hard for you to believe that our only child is a drug addict but it's true! Tell him, Peggy ... tell him! Maybe he'll get it if he hears it from you. Go ahead, tell him!"

"Tell me what?"

As I knew it would be, this conversation is excruciating and my body is trembling. God I wanted so badly to just say how sorry I am, I love you and simply hang up, but I couldn't. Again Dad says, "*What, darling?*"

Holding back tears, with a lump in my throat, hurting, I said, "She's right, Dad. I am a drug addict and if I don't get some money, I'm going to go into withdrawals tonight. I am so sorry. Will you send me some money?"

"Of course, darling. To Western Union?"

"Yes, Dad. Thank you so much; I'm in LA. Send it to the Wilcox office."

"How much do you need?" he asks sweetly.

"Will you do $500?"

"Ok, Honey. Can't you try to stop using this drug . . . isn't there help for people on drugs?"

"Yes, Dad, there is . . . and I will try again, I have before, but the problem is . . . that as hard as they try, they're only able to fix you physically, whereas the real addiction seems to be mental. I don't know, but I'm tired . . . so tired and I'll try anything about now. Thanks so much, Dad."

I can faintly hear my mother crying in the background. Dad says, "Honey, you've made your mother cry. Please don't do that anymore, ok?"

"Ok, Dad."

Within two hours, the money arrived and within less than 72 hours, it was gone.

And the endless cycle continued.

※

While I was in LA, alternately getting loaded, getting high, getting sick, and getting just well enough to ward off withdrawal, the rest of my world, the one I'd left behind in San Francisco, crumbled. Piece by piece, I had to close or sell off at a loss, all the stores and other ventures I'd once been a part of. Profits ceased, and anything in my numerous bank accounts was gone, gone to heroin. Only the house in Stinson was left, but I didn't dare touch that. Somewhere in my addicted, desperate brain, I knew that was my safety net. But all the rest of it disappeared into my arm.

I met Dr. Roseberg in LA, and he seemed a bit smitten with me, at least enough to be willing to write prescriptions for Dilaudid to keep me off the street dope. This began a whole new era and a short respite from the daily hustle. Dee and I began a routine of staying in a hotel room because we could simply sell a few pills each day to cover the nightly fee. Hygiene was better that way, too. By God we almost felt like normal folk thanks to Dr. Rosenberg and our substitute drug. He wrote and wrote and wrote and wrote scripts for us, and we introduced so many junkies to him that he realized that he could make oodles of money by starting a kind of faux detox program. His idea was to detox junkies off heroin, and switch them to Dilaudid. Of course, we were still strung out, but on a safer, more predictable drug.

It wasn't all a con. Dr. Rosenberg would make his charges run on Santa Monica beach. Oh yes, *running!* Running for our Dilaudid. There were ten or fifteen of us in the beginning. Sniffling, skinny, tracked-back, long-sleeved, junk sick or loaded, we would run from lifeguard station to lifeguard station, and back. We had to, to get our 'script. We would be cursin' the whole way, "That son of a bitch, I'm gonna have a talk with that mother fucker." But at the end of the run, we got it. He claimed that he had to do it that way to show the feds that this was a legitimate program.

Once switched over, most junkies could scratch up twenty-five, thirty-five, forty dollars for a hundred or so Dilaudid pills, a big improvement over fifty dollars for a single hit of heroin. We'd have way, WAY more hits. We all had to run twice a week for our script; our little "Run for the Doses" or "Fuckin' Junkie Derby" started to gain attention from the normal, regular beach-goers. Eventually people wanted to know what was happening on Santa Monica beach every Tuesday and Friday morning. A bunch of scraggly people running from lifeguard stand to lifeguard stand?

Word got around, and next thing you know, he had a hundred junkies standing in line waiting to run. Eventually he got busted. It made the evening news: him screaming and yelling, kicking at the cops so hard that they had to put him in a straight jacket to haul him away to the slammer.

Dee said, "I'm gonna figure out a way to get the Dilaudid without Dr. Rosenberg."

She studied the Physician's Desk Reference and realized that the scripts had been written in a kind of shorthand hybrid of English, Latin, and math symbols. One symbol looked like a division sign. It said something like 5mg divided by something and then PRN, which turned out to mean Patient's Required Need. After some practice, she figured out how to scribble the script AND duplicate his signature. If we took the scripts far and wide to different pharmacies, they'd never figure out it wasn't his signature. To keep any suspicious pharmacist really thrown off our trail, Dee would often go in dressed like a cop.

Not only were we scoring enough to keep ourselves high, I was, in some sick way, pleased to once again be using my business skills because we also figured out how to get other junkies to pay us for all the extra Dilaudid we could obtain this way.

We bought the blank triplicate prescription books that we needed for a narcotics prescription on the black market for about $100 a book. There'd be twenty-five triplicates. We wrote scripts for the #4 Dilaudid, often 60 pills in a single bottle, which we paid $80-150 for when filled at a pharmacy. We then broke down the bottle, and sold individual pills on the street for ten dollars each. If you wrote a script for a hundred pills, that might invite scrutiny, but Dee wrote letters from doctors on fake letterheads, or in one case, she wrote a letter from MIT, saying she had cancer and was traveling to Europe and would need bottles of 100 sealed tight from the factory, so they could cross borders. She also wrote prescriptions for Prednisone because if you presented both scripts, it didn't send up a flag that you're after narcotics alone. Of course, we never went to Europe. We went home, unsealed the bottles, shot it, and sold it.

On and on it went. Now we were equal business partners, as well as lovers. Dee wrote the scripts and my job was to scout pharmacies for those most likely to fill without a problem.

After awhile I looked for shops with plate glass fronts so I had a clear line of vision from the pharmacy counter. We would rent a limousine to drive us up in front and let us out, in hopes that the pharmacists would see the limo at the curb, and be thinking not *junkie*, but *money*. And it worked. The limousines were just $25 an hour, plus an optional tip. We'd rent one for twenty-five bucks, go to a pharmacy, get the prescription filled, and we'd tip the driver anywhere from fifteen dollars to forty dollars and we'd have a thousand dollars worth of narcotics. Between the police uniform and the limousine, we did well. Then Dawn, a junkie friend of ours, broke her neck and she had one of those halos with rods drilled into her skull. When she went in to fill a script, no one ever questioned her. Anyone with four screws in her skull, who handed over a prescription for a painkiller, the pharmacist wouldn't even bother to verify. We paid Dawn with ten or fifteen out of the sixty or so she'd help us score.

Write 'script, crack 'script, crush pills, cook, shoot, nod off, feel the tickle in your throat, time for the next shot, run low on 'script, rinse, repeat. It went on and on. It was a monotonous, dull existence. We had ceased to even try and get clean, and simply tried to be the best junkies we could be. No stealing, robbing, or being violent with people. We didn't write bad checks. We didn't rip people off. We weren't really dealing because we never held onto it long enough in any meaningful quantities. Just figuring ways to run illegal prescriptions, pay at the counter for the drugs, sell enough for a hotel room and keep the rest. No joy. No inspiration. No fun. Nothing but the drug. It had finally come down to just that, after so many failed attempts to clean up. So many broken promises to ourselves, let alone crushing the hope that I know my mom and dad endured each time I called to say I'd checked into treatment, only to find out that I was strung out again a few weeks later. For years, we did nothing but keep from getting dope sick. Get high? Rarely. It just became, week after week after week after week after week, month after month after month after month, then year after year of the same despair. That's all I can say. Each day, we sold enough to afford to stay in a motel that night so we'd be sheltered. We'd get high, pass out, and wake up worrying about how we were going to get well, and how we were going to pay the next night's motel bill.

We stumbled on one little trick by accident. If you put your finger in the "2" slot in a rotary dial pay phone, and then "dialed" it, it would sound to the person on the other end of the line like they were being put on hold. We'd figured out that on all the pay phones, there was the area code, the prefix and then the last four digits, and the fourth digit was always a nine. So, when we would print the scripts, Dee would write in a pay phone number for the doctor's office, so if a pharmacist called to verify a prescription, I would be at the pay phone.

"Hello, Dr. Rosenberg's office," I would answer.

"This is Westside Pharmacy and we're calling to verify a prescription for Judy Pentheiter."

"Yes, she's a patient of ours. What's the prescription for?"

"Dilaudid and Prednisone."

"I'll check with the doctor. Can you hold a moment please?" Then I'd put my finger in the "2" circle, pull it down and hold it for fifteen or twenty seconds. Once released, the dial would roll back into position and I was still connected to the pharmacy. "Yes, I checked with the doctor and that prescription is good."

It worked like a charm hundreds of times.

Eventually, I was back in Sybil Brand waiting to be sentenced for running the illegal drug prescription scam. Dee had already been caught, sentenced, and was doing time at the California Rehabilitation Center. It had taken a year or so before they caught up with me. In the meantime, to handle Dee's bail when she got caught, one of her sisters put up the $6000 to the bondsman, but I had to sign the Stinson house over as collateral. I knew Dee might run and skip out on the bail, but I thought that I would have the time to redeem the deed, as I'd once done with Ned. At the time, the property was probably worth around $50,000. Sure enough Dee, knowing she was facing a prison sentence, opted not to appear. A warrant was issued, the bail was forfeited, and without my consent (though within her rights), Dee's sister, Margie, relinquished the house to the bail bondsman and my little sanctuary was gone forever.

Not long after Dee failed to appear in court, we were back to our old pharmacy scams. Sitting up the street from Vitamin Quota on Crenshaw, I had a bad feeling.

"I don't feel good about this, Dee."

"Oh Christ Peggy, they never have a clue."

"The back door to this place is blocked. You don't have an escape."

"I don't need one. Watch." She hopped out of the car in her costume police uniform and strode in. Meanwhile, I moved over to the driver's seat and watched.

About ten minutes later I saw a police car pull in front of the pharmacy and my blood ran cold. The cops leapt out, guns drawn and entered the building.

I started the car, eased it into gear and slowly drove away.

This time, there was no chance for bail. Not that there was anywhere to get it from by then. Dee was sentenced to two to five years at the California Rehabilitation Center (CRC), a prison for drug-addicted women.

I couldn't risk visiting her. We wrote letters, like pining lovers, not realizing we loved the dope more than each other. Since losing my partner in crime, I floundered around the best I could; it never occurred to me to stop. Eventually, I built up a small network of "walkers" or "crackers" who would take the phony prescriptions into the pharmacy. I did well enough to keep myself in plenty of Dilaudid.

An ever worsening problem was nearly running out of places on my body to inject. Looking in the mirror one day I noticed my jugular vein. Hmmmm. I fooled around, holding my breath until I saw the vein pop up visibly on my neck. I cooked up a hit, held my breath again, stuck the needle into my neck, and sweet Jesus it worked! This vein was two to three times as wide as any other vein I had shot dope into. I no longer had to stab and stab at the crusted, scarred lines I had been digging into for years. The downside was, I had to watch myself fix. In some ways, it was easy because the person in the mirror wasn't someone that I liked very much. On the other hand, I was watching someone I hardly knew at all. My reflection reminded me that I had crossed a line into another level of sickness and desperation.

*

Once, after being released from Sybil Brand, I found my car waiting for me, as I'd arranged with a friend—who had stashed some dope and a syringe under the seat for me so I could fix as soon as I got out. A couple of cops were nearby, and yes, I saw them and I knew they could see me. But still, I got into the car, found the dope, cooked it up, drew the Dilaudid up into the rig, and tied off. Then the cops were running toward me, waving and yelling, "No, no, no!" Just as they got to the car door, I shot the dope and loosened the tie. They flung open the door and arrested me right there. Because I'd already injected, technically I was no longer "in possession of" and mouthed off, smirking. "Ha, ha! Now you can only charge me with a misdemeanor!"

"We can charge you with several misdemeanors," one shot back.

"Don't you guys find it ironic, that once I've done what you were afraid I might do, it's a lesser offense?"

"What are you talking about, Caserta?"

"If I still had dope on me, you would charge me with felony possession. Once I get it into my system, it's a misdemeanor. At this point I'm only 'Under the Influence.' It doesn't make sense."

"Well, your probation violation will land you right back in the cell." He grabbed my arm.

"Let's go."

※

I wasn't trying to become a serial inmate, and often I took pains to mask my condition—as either someone completely stoned or as a junkie in desperate need of an elusive fix—but looking back, I can see how ludicrous I must have appeared. On one blazing hot summer day, there I was near Venice Beach in a zipped-up leather bomber jacket. Why wouldn't the cops notice?

At that time, I had been spending my days waiting in alleys behind apartment buildings, or lurking around hotel parking lots, hoping to cop some dope. I constantly rubbed my runny nose and scratched my face. And if I was loaded when the police came, I tried to be cool—not walking too fast or too slow—acting "normal," holding my breath and forgetting to breathe. Or else I was shaking so bad from being junk sick that I could hardly get my cigarette to my lips. The Venice cops knew who most of us junkies or speed freaks were and they lumped us together under the not-so-affectionate term "hypes." The boardwalk was full of us. There was one of the early rehab places on Speedway known as "Tuum Est" which allegedly was Latin for "It's up to you."

I ended up getting busted for possession and being under the influence. It was right when courts were beginning to sentence people to rehabilitation centers instead of jail. My public defender worked a deal for me to serve my time—366 days—at Tuum Est. I really had no intention of staying clean, but I figured it was better than the county jail. Besides, it was right in my neighborhood.

I arrived and as soon as I could, I posted up near a window. It was a couple of stories up, right above the boardwalk. Hot damn! I was like a cat watching birds in an aviary. I could see one junkie friend copping from some guy over by the trashcans and another nodding out, propped up against one of the palm trees. I loved it. As I sat there, my wheels were spinning as I tried to assemble a plan to score some dope, even if I had to buy it leaning out the window of the rehab center. Just then I was interrupted by a tap on the shoulder.

"Peggy. Peggy!"

I turned around and some guy was looking at me, shaking his head.

"What?" I said, annoyed at the interference.

"This isn't going to work. I'm recommending they send you somewhere else."

"What do you mean? Who are you?"

"I'm your case manager here. There is no way in hell you are gonna stay clean being this close to all the action."

"But I wasn't doing anything," I protested. "I'm just checking out the view."

"Yeah right. Your wheels were turning so fast I could smell the smoke. C'mon, I'm gonna make a call and get you somewhere else."

"But what if I don't wanna go somewhere else?""

"Then you can go do your time in Sybil Brand."

"Fuck!"

Threatened by the mention of Sybil Brand, I followed him to his office and he made a couple of phone calls. I was to be transferred to a rehabilitation facility on a farm. I thought that might not be so bad. I could get out in the country and clear my head a bit. I had visions of gently sloping hills, green with alfalfa and cows mooing in the distance, maybe a couple of horses kicking up their heels.

The van arrived with both men and women, who were apparently sentenced to the farm as well. They all looked like garden variety drug addicts: skinny and furtive. I fit right in.

We headed inland near the California's Central Valley. The great concrete mazes of the Los Angeles freeway system gave way to greater expanses of land. I could no longer see or taste the lead in the air.

The scenery eventually turned more agricultural as the miles rolled by. I started to feel a little bit more relaxed and thought maybe the worst this could be would be a mini vacation. We ended up somewhere outside of Fresno.

It was dark as we wound our way through some foothills and through the gates of the property, pulling up to a nondescript, prefab-looking, single story building. I had heard on the way up that we were going to a well-known chicken farm. Some of the buildings had lights on, which made it difficult to make out much of anything else around them. Once the van came to a halt we were led into a kind of barracks. It seemed pleasant enough, except there was no privacy. Processing was simple. I signed in, received my bedding and found my bed. It was what I imagined summer camp would be like, if I'd ever gone to summer camp. There was a shared bathroom with a door that closed and hot running water. Halle-fuckin-lujah! It beat sharing a cell and having to piss and shit in front of another inmate.

At the crack of dawn, we were awakened and shuffled out to breakfast in a mess hall, then had orientation. Oh my God! There were chickens everywhere! As far as the naked eye could see, all around the outside of the building, a half million or more! The smell was something else. A hefty amount of ammonia, coupled with stale gym socks, fine dust and microscopic feather bits rose and hung in an atmospheric bloom. My vision of life on the farm was shattered. It certainly didn't seem healthy to me. Good Lord, the sound! A cackling cacophony!

There was somebody driving a mini tractor that resembled a beefed-up golf cart that shot out chicken feed. As one would expect, a small mountain of chickens, growing larger by the minute, flapped crazily, following this thing. Their feathers flew as they clucked, scratched and pecked their way through the heap. One of the inmates tailed the tractor and pulled dead, smothered chickens out from the bottom of the pile. Thousands, upon thousands of chickens, everywhere. Several of these little chicken-feed-shitting tractors tooled around at set times during the day.

Then there was the plant, which is where I was assigned. Those chickens would enter the building on a belt while they were still clucking, and come out the other end, plucked, washed, sliced, packaged and priced. My senses were assaulted and I decided I'd never be able to eat chicken again.

There was a rumor circulating among the junkies and drug addicts that the chicken feed contained speed because the poultry seemed frantic. I didn't doubt it, but what did I know? I had never been around thousands of chickens before. Some of the speed freaks decided they'd try to get high. How they managed to gag down chicken food, or even get it off the ground before the chickens got to it, was beyond me. It resulted in a couple of them being shipped off to the hospital in the middle of the night in extreme gastric distress—not because they had overdosed, but because they didn't even chew the hard grains. After that, I assumed the chickens were just naturally crazy in such an unnatural environment. But, hey, if I thought there was heroin in that chicken food, I probably would have tried to slam it, if I could've cooked it up.

By day two I was transferred from chicken duty over to care for the pigs. The pen was split rail, so the porkers could stick their snouts and part of their faces through the rails. One of the civilian workers instructed me to see if the pigs needed more food. I entered slowly, while he watched and I immediately noticed that the largest of the pigs had focused on me as soon as I closed the gate. The other two pigs didn't seem to notice me at all.

As I made my way across the pen, this big pig started toward me. I got nervous and picked up my pace. He did the same. The next thing I know this beast let out a tremendous squeal and charged me. I screamed and took off running. I heard people yelling, and all I could think of was how to get my ass between those rails and away from the pig.

I could feel the ground shaking as this shrieking hulk gained on me. I got to the fence, and as I glanced back I could see that there were several people trying to lure this creature away from me. He was having none of it. He stomped and snorted, then squealed and charged. The bottom of my pants caught on the wood. I screamed and cursed because I was half in and half out of the pen, when the hog knocked one of the guys over in the muck. I swear it smirked as it bellowed triumphantly and frothy saliva dripped from its enormous jowls. It wagged its funky curly tail and then launched itself, like a shot, straight at me. At the last second I yanked my other leg through the posts, ripped my pants and tumbled to the ground just as the crazy beast slammed into the fence not three feet from me. He was staring right at me, his eyes lurid and unsettling. Then I heard the laughter and looked up to see a young guy in his twenties leaning over with his hand extended to help me up.

"What's so fucking funny?" I asked.

He looked at me and burst out laughing again. "You." He helped me up, clearing his throat as he shook his head. "Sorry, sorry. It's just . . ." Then he buried his face in the crook of his arm, trying to stifle the laughter.

"There is not one fucking thing I find funny right now. Not one fucking thing!" I grumbled as I dusted myself off the best I could.

"I think that pig wanted to fuck you," he said, and fell into spasms of laughter.

I glanced back over at that porcine devil and recognized the look in his eye. "Son of a bitch," I said, incredulous. "You mean to tell me that I nearly got raped by a four-hundred-pound hunk of horny bacon?" That's when I noticed that there was a curlicued pinkish appendage between its back legs twirling in and out in the air below its belly.

"Tell me that isn't what I think it is. Please God, say it isn't so!"

"Yep, you definitely caught his interest. But hey, don't feel too special. See that big old bucket-looking thing?" He turned his head and pointed with his chin. I nodded, as I followed his gaze. "That is his sex toy. It may not be pretty but he doesn't mind having his way with it."

"Oh, this is not going to work. I'm not farmer fucking Jane! No one should have to worry about getting raped by a pig. No one! This is crazy! I'll take my chances in jail. Jeezus H. Christ!" I blustered as I made my way back to my bunk.

Once I realized this was not a locked facility, I knew there wasn't much they could do to keep me there. I grabbed what little personal effects I had, which amounted to my ID, a toothbrush, a hairbrush, and an extra pair of panties that I shoved into an inside pocket of my tired old bomber jacket and started on my long walk to somewhere. As I hoofed it toward the main gate, I had a confrontation with one of the people who ran the program. She attempted to coerce me into staying.

"You can't leave! You're on the honor system here. If you leave it will be a big mistake."

"Oh yes, I can leave. Watch me."

"But Peggy, wait. Wait! You haven't given it a chance!" she pleaded.

"I haven't given what a chance?"

"Rehabilitation. You haven't given yourself a chance."

"Oh, *that*. Well, to be honest, I wasn't looking for a chance. I was looking for dope when I got arrested. I think I'm going to go back to what I was doing before I got sidetracked into this feathered fiasco. With a rapist pig, no less."

"Peggy, think about what you're doing. If you leave, and they pick you up, you'll have to go back to jail, no other options will be available to you then."

"No, I don't think so. Just tell me where the hell I am."

"You're about 15 miles from anywhere."

"If I start now, I'll be that much closer to somewhere." With that I spun on my heel, headed down the driveway, and out of the gates, muttering to myself about chickens, farming, and crazy fucking pigs.

I was anxious to get away and was walking at a pretty good clip. The weather was very warm—hot, in fact—but in spite of the heat, I seemed to be making good progress. On the rare occasion a car came by, I stuck my thumb out. Nobody stopped. If anything, they sped up. The locals must have been aware of drug addicts tending to the chickens. After several hours I was beginning to think this was not the brightest idea I'd ever come up with. Then, I thought back on the mountain of shrieking chickens and pressed on.

The little two-lane road had no shoulder to speak of, just pavement fading into weeds and miles upon miles of barbed wire fences. I finally came to another road that stretched to seemingly nowhere in both directions. No clue as to where I was in relation to anywhere. Behind me was the chance to stay clean. The option to do my time, and maybe start anew. But what would I even do with my days when and if I did get clean? The days of owning my own business, the days of success, of love, of endless possibilities, were annihilated. Knowing I'd lost everything to dope conjured up more bad feelings than I could bear. I increased my pace, determined to create as much distance as I could from my immediate circumstances.

I figured I'd head towards the sun, which would lead me west. If I could get to the coast it would be easy to get back to LA. I was in my thirties and not accustomed to walking marathons, and my feet were aching in my drugstore sneakers. The sweat was dripping into my eyes, burning them. When a breeze came up, it felt icy so I'd put my jacket on. Then I would overheat, and have to take it off again. On. Off. On. Off. Not being used to feeling much of anything, made all this more intense. Double bummer. I kept on though, and dreamed of how good it was going to feel once I got my hands on some dope.

By the time I reached the I-5 freeway, the sun had begun to set and I was still walking. At least I knew which direction to head, but that was miles and miles away. I had begun thinking about where, or how, I was going to sleep that night when I heard a big truck approaching from behind. I stuck my thumb out and by golly that truck slowed. The air brakes hissed and the diesel engine groaned its way through the downshifts. When it came to a stop, I climbed up and opened the passenger side door. The semi driver had short hair, a five o'clock shadow, and a trucker cap emblazoned with Peterbilt. He grinned. "I'm headed to LA. Where you headed, little lady?"

"LA is close enough to Hollywood for me."

"Hop on in."

This guy could have been going anywhere, and I would have been glad to land anywhere even close to civilization. But to L.A? Oh yes! We chatted and he turned out to be a pretty decent guy who made me feel safe in his cab. He had obviously been indulging in something much stronger than coffee. I could see his pupils were dilated and he talked and asked questions non-stop. At one point he said, "I take Bennies to keep myself alert. Ya don't mind, do ya?" He fished into his pocket and threw what looked to be a handful of little white pills into his mouth. "Ya want some?" he queried before he washed them all down with some liquid from a big green Stanley thermos.

"No thanks," I said, but was truly glad he had even asked. He'd followed the drug addict code of ethics.

Unbelievably, this trucker dropped me off at the corner of Hollywood Boulevard and Vine Street. Statistically, it should have taken me several different rides to even get in the vicinity of where I wanted to go. With one shot, I was back in my element and set out to see a fellow junkie who lived at the Villa Elaine apartments, a few short blocks away, across from the Ranch Market. I loved this area of town, and promptly settled in to work up a good strong drug habit and avoid getting picked up on the warrant I knew had been issued when I left the farm. And I succeeded.

I rose through the ranks of a $100 dollar a day habit back up to $300 and climbing. In the early 1970s that was a heck of a lot of money. The gorilla on my back had an enormous appetite. Without stealing, hooking, or writing bad checks, I did my damndest to keep it fed. By working as a kind of intermediary, a distributor in a sense. I was able to get other junkies to ask me to cop for them and then I'd get my *issue* from the dealer out of that transaction. Exhausting method, and it put me constantly on the front lines of vulnerability for getting busted.

*

Needing money, I finally sold my beloved Shelby Mustang Cobra-jet 350 ragtop with a roll bar, the one really nice thing I had somehow managed to hang on to from my glory days of The Haight. I was desperate for dope, and the Shelby was in need of service I couldn't afford. I think I got $3500. That was a dark day. Watching the new owner drive off in my car, I knew it was pretty much over. Prison loomed; that is, if death didn't catch me first. With Dilaudid, an overdose was practically impossible, so it was high odds prison would win.

With time off for good behavior, Dee was about six to nine months from finishing her sentence at CRC. I wondered if I'd be on the inside when she got out. In a strange way, I was beginning to wish for that. Chances were, I would be sentenced to the same facility. I had not been sentenced to prison before, nor did I have any violent felonies, so I'd likely end up at CRC, and I imagined it would be better with my lover there, too.

I had been staying at the Jolly Roger hotel in Venice Beach, fairly regularly for several weeks, having hooked up with a young actress and a couple of her friends who were gung-ho about walking scripts for me. But Sheila had been busted a few weeks before on some minor charge, and being the good little strung out junkie that she was, had failed to appear in court.

I had just settled in for my afternoon fix with Sheila and some friends.

Boom, boom, boom, boom, boom, "Open up, Venice police!"

"Shit!" we all cried in unison.

"Sheila McKenna, we know you're in there! Open this door, now!"

I slammed my fix closed, since I had an arrest warrant out as well. Somebody flushed the Dilaudid down the toilet.

"You can't come in without a warrant!" one of the guys yelled.

The police shot back. "We have one. The ink ain't even dry! Open up! We're coming in one way or the other!"

"Alright, hold on!" someone snapped back

"I'm fucked," Sheila said.

"Yeah, you're fucked Sheila. You're going back to jail," I said. "This time I'm going to prison." And then I slammed into my neck what I knew would be my last hit of dope for a very long time.

At Sybil Brand waiting to be sentenced, my cellmate was a woman who had put her three-week-old baby in a trash compactor. When she got back from court, she'd received nine months. Nine months for killing your baby? That's all? For something as heinous as that? Dee had gotten three years and had completed over two-thirds of that. My fate would be decided in a few days.

Some days are just no good, you know that. This was going to be one of those.

Hearing that sentence was a real blow. It's all dramatic on television, but when the judge stated my name, what I experienced was a stark, raw fear.

"Peggy Caserta, you are remanded to the custody of the California Department of Corrections for a period not to exceed seven years."

The flesh, blood and bones that held my knees in a locked position seemed to liquefy. I thought I was going to fall, or faint, and I grabbed onto my lawyer's jacket to keep from hitting the floor.

"Did she just say seven years?"

My lawyer said, "Shhhh! Peggy, be quiet. It's not what it sounds like. Don't worry."

Not to worry, my ass. I knew what I'd heard. *For a period not to exceed seven years.* Seven years! I did the math: that was over two thousand days! I whispered, "But I heard her say it. Seven years!"

"Peggy, the CRC is an indeterminate sentencing program; they always give you 'a maximum of seven years.' But if you stick to the program, stay out of trouble, and keep a low profile, you go before the release board. It's possible to get out in about nine months."

Going to CRC was a trip, figuratively and literally. It was the last place I had ever expected to land. The day I was transported they had me in chains on my legs, wrists, and around my waist. Didn't they know that this skinny junkie had no fight left? I could barely drag the chains, let alone put up a fuss. That particular day in Southern California it was overcast and grey—chilly and misty. As the electronic gate of the razor-wired, walled prison, opened, the Kenny Loggins song "This Is It" came on the radio. Maybe that was the CRC theme song? I remember the song, the gloomy day, and the chains. I remember the awful knowledge that I was being incarcerated for a possible seven years.

But what happened there was not what I was expecting. In truth, or at least the truth for a junkie, was that CRC wasn't bad at all. And at times, one might even say it was *fun*—a place populated with a bunch of non-violent middle-class girls who happened to be drug addicts. Sure, tempers flared and there were spats and upheavals. But we weren't likely to kill each other. Most of us allotted a fair amount of time to figuring out how we might be able to get heroin on the inside, because, no matter what, addicts want to get high. I don't drink, but what others went through to get drunk was a hoot. The only real drawback to life at CRC was that I wasn't free to make choices. I had to eat when they said eat and sleep when they said sleep. And, of course, we couldn't get out.

The CRC had been a luxury hotel, in the 1930s. It went broke I think because it was too far from LA. Cars weren't the jets they are today. In 1955, the State of California bought it and converted it into a rehabilitation center for convicted drug addicts. Before that it served as a rehabilitation place for battle-worn soldiers and sailors who were shot up in World War II, and the place had quite a colorful history.

There were no bars on the dormitory windows, but the windows slammed closed on me if I wasn't careful. We were incarcerated, but the supervision was a lot looser than I expected and the atmosphere was less brutal than you'd find in a cement building purposely constructed as a prison, where they housed murderous criminals like the infamous Manson family girls, who were down the road at California Institute for Women (CIW). The authorities threatened that if we were bad, we could get shipped to CIW and take our chances among the real criminal chicks and heavies. I didn't want to do something that would get me shipped.

At CRC, there were eight dorms connected by a breezeway where the women hung out and scoped out other inmates. There were mostly straight women in there, but it seemed even they knew the easiest way to do time was with a partner or lover. Still, it was hard to have sex without a guard stumbling onto the scene.

One of the first things that struck me was the voice level. I was stunned at how noisy it was. Everyone was talking and yelling back and forth from one dorm to another, or down the hall. Or playing loud music. My first thought was that I wouldn't be able to deal the din, but of course I had little choice.

Not long after my arrival I saw a girl who caught my attention. She had on the latest trendy duds and sunglasses, and was listening to a new Walkman. No hand-me-down County jumpsuit or State-issued attire. I asked one of the women, "Who's that?"

"That is Katie Elwood. Katie wouldn't know she was locked up if it weren't for the fact that she doesn't have her Corvette."

I introduced myself to Katie, and we became good friends. She showed me what life could be in there. She had somebody on the outside "running for her"—sending her everything she wanted, including smoked oysters and caviar. She had everything she wanted except her freedom, and her Corvette.

One day, someone asked, "Do you want Katie to grill a cheese sandwich for you?"

"What? How is she going to do that?"

Katie had a clothes iron, and bread and cheese, and she was making grilled cheese sandwiches with the iron. I ordered one and paid with the dockets the prison issued instead of cash. Not long after the Katie's Deli Experience, she whispered, "Peggy, come here. It's not going to be too long before we have some hooch."

"That's cool, Katie. I don't drink but that ought to liven things up around here."

Late one night, I heard a loud noise and thought a boiler had blown up. Turned out, Katie had squirreled away giant mayonnaise containers from the cafeteria, cleaned them out, and filled them with fruit and yeast she had scrounged up. They swelled and swelled and swelled and finally blew up, spraying fruit all over the ceiling and the walls of the library where she had them hidden. The cops weren't happy. My cellmate said, "We are in trouble now."

After that, we couldn't cruise on the breezeway or buy Snickers bars, or even toothpaste, in the canteen. Finally, Katie came forward and said she had done it. She wasn't the sole instigator, but told me later, "I didn't want everyone to suffer, so I took the rap. No big deal."

I think they issued "demerits" for such acts; too many demerits and they could bring you in front of a board that would decide whether or not your shenanigans warranted more time.

Everyone had a job and mine was in the kitchen, though I hated washing dishes for six hundred people. The pots were large enough that I could have gotten in one and rowed my way to freedom. I used to fantasize about grabbing one of those enormous spoons, finding a body of water, sitting down in a gigantic pot, casting off and paddling like hell—except there was no body of water nearby.

I didn't want to work on the grounds or mop the floors or anything like that. I was much more cerebral than physical. I finally agreed to become what they called a pre-release agent, helping people to obtain driver's licenses, marriage licenses, social security cards and divorces before they left CRC.

Katie managed to get us some heroin on occasion. One day in particular, we were by the tennis court, sunbathing. She asked, "Do you want to get high tonight?"

"You bet, but fat chance of that."

"Well . . . maybe not. Are you sure you're in?"

"In what?"

"Just watch."

In a few minutes, a couple of Mexican guys in a low-rider drove down the frontage road and lobbed a tennis ball full of heroin over the wall. She grinned at me as I sat with my mouth open.

"Ok," I laughed, shaking my head. "I'm in."

So, I waited until the guards were changing positions. Katie whispered "now!" and I ran down into the ice plant and grabbed the tennis ball.

Now, I thought, I'm really in.

Just down the hill from our facility was the men's unit of CRC. One day I saw a girl hanging out the window with a day-glow hairbrush in her hand waving it frantically in the air. I could tell that she wasn't just simply waving a hairbrush. There appeared to be intent and purpose in her flailing.

"What is she doing?" I asked.

"She's flagging," an inmate named Angela said.

"Flagging?"

"Talking to her boyfriend down the hill."

"Talking to her boyfriend?"

"Yes. Many of us have husbands or boyfriends doing time down the hill and we flag them. The cops don't like it because we could be planning anything . . . an escape," Angela explained.

"How exactly does flagging work?" I was now intrigued.

"We write the words in the air backwards. The day glow brushes create a kind of tail when they are moving fast. We write it backwards but they read it forward. It's like a mirror. For example, I'll write, 'I love you.'" At first it just looked like frantic streaking colors. They would write backward letters in the air and then wave a line underneath so you would know that was the end of a word. Then they would start the next word. The woman I saw flagging that day had been in for a while and could write that shit in the air like I couldn't believe.

Angela said, "Now watch her boyfriend answer." It was actually an art form. They would write whole scripts to each other: "I got a letter from Aunt Susie." "How's your cough?" "I miss you." If they got caught the guards would confiscate the brush; big deal, the girl would just get another one.

Because I was looking for something else to do that would be more fun than processing documents, I told the staff that I was a writer. The proof was my book—*that awful* book. They didn't have a copy, thank God, but they knew it existed. I somehow convinced them that if I didn't have to work at a regular job I could write a play for the institution, cast the inmates, and stage it. I made sure that the playwriting and production would take me the rest of my time—however long that might be. Months went on and I did nothing but lie in the sun with some of the girls in our bathing suits. Because this had been a luxury hotel, there was a swimming pool across the blacktop from the administration building.

Katie would ask me, "Are you writing the play?"

"Not yet."

"Peggy, they are going to keep you longer because they're going to figure out you conned them. They aren't going to like that. You're not going to get released. You can't con the staff."

"Don't worry about it, Katie. I'm going to write it. I have it all in my mind."

She said, "Well, you better get it all down there on paper because you are coming up to the parole board soon. They are going to say, 'Did you do what you said you were going to do?'"

Katie was right. In the next two or three days I wrote a play called "Ain't Love a Bitch," using Rod Stewart's song by the same name as the opening background music. What I'd noticed while I was in there was that a lot of those women—especially the straight women—were doing time for a man. They had either taken a fall for their boyfriend or they went along with some illegal activity that was his idea, and had been the only one to get busted. That idea kept rolling around in my head and eventually that's what I wrote about. I had one of the main characters doing time behind her boyfriend's rap. He had done two years and she was being readied to be released, then a week before she got out, he overdosed.

I cast the inmates, and they were incredible. I gave them the scripts and right before they would go on stage in rehearsals I would say, "Do it like this," and they would follow my directions. Then came the day to put the play on. They were nervous; I was nervous. Somehow it flowed and came off spectacularly. I was called on stage for a standing ovation, took a bow and felt the rush.

I hadn't known I could pull it off until I actually did it.

Not long afterwards I went before the parole board and they asked me about the play. I'm certain they already had the information, but it was almost like a job interview to get out of prison, to see if you "qualify" to rub elbows freely with the rest of humanity.

"Well, Miss Caserta, we see that you wrote your play and cast the inmates and we understand that it was a smashing hit." Then they talked among themselves for a little bit and someone said, "Alright. We are going to put you out for an early release."

I had just written myself out of jail!

The day arrived when my papers came through and I was asked where I wanted my parole to be assigned. While in prison, I met an inmate who was later paroled, and she was willing to help me, so I asked to be assigned to Monterey, California. (Of course, felons are not supposed to associate with other felons, but they are often the only people willing to have you around, especially if you have little or no family in the area.)

I was released with a brand new driver's license, the clothes on my back, some hand-me-down prison shoes, the name of my Monterey parole officer, and a couple hundred bucks for a bus pass.

If anyone has an ego when they enter prison, it will get kicked out before they get out. It begins with multiple stays in the County Jail. The first time they deloused me and slammed the bars behind me, it knocked me down a notch. Then, you face a metal bunk with a thin cot and a cellmate who isn't thrilled with your mug a few feet from theirs for days, weeks, or months at a time. After multiple visits to the County facility, the felonies pile up enough to get sent to prison. By the time you leave prison you are made to know you have nothing coming to you. I came out of CRC believing I wasn't anything special.

I had not gotten beaten or raped in there. In fact, I had quite a good time over all. Still, something happens. No one gets to, or out, of prison easy. No one.

When I initially went in I thought either I had something on the ball, that I was smart, lucky, or all three. Prison killed that and I've never recovered from the feeling that I amount to next to nothing.

When you are restricted to when you can eat, bathe, sleep, read or do anything, you don't come out of that with a lot of self-esteem. It's not about being physically beaten. They just made it clear that all that was left of me was a number.

Later—and I mean decades later—I believe that, through years of staying clean, and repairing the emotional damage and physical toll on my body, that my 'thing'—whatever that is—is coming back around. But on the day of my release, flattened and scared, I did what I'd always done.

✶

I got strung out again right out of prison. Big surprise. The woman I joined in Monterey was, of course, using heroin. I attempted to be clean, which lasted about a minute. I got hooked again, so hard and so fast, it even blew *my* mind. I knew it was just a matter of time before I was going to get violated because, as part of my parole, I was subject to random drug testing. If caught, I would have three to five years hanging over my head. Fear weighed heavily on me day in and day out. Even the dope couldn't take it away.

One day I remember walking across a street in Monterey, feeling an overwhelming rush of desperation and despair. I prayed, "Oh God, please! How am I going to get a grip on this addiction?" I felt truly helpless. I looked up at the sky. *If there is a God and you're out there, please, please . . . I need help.* I thought that it was futile but I kept begging. The next thing I knew, I began to feel a mild trembling sensation, then I suddenly felt weak in the knees. I stumbled the last couple of yards to the curb and literally fell down on the grass between the street and the sidewalk. I felt myself shaking as if my body was crying but without sound or emotion. A short time passed and the shuddering stopped and a sense of peace flooded into what felt like every little cell of my being.

I know this will sound ridiculous, or naïve, or simply a lie, but at that precise moment I just knew I wasn't going to use anymore—that it was over. I had never been a religious person, and anyone who knew me then would have laughed at the suggestion that I would turn to God, and—more unbelievably—that by doing so, I would experience some kind of real, tangible, and lasting change come over me. Yet, that's exactly what happened.

From that moment, things changed.

I wanted to get in touch with someone who knew me when I had been successful. I tracked down Stella and she was incredulous. The call went something like this. "Stella?" I began, "this is Sam."

"Sah-*man*-tha," she gasped, "where are you?"

"I'm in Monterey, and I'm *clean*," I said enthusiastically.

"Really? *Really*? she exclaimed, sounding excited. Then with a bit of skepticism she added, "At least you sound like it. What happened?"

"I just got out of prison a few weeks ago and got strung out again. I was feeling desperate, just so desperate and I said a little prayer. Ya know I had to be desperate to pray!"

"Prison? Oh Jeezus!"

"Yeah, prison. But listen." My tone got serious, "I think I got struck clean. Like God sent down some kinda energy and made me clean."

There was silence.

"God? God struck you clean? Are you fucking kidding me?" Stella yelled.

"Yeah, I think so," I said, taken aback at her fury. "I mean, Stella, really it was *so* huge it shook me to the core. Fucking to my *core*. I'm as stunned as you that I don't shoot dope anymore."

"Jeezus Samantha," she said, her tone exasperated now. "All the times Ned and I dragged you out of some crappy situation and nursed you back to health and you were struck, *struck clean?* With a prayer? A prayer is all it took?" She was quiet for another moment.

"How was I to know? I mean, I'm not religious, but something happened and I'm glad it did."

"I'm glad it did, too," a deeper pause, "but do ya think you could've fucking prayed a little sooner?"

Next I called Kimmie, who was now living in Santa Barbara. Though our romantic relationship had been over for years, we'd remained friends of a sort, and I hoped by being around her—Kimmie had never tolerated hard drug use—it would be a good influence on me.

I had my parole transferred there and checked into a hotel downtown called the Schooner Inn Hotel. My room was right above the "T" in hotel. It was also above a Mexican dive called the Office Bar. On rowdy weekends fistfights and knife fights were not uncommon. Across the street was a place called Maggie McFly's, which had big picture windows so that both the patrons and the passersby had a clear view of one another. The local gay bar, The Unicorn, was around the corner on Cota Street.

One night I'd gone down the street to Joe's Café—across the street and down a ways from the hotel—to get some dinner. On my way back, I stopped in front of Maggie McFly's, where a drunken woman was doing an inebriated version of the "Can Can" except she had no panties on. There she was, with her skirt lifted practically over her head, flashing the patrons with her low-budget burlesque routine. Across the street there was a commotion outside of the Office Bar. People spilled out and a couple of guys were brawling on the sidewalk. Then I saw the glint of metal as one of them pulled out a knife. I didn't want any part of that, so I made a b-line to my hotel. Unfortunately, by doing so, I crossed in the middle of the street.

Two police officers approached me. "M'am do you realize you just illegally crossed State Street?"

"I was trying to avoid the knife fight and . . ."

"M'am, let us see your identification."

"Are you kidding me? There's a knife fight going on right . . ."

"M'am, I don't want to ask you again. Do you have any identification?"

How much more surreal could this get? There was a lewd woman dancing on one side of the street and a full-on knife fight 100 feet from where the officers and I were standing, and these two are focused on *me*?

"Here." I handed them my I.D.

"Is this your current address?"

"No. I live right here at the moment." I pointed down the street in the general direction of the Schooner Inn.

"Where?"

"Right there, at that hotel."

By then the burlesque dancer was doing her special moves while facing me and the cops.

"M'am, you need to notify the DMV within ten days of an address change. Have you done this?"

I heard the sound of breaking glass and I could see one of the guys outside the bar had just broken a beer bottle and lunged at the other guy.

"Um no, not yet. I will as soon as I have a more permanent address."

Cars are honking at the dancer who had, literally, taken her act on the road.

The whole time, one of the two cops had been looking across the street, hands on his belt, at a right angle to me so he could have a clear view of the dancer and of the bar scene. He showed not one flicker of interest, amusement, entertainment, or acknowledgement. The other cop heard on his walkie-talkie that I had no warrants. Another roar goes up from the crowd outside the bar as someone comes close to getting sliced.

"I'm citing you for jaywalking. I won't cite you for not updating your license. But if I see you again and you haven't done it, I will happily write you up."

The burlesque gal stumbled and almost got run over. Brakes squealed and the driver laid on his horn.

I wanted to scream at them! All this crazy shit going on and they are gonna land "the big fish"—the fucking jaywalker? Yet, I knew better than to mouth off after all the time I'd done.

"Yes sir," I said.

The bar fight spilled into the middle of the street. The cops turned away. I walked into the hotel lobby. Another day in paradise.

Soon, I considered moving from the Schooner Inn and asked Kim to let her friends know I wanted to rent a room or tiny apartment. A couple of weeks passed and one evening I got a call from the desk clerk. "Miss Caserta, we've caught someone creeping up the stairs to your room. She had asked us earlier to ring you. Now she just won't say a word." I'm thinking, "Oh great! Another fucking freak."

"Well, who is it?"

"She won't answer, but we know her. What do you want us to do?"

"I'll be down"

I went downstairs to the desk and there she was, green eyes ablaze, a beat-up felt hat pulled down low, and a little Lord Fauntleroy haircut spilling out underneath. She was familiar. I had met her at Kim's a couple of times and seen her at the local bar. From what I had heard, she basically lived on the streets and always had a guitar with her.

"Why are you here?" I asked.

"I heard you were looking for a place to rent."

"Why didn't you have the desk call?"

"They refused."

I turned to the desk clerk. "You refused?"

"Yes, Miss Caserta. We've had trouble with her before. We've asked her not to return to this establishment."

"Really? What did she do?"

"She has been drunk, singing loudly on the roof at all hours on numerous occasions."

I turned to her and asked, "Is this true?"

"Yeah."

"C'mon up, we need to talk."

The desk clerk protested. "Miss Caserta, you can't do that. She is not welcome here."

"Excuse me, I pay my rent a month in advance, and I will be responsible for her."

"Miss Caserta, if you have any trouble or if we have any complaints, we will not hesitate to have her removed."

"No problem. I'll have her removed myself if there is any trouble. C'mon," I said as I turned to the little creature in a hat. "You're Maggie, right?"

"Yeah."

She shot the desk clerk a "hmmmph" and followed me to the elevator, an old-timey one where I had to pull a grate across the opening before I could press the button. I pressed 3, folded my arms across my chest, and studied her. "What in the hell were you doing, and why the fuck were you creeping up the stairs?"

Her pupils were huge and she took a minute to answer. "Look, I'm high on mushrooms. The desk clerk hates me. I tried to get him to call, he wouldn't, so I thought 'fuck him' and tried to sneak up the stairs instead of using the elevator."

"You didn't think this could wait? Especially until you weren't high anymore?"

We arrived at the third floor and went into my suite. "So, you have information for me about a rental?"

"This guy I sometimes work for doing roofing and stuff has a couple of places. One is for rent right now. If you wanted it, there's not all the usual stuff to fill out. You could pretty much have it if I told him you were a friend of mine."

I wondered how this little ragamuffin could have any housing connections. From what I knew, *she* didn't even have a place to live.

"Why don't *you* rent it?"

"I can't afford it. Sometimes I stay with my girlfriend, sometimes my car, whatever. I'm not really homeless all the time."

"Alright, give me the info and I'll look into it."

She wrote down the name and number. "Don't forget to tell him I sent you."

"I won't. Thanks."

"Ok, cool. See ya," Maggie said, and walked out the door.

Immediately I got on the phone to Kimmie. "Who the hell is this Maggie woman? The clerk caught her crawling up the stairs to my room, high on mushrooms. Is she a freak? Is she dangerous? What the fuck, Kim?"

"No, she's just young, kinda flakey, lives on the street half the time and has a bad relationship with some crazy woman from LA. She's harmless. She's also a really good singer and songwriter, Peg."

"You sure she's no problem?"

"No, she's no problem. If you want me to tell her to stay away from you I will. She'll do it."

"No, that's ok. She says she knows some guy with a place for rent."

"She probably does. She grew up here. She could know anybody."

In the end, I decided I was just fine staying at the Schooner Inn. The location was perfect, two blocks from the place I had wanted to lease: my plan was to open a lesbian bar, and since I had no wheels, it helped to be close. I drank Cokes at the Unicorn and got to meet some of the local dykes who had, by then, commandeered the back room with the pool table, much to the chagrin of the owner. Those dykes were spending money, though. I began to see Maggie around more and more, dragging a guitar with her, and occasionally her girlfriend. It rarely looked as if things were going too well with her. She seemed to be out on the streets way too much.

While I was trying to retool myself as the smart business owner I once was, I went out to see Gloria Steinem speak at the University of California, Santa Barbara. They had overbooked the event and were seating people in the aisles. Before Steinem spoke, there was some warm-up entertainment happening up on the stage, a woman playing a guitar and singing. I found a place on the floor in an aisle about midway back from the front, and finally noticed: damned if it wasn't Maggie, playing her heart out, surrounded by about a dozen people in chairs. I felt bad for her, as there must have been some glitch with the mic because I could barely hear her.

I noticed, however, that the people on the stage were bobbing their heads in time, but I could barely hear a thing. Then I could see that there was a woman gesturing in the air—sign language, it appeared. I realized the people sitting in the chairs were hearing-impaired, but they seemed to be the only ones who could "hear" Maggie. Seeing Maggie up there, giving it her all, made me more curious about her. How the hell did she end up opening for Gloria Steinem? She sure seemed to be something more than a street waif.

Not long afterward I saw her walking down the street with her dog.

"Hey, where's your guitar?"

"Um, I lost it."

"You lost it? Did you leave it somewhere?"

"I used it for collateral for a cab ride."

"And you couldn't pay?"

"I got the money the next day and tracked the driver down. He laughed and said it was gone. Fucker," she scoffed, shaking her head. "He got a $50 guitar for a $10 fare."

"What an asshole."

"Yeah, a real fucking sweetheart."

"What are you going to do?"

"I'll figure something out."

Next time I saw her, she had a guitar. I asked her where she kept it. She said sometimes she would hide it in a dumpster if she couldn't keep it with her for some reason. In the process of trying to open the bar, I had been holding music auditions. I really wanted to have live music there. The first time I was actually able to hear Maggie was when she auditioned for me. I was impressed by her voice, but more so by her lyrics. She was a helluva writer. I admit I was becoming a bit smitten. As I was talking to her about her songwriting, I suddenly gasped. "Where did you get *that*?" I said, pointing to her middle finger.

"What?" she said, looking down.

"That ring, that little blue heart ring."

"Oh, I thought you knew," she said.

"Knew what?" I said.

"Kimmie gave it to me, a couple of years ago. We had been partying all night up at her and Annie's place on Mountain Drive. She bestowed it on me in the wee hours. Somewhere in the midst of cosmic, philosophical, musical musings and Tequila. Or Red Mountain wine. Or both. She said she'd had it since Stinson and had never known what to do with it until that moment."

My head was swimming. I reached back into my memory and saw myself putting that ring into my jewelry box the day Janis had come to lie on my deck. I had never gotten a chance to get it back to her because she had died a few weeks later. I had not thought about that ring for so many years; in fact, I tried, often in vain, never to think about Janis or The Haight or any of it. Yet, here I was, staring at Janis's ring, on the fingers of another young female musician, ten years later.

I offered to keep Maggie's guitar at the Schooner Inn where it would be safe and told her she could come get it anytime she wanted. She hesitated and said she'd let me know. I saw her a couple days later. She asked if the deal was still open and I said it was, so she left her guitar.

To be honest, I knew if I had her guitar, I was sure she'd come back, which of course she did. Then she began to stay. She had this wild, dingo-looking dog named Blue who was with her most of the time. Blue had one blue eye and one brown eye, and didn't move or act like any other dog I'd ever known. I didn't know what to think of the dog. She wasn't overly friendly but she seemed in tune with Maggie's every move. Blue seemed like she was from another world. Then again, so was Maggie.

It's a summer afternoon, not too hot or humid, a warm gulf breeze touching us and Mom turns to me and says, "Darlin', when you were just a little girl in grammar school, and later in high school, your teachers used to tell me and your daddy how smart you were. We were so happy to know that we had a brilliant kid."

"Awww Mom, that's so sweet but I'm not brilliant. At best, I hope I'm above average."

"No, Peggy . . . we think you're brilliant."

"I love that you think that much of me, but Ma, there are people out there tirelessly searching for cures for diseases thus far incurable, really brilliant folks. Somebody even identified genetic markers, making it possible to catch the guilty person and exonerate the wrongfully convicted! Major stuff."

Since she appears to be listening, I figure that while I got her, I'll drive it home with one last example of "brilliance."

"Did ya know that some extremely brilliant people came up with the science to launch a probe that is transversing the galaxy? This thing has to withstand incredible tasks, radiation belts, star clusters, meteors and lordy knows. I've heard that it's taken 22 years but it actually is alleged to be at the outer galactic limits ready to enter into deep space!"

I've dazzled myself with this story, now hoping she gets it, I say, "See Mom, those are the accomplishments of brilliant people; I'm not one of them, but I'm moved that you and Dad thought that I'm smart."

I think I've finally brought it on home when she turns and says, "Not smart . . . brilliant."

I'm enjoying the breeze, she's sort of brooding and then she says, "Ya know, Peggy, just because you can't do some of those things, doesn't mean that I don't have a brilliant kid."

Part Six

I WAS NOW CLEAN, and working on opening the bar which I planned to call Flames. Santa Barbara already had two gay bars at the time but they catered more to men: The Unicorn, and a much larger dance club on the beach side of the 101 freeway called The Pub. In order to get my bar open, I had to deal with the prickly licensing department in Santa Barbara. I had a business partner who could be the "straight" owner, in order for the liquor license to be legal since I was a felon. It was a far cry from having rented places to sell jeans and tops. I had no idea a bar would be such a hassle. I bought all the equipment and was getting ready to open; about a hundred people promised to show up for opening. The city then decided I needed to have private parking. But none of the other nearby businesses were open in the evening, so I'd assumed there would be enough street parking. Wrong. I sat out on the street for a couple of weeks counting cars coming and going, and tried to use reason and real-world statistics to support my case that there was indeed enough parking to sustain the bar's capacity. No. They decided I needed to build a parking structure on the roof of the building I was renting. No matter that there were over 100 available parking spaces on the street within a two-block radius and the bar capacity was seventy-five people maximum. The city planners decided the rooftop solution was the only viable option.

I actually considered it and was working to draft a plan when I had my inspection by the fire department. They insisted I have two entrances, but that the emergency exit door be positioned practically next to the regular entrance. However, access to that door could only be had from the back of the room, down a hallway that wrapped around on the other side of the wall behind the bar. In other words, instead of going straight out the exit/entry onto the street, people were expected to enter a corridor that kept them in the building, winding around the perimeter of the bar to be deposited, *where?* Right next to the entry/exit where they started. So in case of emergency, someone would have to spend a couple of precious minutes running in a crowd through a virtual tunnel, circle the entire bar, only to exit a mere five or six feet from where they entered. It made no sense to me, but the wise people at the Building and Safety Department insisted this corridor be built. I am tenacious, but after all I'd been through, I knew when I was fighting a losing battle. I was fresh out of prison, had no job, and I'd used up all my assets fixing up the place.

Finally, I had to admit to myself that I wasn't really that passionate about opening a bar. I mean, why? I don't even drink. I let the lease run out and sold most of the fixtures except one of the pool tables and a couple of the pinball machines.

*

Maggie was living with me full-time by then, and we moved out of the Schooner Inn and into a little Craftsman house on Laguna St, along with the pool table and the pinball machines. It was a rather sedate neighborhood, yet somehow, we managed to sell a lot of pot from there, mostly to dykes in town.

One of the little old ladies who lived across the street caught me in the yard one day. She said, "Your daughter sure has a lot of suitors."

"Excuse me?" I couldn't think for the life of me what she was talking about. I had no daughter. And what in the world could she mean by *suitors*?

"Your daughter . . . I see she has a lot of suitors. I see them coming over almost every day. It must be nice to know she is so popular with young men," she said with a sincere smile.

I started to explain I had no daughter. Then it dawned on me. She must think Maggie is my daughter and all these butch dykes coming to buy weed are young men! Fucking brilliant! It couldn't have been a better setup if I had tried!

"Yes, M'am," I said. "She sure is lucky, isn't she?"

"Oh yes," said the elderly woman. "It's nice to see people doing things the old-fashioned way."

"Indeed it is, M'am. Indeed it is."

Word got around town that our place was called the Laguna Girls Club. People would come over, buy some pot, hang out, play some pool and then go on about their business. The small house had beautiful wood flooring, the quintessential Craftsman porch, and an ironing board that folded down out of the wall. A floor furnace dated around the 1940s that modernized the heating from a mere fireplace. In the kitchen to the left and below the sink were screen-like grates set horizontally inside the cupboards and behind them, a small trap door which opened to the outside where the iceman long ago must have delivered a block of ice. An old-fashioned icebox.

The floor heater required some ingenuity to work. We discovered it to be a two-person job. One person had to switch the wall thermostat to the "on" position while the other jumped up and tried to land with enough force to trigger the pilot to light the gas burner. If we were successful, there would be a loud *woosh*. Over time it became more and more difficult, requiring a lot more jumping and timing. Finally we called the landlord, who passed the buck along to the gas company, which sent out the serviceman. We explained and proceeded to show him our method for igniting the heater, which we were quite proud of, and the heater started on the first try with its signature WOOSH.

"I would suggest you don't do that anymore."

"Why not? We've been doing it all winter."

"Seriously, you really don't want to do that anymore."

"Why not?"

"Maybe boom."

"Maybe *boom*?"

"Maybe boom," he repeated.

"What do you mean? It's winter. It's cold. What will happen?"

"Maybe boom."

∗

"Peg," Kimmie said in a whisper, "Peg. Ya gotta help me."

I held the phone receiver closer to my ear. "What's wrong, Kim?"

"I'm in the hospital."

"Oh shit, what for?"

"I think, I'm a little stressed. You have to come here."

"Ok, where are you?"

"Third floor. Room 2018. Bring a bag. A big one."

"What for?" With Kim, it could be anything.

"I have a bunch of green shirts you need to take out of here."

"Ok. We'll be there in a little while."

"Green shirts" was code for marijuana. She must have brought some pot to the hospital with her. So, I grabbed a small lunch-size brown bag, and another larger purse-like carryall and Maggie and I headed to the hospital. Arriving on the third floor we headed down the hall towards Kimmie's room, when Maggie turned to me.

"Do you smell that?"

"What? I smell cleaning stuff."

"Smell again."

I sniffed again. "I smell cleaning stuff, and, and hmm . . . it can't be,"

"Fucking Kimmie." Maggie chuckled.

Kim was lying in bed with her black Wayfarer sunglasses on, hooked up to an IV and a Walkman. The sweet scent of fresh, sticky ganja buds enveloped the entire room. Kim's head was bobbing as she sang along to a reggae song.

Maggie and I shook our heads as we flanked Kim on either side of the bed.

"Kimmie," I said, still laughing.

Her gyrations stopped and she bolted upright, grabbing my arm. I could hear the tinny voice and beats escaping the headphones, as she pulled me closer.

"Peg. You gotta help me get this pot out of here."

"I should think so. We could smell it all the way down the hall."

She fell back flat on the bed, then bounced right back up.

"Really?" She grabbed my arm again, looking around conspiratorially. "I couldn't trust the little one, ya know?"

"The little one?" I wasn't sure who or what she meant.

"You know, that girl. She's just too *something* to be trusted."

I realized she was speaking about her latest fling.

"So . . ." I looked around. "Where is it?"

Kimmie pointed to a closet.

"At the very bottom. In the back."

I walked over, opened it and immediately shut it.

"Oh Jeez-us, Kimmie! There's at least a couple of pounds in there!"

"Shhhhhhhhhh!" she hissed, her index finger to her lips "There's ten pounds." Then she giggled a literal "Hee, hee, hee."

"I didn't bring a bag big enough. How the fuck are we gonna get this out of here?" I'm looking at the terribly inadequate bags I brought. "How in the fuck did you get it in here to begin with?"

"Well I drove myself here and had it stashed in the car. Once they settled me in this room, hooked up to the IV bottle, I started to worry about the car getting stolen or something, so I dragged myself down there, IV pole and all. I couldn't bring it all up at once," she explained. Adding pragmatically, "So, I did it in two trips, and I'm sick, ya know!"

The pot was already in two heavy duty garbage bags, so Maggie and I decided we would carry one each, and opted for the stairs instead of the elevator. We got the stash out without incident, and hoped my parole officer wouldn't decide to search the house.

On our way back home from breakfast, a few days later, Maggie said, "Isn't that Kimmie?" as she pointed to a white station wagon that crossed the street ahead of us.

"Sure looks like her," I said, deciding to follow.

"Yep, that's her," Maggie said, adding, "Is that an IV bottle hanging from her sun visor?"

"Sure is," I replied as we came to a stop behind her.

Smoke was billowing out of the driver window. Maggie jumped out and began to jump up and down on the bumper of Kim's wagon. Clouds puffed out like smoke signals. Puff. Puff. Puff. I could see Kim's arms flailing and her head twisting around trying to see what the hell was going on. Then Maggie jumped in through the passenger door and Kim pulled over in the next block. Maggie was laughing hysterically when Kim blew a lung-full of pot smoke in my face as I approached the driver side.

"What are you doing?" I asked. "I thought you were still in the hospital."

"I *am*," she emphasized. "But I had some business to do."

"Business?"

"You know. My people need stuff. Which, by the way I'm glad I ran into you. I need to pick up my stuff."

"You mean, the stuff we took home for you?"

"Yeah. I need it back if I'm gonna stay in the hospital any longer."

Maggie and I glanced at each other. Maggie shrugged and grinned.

"You wanna come get it now?"

"I'll be there in a half hour. I have to make some deliveries. I'm busy, ya know. Gotta take care of business." She relit a joint, took a hit and handed it to me. "See ya later." And drove off.

✳

Maggie had a couple of friends and boyfriends in the pot trade and we were dealing hand over fist. When my friend, Ned, whom I hadn't seen since before I went to CRC, came to stay with us from Hawaii, he brought some Kona Gold with him, and boy was that fun! He was glad to see I wasn't strung out, and so was I. It was great to have him back, a lot like old times. I was still on parole and subjected to random testing; my P.O. could show up any time, and often did. However, there was no test for marijuana in those days.

One day Rickie, a friend of Maggie's, was dividing up a pound of the good Hawaiian bud. The scale was set up and he was doing pirouettes and flinging the buds onto the scale. Then he was doing NBA imitations and all kinds of gyrations. I was getting nervous and telling him to just get it done, when Maggie came in and announced, "PO!"

I growled to Rickie, "Clean that shit up now!" He stopped in mid-slam dunk. Maggie grabbed the scales and started shoving stuff in bags, and told me to go out in the living room and meet my PO.

Rickie asked, "What, what?"

Maggie told him, "Cop, fool! This shit needs to be packed up NOW. This woman can search this house any fucking time she wants to."

It finally hit him. "Shit! Shit! Oh shit! Oh this is fucked. I gotta go." He opened the back window and crawled out—all six-foot-something of him folded and contorted to fit through the two-foot by three-foot window opening. I headed to the door to let my "guest" in. My Parole Officer wanted a cup of coffee.

I poured the water into the pot.

As I was measuring out the coffee grounds Marilyn, my PO, began. "I'm ruined," she said, her affect flat.

"Oh, why is that?" I asked.

"My boyfriend got arrested last night."

"Drunk driving?" I guessed, thinking that might be a realistic, conservative bet.

"That would have been better."

Just then Maggie came through the front door.

She turned to my PO, "Oh hi, Marilyn."

Marilyn hardly looked up, "Hi, Maggie."

Maggie gave me a barely perceptible nod, letting me know all was clear.

"Well, I'll leave you two kids alone," she said and headed back to the bedroom.

Marilyn raised her head and looked at me pitifully.

"Oh, it's awful. Just awful. It can't be true. It just can't," she said cupping her face in her hands as she shook her head.

"What? What can't be true?" I was starting to get irritated.

"He got busted." She hesitated for a minute wringing her hands. "For . . ." She began to almost hyperventilate. "For, uh, for uh, for . . ." she took a big breath in and held it, as she appeared to teeter on what looked like the very edge of her own sanity and in a voice a bit too loud for normal conversation, she blurted out, "Groping a cop!"

"He what? A cop? Groped . . . oh my." Then I was all ears.

"Not only that, he was driving my car. My work car!"

"That one?" I say pointing out the window to her County car parked at the curb.

"Yes. They opened the trunk and found shackles, and handcuffs."

"Well, isn't that part of your tools of the trade, so to speak?"

"Yes, I do carry handcuffs. But not *these*, not leather. Not chains. Not . . ." Her voice trailed off.

I was attempting to keep a straight face, trying hard not to laugh.

"It had to be a setup! He's not gay! Not like that! The cops set him up! Anybody could walk into a bathroom in the park. It's a public bathroom! All you have to do is say 'Hi' and they think you are gay!"

"Well, you did say he 'groped' the cop. That's a far cry from a conversation."

"Do you know how embarrassing this is to me? My supervisor called me in to tell me what they found in the trunk. MY trunk! Whips, chains, shackles, handcuffs! It's nobody's business." She suddenly stopped.

"Oh, yeah . . . nobody's business. They were yours?" I ask gently.

"They were . . . found . . . on top of the pee bottles, you know, the ones I use for testing. He says they weren't his." She slumped in her chair.

"Want some more coffee?" I offered, just to change the subject.

"No, no thank you. I have to . . . here . . ." She shoved a jar at me to piss in.

"Yeah, right. No problem." I head toward the bathroom.

"Wait!" she yelled. "I have to watch you!" and came stomping after me.

I filled the jar as she stared at my crotch.

✳

I lost track of all the close calls we had. After Ned arrived, we all were stoned on pot 24/7. Every day we'd do what people call "wake and bake"—start our morning with a cup of coffee and a joint. Maggie would often have a beer, too. It all seemed so normal. One time Ned, Maggie, and I went to see a double feature at the movies. We were passing popcorn back and forth, and I'd had enough. Maggie kept insisting, being strangely emphatic and I kept saying, "No, I don't want any."

"Are you sure? *Really* sure?"

"Yes, I'm sure. Don't ask me again! I don't want any!"

"Ok, ok," she said and we watched the rest of the first feature. At the break, we went outside to smoke a cigarette. I looked at Ned and then at Maggie and back at Ned.

"You fuckers, you're high! What the fuck are you on? Why the hell didn't you offer any to ME?"

Ned said, "Sam, Sam I did. I passed it to Maggie and she passed it to you and you kept refusing." He smiled his charming, handsome smile, but I felt betrayed and wanted to slap him.

"You two got high without me? How dare you! I would never, never you hear me, never do that to you, Ned!" I turned around to Maggie. She just stared at me with her huge pupils, and shifted back and forth on the little silver heels she had just gotten at the thrift store. "Why didn't you tell me? Why, Maggie? Why?"

Maggie was silent, so I focused back on Ned.

"Sam, Sam I would never not offer you my best bud, my best acid, my best mushrooms."

"What the fuck are you guys on anyway? Acid?"

"No," he said, laughing. "Psilocybin mushrooms. Do you want some now?"

"No. No I don't. I'm so fucking pissed at you guys."

"C'mon Sam, don't ruin my trip."

Wrong thing to say.

"Don't ruin your trip? Don't ruin *your* fucking trip? I wouldn't ruin your trip if I was tripping, too. Dammit Ned you don't get how much you hurt me, do you?"

"Oh c'mon Samantha. Really. I'm sorry. If you want to trip I will give you as many mushrooms as you want. Otherwise c'mon . . . let me trip in peace."

"I don't want your fucking mushrooms. Not now. I probably wouldn't have a good trip. I want to go home. Where's Maggie?"

"I don't know. Maybe she went to the bathroom?"

I went to the ladies room. No Maggie. I went back into the theater where we had been sitting. No Maggie. I came out and told Ned, "I can't find her."

"Maybe she went to the car."

We headed to the car. No sign of her.

"Great. She's trippin' and God knows where she is."

"She'll be fine, Sam. Maybe she went home. Let's see. If she doesn't show up or call the house we can then go look for her."

The theater was three miles from home. When we got there, no sign of Maggie. Ned and I went in, fired up a joint, and waited. About an hour or so later Maggie showed up. She flung the front door open, walked in, slammed the door behind her and came straight up to me. "Don't you say a fucking word."

I opened my mouth to ask where she'd been.

"I said," she hissed, her eyes ablaze, "don't you say one fucking word. You have no idea how hard it was to get here tripping my brains out, in fucking heels no less! No. You don't get to say anything. Not. One. Fucking. Word." With that she whipped off her heels and limped into the bedroom, slamming the door behind her.

Ned said, "I think you kind of overdid it at the theater, Samantha."

"Maybe I should go talk to her?"

"Didn't you hear her, Sam? Jeezus, I'm a guy and I know when you do not talk to a woman. Now is definitely one of those times! Leave her alone."

Just then Maggie came out of the room, glared at me, went into the kitchen, grabbed a beer, and came out to sit on the couch.

Ned and I were quiet. Maggie popped the cap off her beer and downed it.

"I would like to enjoy what's left of my trip, if you don't mind," she announced, and lit a cigarette.

Maggie started to chuckle, then both her and Ned started laughing hard. I was miffed again that I wasn't included.

"C'mon you guys. I'm feeling left out here." I turned to Ned who slowly unrolled the top of a big paper grocery bag, "Have as much as you want." He scooped out two big handsful and held them out as if it were diamonds.

"I don't want it now. I wanted it *then*."

Ned sighed and rolled his eyes, putting the 'shrooms back in the bag.

"Stop it. You're being impossible!" Maggie said exasperated, and stood up. "I just endured three miles of psychedelic traffic lights, melting sidewalks and police cars that stretched around the block at every street crossing. All while wearing silver heels that looked like snakes on my feet." She grabbed the bag from Ned and held it in front of me. "Take the ticket. Get on the train. Or forever hold your peace!!"

I wanted so bad to fight back. I didn't *really* want to trip. I just wanted to be asked. I realized maybe I was being just a tiny bit unreasonable.

But I wasn't going to admit it.

Ned had what turned out to be about a pound or so of Magic Mushrooms; mushrooms are extremely light, so a pound is a lot. He and Maggie took them often in the ensuing days. I chose to abstain as I didn't want to run the risk of being that kind of high when my Parole Officer might show up at any moment. Other than that, it was a nice respite and a great time having Ned around. We reminisced, laughed a lot and talked late into the night. Stella was at their home base, tending to family matters, so couldn't make this trip. Ned gave me her contact info. Having the two of them back in my life meant so much. Very few people had seen me through the heights and depths in the way they had. Being in touch with them began to give me back a sense of "home."

After another month or so, Ned organized getting some pot across the border from Mexico. My parole was ending and I was soon to be put on summary probation, which meant that they thought I had been a good girl, and unless I got into some real trouble, the state didn't have enough time or resources to keep an eye on me. Ned had taken me to my final meeting with my Parole Officer, which took place at her home; I thought that was kind of strange, but didn't really know what to expect anyway. I told him it shouldn't take me long and had him wait in the car. But it seemed oddly emotional, and I have to admit I was a tiny bit choked up as it had been a long fucked-up road to get out of the clutches of the authorities and to leave my heroin addiction behind. She had to sign off on some papers that would "Gold Seal" me off parole. Since everyone at CRC, and my PO in Monterey, and Marilyn in Santa Barbara County had all reminded me often that I had a 98% chance of returning to prison, this piece of paper meant something to me. She went on and on, telling me told me how much I had meant to her, what a pleasure it had been to work with me, blah, blah, blah.

And all I could think of to say was, "Are you gonna sign those papers? Cause I've got someone waiting for me in the car."

She became indignant, and started screaming at me as she wrote the final signature, then shoved the papers into my hands. "You never got the one thing I was trying to give you! Never. You wouldn't let me give it to you!" Her eyes were wild and she was in my face.

I was backing away and defending myself, "What? What are you talking about? You gave me pee bottles. I filled them. You examined my arms with a magnifying glass a hundred times. What was I supposed to get from you?" I asked, becoming alarmed.

"You just don't get it, do you?" Her face screwed up between anger and sadness. My hand reached for the doorknob and I threw the door open. She was right behind me. "You never got it, did you? Did you? The ONE thing I wanted to give you!" She was yelling now.

Ned was standing wide-eyed in the driveway. "Is everything ok?"

I shook my head and headed for the passenger door. "No Ned, let's just go. Get in and drive."

"Why Peggy, why? Why didn't you let me give it to you? Why?" She broke down sobbing in the driveway.

Speechless, Ned glanced from me to her, his Camel cigarette dangling between his lips. The ash grew and then dropped off as he put the car in gear and took off.

"What the fuck was that all about, Sam? If I didn't know better I would've thought it was a lover's quarrel." Ned's eyes were still wide and he shook his head. "It's not, is it?"

"I have no fucking clue, Ned. But whatever it was, I'm pretty sure I don't want it."

※

Being off of parole allowed me to breathe. Maggie had gotten friendly with a musician named Jerry who lived in the Los Angeles area and we decided relocating to LA would be a good move for her music career. With $60 between us, we stuffed the orange Audi 100 full—Maggie's dog Blue, some clothes, her P.A. system, guitar, amp, and some good bud. Jerry had a little bungalow in Lomita and had invited us to live with him while he and Maggie put a band together.

Within the first two weeks we found out a couple things. One, his mother owned the bungalow, and she hadn't expected us to be moving in. She was just this side of cordial, and would show up throughout the day, fuss at and over Jerry, and quiz us about our activities. Second, he was on Methadone. I don't know how that escaped my dope radar. This made me uncomfortable since I was still on probation and really didn't want to start using, or even be around junkies, nor heroin.

One day, Jerry's friend came looking for him.

"Hey, is Jerry here?"

"No. Who are you?" I asked.

"I'm Fred. Will Jerry be back soon?"

"Yeah, I think he just ran to the store."

"Do you mind if I use the bathroom?"

"No, come on in."

A few minutes later Jerry comes back.

"Hey, your friend Fred is here. He just went to the bathroom."

"Oh fuck!" Jerry said, bolting for the door and pounding on it, screaming, "Fred! Fred you fucker! God damn it, Fred!"

"What the fuck?"

All became clear when Jerry kicked the door open.

Fred was face down and blue. Maggie and Jerry rolled Fred over. Not breathing. Needle still in his arm. Jerry slapped the shit out of Fred while Maggie turned on the shower. Still no breath. Check for the pulse. No pulse. Cold water in the face. More slapping. Nothing.

"Call the ambulance!" Jerry shouted. "Fuck! Fred, you fuckin' asshole. Come to, you fucker . . . c'mon Fred . . . c'mon . . . you fucking asshole!"

"I gotta get outta here" I said. "I'm on probation. When the cops come, they'll violate me for sure."

"Do what you gotta do, Peg," Maggie said as she dialed the emergency number. Meanwhile, Jerry was still slapping Fred around, pushing on his chest and screaming at him.

I took off and within minutes I heard the sirens, but I was now a few blocks away. I walked into Norm's Diner on Pacific Coast Highway and grabbed a seat at the counter. The sirens stopped abruptly. I was left wondering if Fred made it, if somehow my name would come up and trigger the system. "Fucking Fred," I muttered while I stirred some cream into my coffee and waited.

I called the house after about an hour and Maggie said it was clear for me to come back. Fred had had a close call. His face, hands, and feet had turned that weird blue/grey/green color and he hadn't drawn a breath despite Jerry's CPR and shake, slap, scream efforts.

According to Maggie, the firemen immediately began CPR. Then the ambulance arrived and the EMTs started an IV while continuing to do chest compressions. They didn't mess around. Fred was still lifeless on the floor, soaked from the earlier cold shower attempts to save his life. After consulting with the hospital they administered the opioid antidote drug, Narcan. The paramedics said they hoped it wasn't too late. Then everyone held their breath and waited. And waited. Finally, they could see Fred inhale. In less than a minute he began to breathe normally and move his arms and legs around. Once he came to, he looked around again with a scowl on his face and said, "Who panicked?"

*

I was feeling nostalgic.

After Fred's overdose and the uncomfortable dynamic of Jerry and his mother, Maggie and I rented a room in a motel and looked for jobs. I hadn't sought employment since I had worked at Delta Airlines, and back then I didn't have a prison record. My ego was so deflated. I figured I could run something, be a manager of something, but knew it was unlikely anyone would let a felon run amok with their business. Nevertheless, I applied for a bookkeeping job in Palos Verdes, and to my surprise, they hired me. Viola and her husband Joe were very kind and treated me well.

Maggie and I found a little house to rent in the South Bay area where we could have Maggie's dog. The place was two blocks from the railroad tracks and just a few blocks to either the 710 or 405 freeways. The Arco oil refinery, the city of Compton and Flo's Broasted chicken triangulated our new-found home.

As grateful as I was for the work, it ate away at what little self confidence I still had. After my first year, I had earned a vacation. What a concept! So, in June of 1984 I decided to go to San Francisco and see if maybe I could find some of my old business connections, and get a sense of what it was like to be in San Francisco after all this time.

Maggie and I had budgeted just enough money for a cheap hotel room, but the car was in questionable shape, grinding and screeching as soon as we'd exited the freeway and tried to climb one of

San Francisco's infamous hills. We couldn't figure out what it could be, but thought for sure it wasn't a good sign. Finally, we came to a sputtering halt. People on the sidewalks and in nearby cars looked on with shock and concern evident on their faces.

"Maggie, San Francisco seems way more crowded." I remarked. "We sure are attracting a lot of attention with this damn noise."

Maggie surveyed the scene. "Yeah, there sure are a lot of people. And they all look really festive, too!" She pointed to what looked like a small cadre of obvious butch lesbians crossing the street in front of us.

We chugged on for another little incline, another decline and then pulled up to a stop light. The crowds were particularly thick here and that's when we noticed hundreds of men in drag. Hot, young things in tight shorts and little else. Big men in leathers, nipple piercings glinting. The light changed and the car died in the intersection, disco music blasting in the background.

That's when we looked around and realized we had broken down in the middle of the Gay Pride Parade. A float loomed ahead. To my right, a bunch of nuns and for a moment, I thought, how nice of them to support our gay brothers and sisters! Then the sisters who weren't sisters started yelling at us to get out of the way.

"We're gonna have to push it. It's not going anywhere. Trade places with me, and I'll get out and push."

But before we could try, someone yelled, "Get back in the car!" And the next thing I knew we went rolling past the rest of the "sisters" and were deposited on the curb at the other side.

We chugged along until we got to a gas station that had a repair shop attached, and were quoted several hundred dollars. We didn't have the cash, and neither of us had a credit card. I ended up calling my mother.

"Oh, darlin'. Are you in an orange car?" she asked.

"Yes, we are. But how did you know?"

"You know they having some kind of Gay Parade thing. Your father and I saw you."

"You saw us?"

"You was on the news, Peggy. You and that orange car, right in front of a bunch of guys dressed like nuns! What are you doing there, Peggy?"

"I came up for a vacation. We just happened to break down in the middle of the parade."

"You just happened to? Peggy, I don't believe you. Every time you go to San Francisco, you get in trouble."

"Well, I didn't try to break down in the middle of a parade, mother. Anyway, can you send some money via Western Union?"

My mother started crying. "Are you using that stuff again, Peggy?"

I felt so bad that my drug use had hurt her and my dad so much over the years, and that she didn't feel she could trust me.

"Mom, I'm clean. Every time you've called lately, I don't sound loaded, do I?"

"No. You haven't sounded like you used to. But I still worry."

"I know, Mom. But the money is for the car, really."

"Ok, I'll get over there tomorrow morning and send it."

"Thanks, Mom. I can pay you back from my next couple of paychecks."

"That's alright, Darling. Just please don't be doing that stuff anymore. Please." She broke down again.

"I promise, Mom. I promise." I got a little choked up, too. God it was hard facing how much my using had affected my family. Thank God they never stopped loving me. I never felt like they didn't. Guess I was lucky in that way.

We decided to just sleep in the car that night in the Castro District, which I knew had become a mecca for gay men, and parked outside of a 24-hour donut shop. I figured a place like that would mean a lot of activity, making it a safe place to park overnight.

But instead of the slow pace we expected, we saw a large group of young guys posing outside the donut shop, as other guys cruised on foot and in cars. Shortly a wagon cruised by, then stopped along the curb. A couple of guys got out, chatted with some of the boys who were leaning up against the building feigning an air of aloofness, looking ever so bored, and smoking cigarettes. It appeared as though they negotiated a reason, if not a price for vacating their spot along this particular stretch of sidewalk. About an hour later it looked as if that same station wagon came back, dumped off the first load of guys and picked up the next set who had filtered out along the street to take up the slack left by the first group. This continued throughout the night. At one point I said to Maggie, "My God, I'm surprised they don't get sick or something. That's a whole lot of suckin' and fuckin'. I bet this goes on every night."

"Yeah, I'll bet you're right." Then she added, "I guess we could take bets on whether a pickup is gonna happen or not. Like that guy with the hat. I think he's gonna say yes."

Just then the guy with the hat got his dick grabbed. He leaned back against the wall, obviously getting comfortable.

"Hmmm, yep. I'd say that was a yes."

We dozed in short snippets throughout the night, as the boy parade grew less interesting. Finally, I opted for a cup of coffee just before dawn and we got a donut and a couple of refills by the time the sun came up.

By 9 a.m. we were at the Western Union, and gingerly made our way back to the mechanic. It took most of the day to get the car fixed, as they had to order parts from across town. Finally, we found a little motel in the Union district and I tracked down Brian Rohan of The Haight-Ashbury Legal Organization fame. Brian and I reminisced a bit, and I gave him a tape of Maggie and her band. He was now the official attorney for the Dead. Michael Stepanian was out of town, and had recently made a cameo appearance in the film *Where the Buffalo Roam*, which was, I believe, based on his misadventures with Hunter S. Thompson in the book *Fear and Loathing in Las Vegas*. Such a cast of characters had emerged from our movement!

The conversation turned to Bobby Boles. I'd given him the Boot Hook years ago, because he deserved it for helping me build my business. But the last I knew he had become incredibly successful, buying homes abroad, and opening a well-respected nightclub in San Francisco called The Palms, which had launched the careers of some of the greatest musical acts of the 1980s. Through Brian I learned that a woman had had an accident in the club that resulted in an injury and the lawsuit brought against him brought about financial demise. Word on the street was Bobby had then, along with his second wife, finally succumbed to the temptations of substances. Brian had seen him last eating pizza on the floor with his three kids. I asked Brian if he had any contact information and he said he didn't, but that he would put out some feelers and let me know if he came up with anything.

Later that day I had lunch with Terrence Hallinan, someone I dated for a brief time when I owned Mnasidika. He was running for a local office in the City and told me of all the great things he had helped to bring to fruition for the less fortunate citizens; later he would become the San Francisco District Attorney. After leaving Terry, we went through The Haight and stopped in the drugstore, and I heard a familiar voice.

"Peggy? Peggy? Is that really you?" I turned and saw it was Bernie. He gasped, "My God, it *is* you! Alive. Wow!"

"Yeah, it's me. Boy, you've seen some changes, eh?" I was amazed he had stuck it out all these years.

"Remember when you told me I should buy this building?" He shook his head, and grimaced. "My wife harps on me to this day about 'if only you'd listened to Peggy. You might've been a millionaire.'"

"Well Bernie, I've certainly made a few mistakes myself since then," I said, ruefully.

"It got real bad for awhile. Way worse than it was when you left," he explained further. "It was sad, really. People urinating all over. Crazy people, talking to themselves. Up and down the sidewalks, little lumps of filthy blankets and clothes that covered people sleeping in any crack they could wedge themselves into . . ."

"Yeah," I said wistfully. "Sure was a long way down from those innocent days."

"Yeah, sure was." He motioned outside. "The district is coming back though. Much better now." He smiled.

"You gonna stay?" I asked.

"I think I'm going to sell the business soon," he said, contemplating for a moment. "I was old compared to you all," he added laughing. "But I'm *really* old now."

"Well, I hope you are able to enjoy it. You certainly worked for it!"

"I guess I did, didn't I?" His eyes gleamed, then he grew serious. "You know, no one thought you would make it back out of . . . well, you know." He looked down for a second then back up at me, to see how I may have taken the last comment.

"Yeah, I know." I sighed. "It's no secret I went off the deep end. I survived though. I'm ready for whatever's next."

"I'll bet you are." He nodded.

"Well, it's been great seeing you," I said, shaking his hand and hugging him.

"Yeah, you, too, Peg. You, too."

As we started to make our way out of the City, I began to be overwhelmed with so many different feelings. Fondness and nostalgia gave way to a jarring moment of desperation. It was like seeing a hundred different ghosts of myself. Some terrifying, some gentle, some happy, some innocent. Some leapt from my memory, reaching desperately from the gates of hell. I did feel a bittersweet sense of relief as we drove out of the City onto the southbound freeway back towards my current life and home.

*

One afternoon in 1989, I was reading the newspaper and I ran across a review of a novel titled *Homeboy*, written by none other than Seth Morgan. Last time I had seen Seth was in 1971; he had asked me to find heroin for him and was threatening to burn Janis's Hollywood heroin connection as payback for her death. I don't quite know why but I looked up the publisher and tracked down a phone number. I spoke to someone there and cajoled and threatened, insisting they tell Seth that he needed to call me. Less than six hours later my phone rang.

"Peggy. It's Seth. You fucking bitch, I love it that you harassed my publisher to get me to call you." He chuckled in his gritty, throaty way. "So, how the hell are you?"

"Uh, ya know, after ripping and running for many years, I got busted and went to prison. I've been out a few years," I told him, then exaggerated, "I'm living a straight life now."

"Yeah, I'm trying to do the same. Did a few years up in Vacaville. Fucking nightmare, but that's where I wrote the book. Well, a lot of it. Got some discipline. That's one thing it did for me."

We caught each other up on the many years since we had been in contact. I mentioned that Maggie had a gig up in Berkley in a few weeks, and it turned out he was having a book signing there on the same day. We agreed to meet at Larry Blake's Blues Club and in the meantime, I asked him to send me a copy of his book.

I'm not much of a reader, but I found his book grabbed me. In fact, it was really good. Although it was fiction, some of the characters were clearly fashioned after Janis, me, and some other personalities from our days in San Francisco Bay. It brought back some good memories, and many that weren't.

Seth showed up just as Maggie's band launched into their first set. Another mutual friend from The Haight joined us. Seeing Seth aroused mixed feelings. But mostly he infuriated me. I did begin to see, finally, what it was Janis saw in him. He had a rugged charm, he was whip smart, funny, and very much a man. He talked that day about his current girlfriend, about whom he seemed to care a lot. He had a few more stops on his west coast book tour and then he was heading back to his home in the New Orleans Garden district.

Over the next few months we were in touch regularly. Maggie had gotten particularly friendly with him and was helping to find an art school for "his" kid out in California. (I believe this boy was the son of Seth's girlfriend, Diane, and he wanted to help out.) Maggie had found the Idyllwild Arts Academy, which Seth loved. He was hoping we would help look out after the boy if he enrolled. It all seemed like things were turning to the positive after all these years, and it felt good to be part of something good in a young person's life. Seth was supposed to finalize the paperwork, pay the tuition and send the boy out to us. He and Maggie talked nearly every day and then suddenly there was silence. He wasn't answering the phone and we weren't hearing from him. I thought maybe all this was bullshit, and that he had run it as far as he cared to and was off on some other sleazy adventure. But he seemed too up, too interested, to just disappear like that. Finally, someone picked up the phone when I dialed his New Orleans house.

"Hello." It didn't sound like Seth.

"Hello. Is Seth there?" I asked.

"Who is this?"

"It's Peggy. Who is this? Where's Seth?"

"I am Officer Howell with the New Orleans Police Department.

M'am, don't you read the morning news?"

"No, I'm in California." A chill ran through me.

"He went sailing into the Saint Claude Avenue Bridge last night on a motorcycle. He's dead."

"*WHAT!* Oh my God NO! He didn't!" I yelled, but I knew it was true. "Diane?" I asked.

"She was with him."

"The kid?"

"His next of kin has him. Sorry, M'am."

"Me, too. You have no idea how sorry," I said as I hung up.

What fucking timing. And that girl. That kid. The collateral damage? Immeasurable.

*

The brief vacation to the Bay Area shook me up. It gave me a boost being in touch with people who knew me before prison, jails, and the worst years of my drug addiction. It felt good to be received so kindly by people who remembered me as a business owner, fashion trendsetter, and contributing member of a community.

The same sort of gnawing that accompanied me while working at Delta so long ago, met me when I returned to Southern California and the nine-to-five bookkeeping job I had finally taken, and I realized it was time to give up the scattershot approach to making a living by selling pot.

I worked at the small family business for several months, but because they had no room to continue increasing my salary, I put out some feelers and got a tip on a job at a manufacturing company who hired me and gave me a decent bump in salary. During that time Maggie and I saved and scrimped and bought our little home in September, 1985. It was on a lot with another house so that rent would help us qualify for the mortgage loan and make the monthly payments. While pleased to finally be a homeowner again after so long, I felt genuinely stifled by those normal jobs with little call for any creativity, yet I soldiered on for another few years, masquerading as a normal office worker, paying bills, and staying clean.

Eventually, we bought the house behind us when it came up for sale and rented that out, after selling the smaller rental house next door once we'd discovered that the tenant was hoarding nearly 100 cats. That move allowed both of us to quit our day jobs. For a while, we sold hot dogs from a cart that we parked outside a home improvement store.

*

I had been keeping in loose contact with Brian Rohan, one of the cofounders of the old Haight Ashbury Legal Offices, when he turned up contact information for Bobby Boles. I was excited to reach him. We had been so close in those early days and were a dynamic team. I called the number and someone said that Bobby wasn't in but that they would leave a message for him. I told them to have him call me collect at 6 p.m.

At six o'clock the phone rang. It was so good to hear Bobby's voice, to be in touch again. But things turned awkward when he started telling me about his drinking and drug use. It was heartbreaking to hear. I never in a million years thought the tables would turn, yet there we were. Me clean, and Bobby strung out battling for his life. Alcohol, cocaine, and heroin had taken a mighty toll on my dear Bobby. I invited him to come stay with us and kick. He only hesitated for a minute then agreed. We arranged to get him out of San Francisco and bought him a plane ticket down to Long Beach. He and Maggie got along incredibly well. She fixed a gazillion pots of chicken soup to get his strength up.

Within a couple weeks, he really started to perk up. The sores that had been festering on his legs and arms cleared up. His eyes were bright and he had finally kicked. Weeks went by and then months in a Norman Rockwell-meets-Salvador Dali kind of way. He loved to watch the game show *Jeopardy*. Maggie and I would barely tolerate it, the three of us sitting on the bed every night, watching *Jeopardy*, then *Wheel of Fortune* and eating ice cream, like a little family.

One night just after sundown Bobby said, "I'm gonna go to the store."

"You're going now? What do you need? Me or Maggie will drive you."

"Nah, that's ok. I want to take a walk anyway. Get some cigarettes and some ice cream."

I RAN INTO SOME TROUBLE

"You sure, Bobby? Don't you have enough smokes until morning? It's not the best neighborhood to be wandering around in at night."

"You know me, Peg. I can handle myself."

He put on his jacket and was out the door. About twenty minutes later we heard sirens, not unusual in the north part of Long Beach, bordering Carson and Compton. Sirens and helicopters were just white noise, the soundtrack to every day.

After a couple hours, I started to get uneasy. Then I thought maybe he'd picked up some chick, and was having a good ole time now that he was feeling better. When we still hadn't heard from him by the next afternoon, I called the Sheriff's department to report him missing. But we couldn't file a report for an adult until he had been gone 72 hours. I called his ex-wife, Marty, but she hadn't heard from him. The timing of those sirens was now alarming. On the third day, we were able to file a missing person report. Two days later, the phone rang.

"This is Sheila from Long Beach Memorial Hospital. Did you file a missing person report?"

"Yes, yes. Did you find him?" I motioned to Maggie and mouthed, *I think they found Bobby*.

"We need for you to come down and identify a man who may be your missing person."

The blood drained from my face.

"He's," I choked out the next word, "dead?"

"No. He's not dead. However, he is in a coma. He was picked up on Harbor View with a fracture to his skull from a pipe. The weapon was found nearby. Witnesses said there was an altercation. He was unconscious when the sheriffs arrived. When can you come down?"

"Within the hour. Where do we go?"

"Come to the main entrance. Tell them you are there to identify a John Doe in ICU."

John Doe, Bobby is a fucking John Doe now.

We took off to Long Beach Memorial. At the main entrance there were a couple of elderly volunteers and a younger nurse.

"We're here to identify a . . . a . . . " I took a deep breath, "a John Doe in ICU."

Her face registered the practiced compassion that hundreds of hours of dealing with an emotional public produced. The very, very kind yet blank deer-in-the-headlights look.

"I'll have someone show you to ICU."

A nearby nurse said, "I'm going that way, I'll show you."

"Oh, good. Thank you, dear." The elder woman beamed.

I had all kinds of visions in my mind as to what we were going to see, including it not being Bobby at all.

The ICU nurse asked, "Are you family?"

"Kind of. He's like my brother."

"Well, he's unresponsive but you should be able to tell if it's him or not." She led us down the hall. "There he is."

I walked in first. The room was dimly lit. I saw a skinny person covered with sheets. A few strands of curly black hair stuck out of his bandaged head.

"Oh Jesus, Bobby." The tears welled up as I turned to the nurse. "It's him. It's Bobby. Bobby Boles."

"Ok. Good. You can sit with him a while. It may help him come around. We will need you to fill out some paperwork and answer some questions."

"How bad is he?"

"He's been unconscious since he was found. We won't know anything until he wakes up. He did have a lot of hemorrhaging in his brain. They caved in his skull . . ." the nurse's voice trailed off. "They caved it in good."

I stepped closer and took Bobby's hand.

"Bobby it's me, Peggy. We found you. We were so worried! I know you're strong, Bobby. We're gonna get you through this." He was still, no response. "Bobby, you remember Maggie don't you?" All of a sudden his knees drew up and he spread his legs and then clapped them together several times. "Hey Bobby! Yeah it's me, Maggie. That's a helluva hello. You think you're gonna get lucky or something?" His legs moved faster and a flicker of a smile moved across his face.

"You're waving your legs at my girlfriend?" I chided him. Now there was a definite grin on Bobby's face.

Maggie went to the other side of his bed and took his hand. "Hey handsome, it's good to see you."

His eyelids flickered and fluttered, opening for a few seconds, then closed again. The monitors started to beep.

"C'mon that's it," we encouraged him. "C'mon Bobby. C'mon."

His eyes stayed open a little longer . . . then a little longer, and it was apparent he was trying to focus. God, he looked so far away. His mouth was moving but no words came.

Maggie looked at me. "I'm gonna get the nurse." She whispered to Bobby, "I'll be back, don't you go anywhere." She patted his hand and left.

A few minutes later she returned with the nurse. "Welcome back, Bobby. Now we at least know what to call you."

The drive back home from the hospital was bittersweet. We were so glad we had found him alive—in bad shape, but alive. At that point the prognosis was still unknown. Something was bothering me, though, that I couldn't put my finger on when Maggie said, "He got hit really, really hard. They hit him so hard it knocked the blue right out of his eyes."

"Oh my God you're right! I've never heard of that happening, have you?"

"No, I haven't. I don't think it's good. Now they're like a weird brownish color. Freakish."

I sighed.

"I wonder if . . ." Maggie paused. "I wonder if, oh God this would be awful, if maybe somehow it's blood? Like it seeped up into his eyes making them that unearthly color?"

"Jeezus, I don't know. That can't be good."

When we went back the next day, he was more coherent though he still had a tremendous amount of difficulty speaking. Each subsequent day brought another degree of improvement. A twinkle of humor here and there began to pepper the conversations. But his eyes stayed dark.

When he was finally able to talk, we wanted to know what had happened that night. He said he had decided to get drunk and had gone to the store to buy a bottle of vodka. He drank it outside the liquor store, then had an ice cream thinking it might mask the vodka. On his way back he encountered some young gangsters driving by. They said something and he yelled back something about them being pussies and that he'd kick their asses if they had the courage to get out of the car. Well, they did. One of them was swinging a steel pipe, and slammed it into the side and back of Bobby's skull. Bobby spun around and his head struck the concrete curb where he collapsed unconscious. A neighbor had witnessed most of the melee and called the cops. Understandably, that person wanted to remain anonymous.

Maggie and I used to joke about our little 'hood when we first moved there. I had gone to get our Audi some insurance. When I told the agent our zip code he said, "You're kidding?" I told him no I wasn't and asked why would he say that. He said, "You're lucky. That is the lowest rate for insurance in Los Angeles County. Lowest for auto theft."

We soon realized the reason insurance was so low was that all the thieves lived here, thug city. One night early on, we fired up a joint while sitting in bed and all of a sudden there was a helicopter over the house and a voice boomed out, "Put it down! The party is OVER!" We both froze and looked at each other, mouths open. "How the fuck can they see us?" Maggie just shook her head, shrugged, and whispered, "They can't mean us, can they?"

The helicopter was still circling and we could see the light sweeping across the windows.

We heard the voice again. "Do not move. I repeat, do not move!" We could hear the chopper widening its circle. Then sirens wailed, came closer, then stopped a few blocks away. I picked up the joint, took a hit and passed it to her as the Ghetto Bird kept circling.

Bobby continued rehab in Long Beach Memorial. He joked that the blow to his head had completely made him forget he was ever an alcoholic; now he no longer thought about drinking. Eventually the hospital said they couldn't do any more for him, which we realized meant his insurance wasn't going to pay for any more care. Since Bobby's family was in the San Francisco Bay area, it was decided he was going to go up there. He had to be transferred via air ambulance due to the level of brain injury. It was sad for us, but it seemed the right thing for him. The doctors weren't sure how much better he could get, but felt a live-in program was best.

A couple of months later, Maggie and I traveled to visit him at a rehab facility for people with brain injury. It was a modest ranch style home in a residential neighborhood. By now, he had remembered he was an alcoholic and wanted us to take him to a liquor store. We refused and he lost his temper. He'd lost the sparkle and sense of humor that had been such a part of his character prior to the injury.

Sometime within the year we got a call from Marty that Bobby had been found dead in the water at Fisherman's Wharf after he'd been missing for a couple of days. His body was fairly bloated and the fish had gotten to him. Marty was terribly upset because the Catholic Church was not going to allow him to be buried in their cemetery, because the police report had indicated his death as a possible suicide. For Bobby's family, Italian Roman Catholics, to have him refused burial by the church was heart-wrenching.

Those who were around Bobby in those final weeks said it was more likely he got into an altercation and had been rolled, that it was unlikely he'd taken his own life.

His eyes never did return to blue.

*

We found our next creative venture by focusing on Maggie. Maggie was a musician, a good one, and she was an especially good songwriter. She was a brilliant lyricist, who wrote an impressive repertoire of songs, arranged the melody, and delivered them vocally, reminiscent of Janis's style—clear and from the soul.

When my father died, and I was rushing to book a flight home, she wrote a lovely song, "May Everything Be All Right," which she played before my departure. I was so grateful (still am); that song wrapped together my damaged heart and soothed my aching soul. I made it home to say goodbye to Dad.

Forming a band was challenging, with a varying array of personalities and egos, and the songs and players changed frequently. The most enduring of her bands was Maggie and the Midnight 30, which played around different clubs in the South Bay area of Los Angeles and the beach towns, gathering a following of sorts. At that time, a very disturbing trend began to unfold. It dawned on some club owners that there were, in fact, more bands trying to get booked than there were clubs. Aha! This reality birthed the "Pay to Play" idea and it took hold. Club owners knew bands needed a venue more than the clubs needed quite so many bands. Bad news. So now, in addition to all the capital funding a group required, they needed to "pay to play," forking over a fee to the club owners each time they were booked. This was a death blow to some groups who were struggling already—like Maggie and the Midnight 30. We stumbled and floundered on for a while, and managed to keep on playing. But funding and polishing a band takes an entire litany of coordinated efforts, repeatedly, over the long haul. As the music struggle wore on, so did the stress.

It seemed like we were freefalling into an irreversible state of contrariness. We discontinued living together but remained somewhat connected. I wasn't feeling well about this change in my life and figured that the best way to deal with heartache is to make myself so busy, and create for myself such a challenge, that I'd hardly have time to think about the loss and what I might could've . . . should've done.

✹

Slowly at first, I notice Mom's world becoming smaller. She had reduced herself to staying mostly between her bed and her chair in the living room, where she sat to watch T.V. Determined not to let her world become a mere microcosm of a normal existence, I would offer to take her out for a ride on Sundays—she loved it. This Sunday went like this.

"*Mom, wanna go for a ride today?*"

"*Oh yes, Honey, I'd love to go for a ride.*"

"*Great. Where ya wanna go? Ya know?*"

"*Anywhere you decide is good with me. Just pick a place and I'm ok with it.*"

"*Fine. What about the Arboretum?*"

"*I love the Arboretum, but didn't we just go there?*"

"*Eh, well a few weeks ago...we did. Ok, it's been a while since we drove out by the old airport and looked at where that tornado cut through the woods.*"

"*Tornados in the South! Never had those before. Gives me the willies.*"

"*All right then, wanna take a ride down River Road and look at the fabulous homes?*"

She hesitates on this one and I think I've got it 'til she says, "Nah, I've seen those houses enough."
"The Coast! Yeah! You love...tha..."
"Too far today."
"Well Mom, WHERE do you want to go?"
I don't know...anywhere you suggest I'm good with."

※

My next venture was opening an espresso/cappuccino coffeehouse in Long Beach called The Tropics. True to my expectations, it absorbed me, especially because I was still of the mistaken belief that I could pull anything off *underfunded*. My old friends Stella and Ned were part of the startup business. Stella painted an amazing tropical scene on the walls and I hung some of her watercolors.

One day, not long after opening up, I heard a voice that stirred my memory from someplace a very long time ago.

"Peggy? Holy shit! They weren't kidding! It *is* you!"

I looked up and walking towards me was Danny Rifkin, co-manager of the Grateful Dead.

"Danny? Yeah, it's me," I said as I came out from behind the counter and hugged him, hard.

"Wow, Peggy. You're doing it again, I see."

"Not quite the same, Danny. There is no cultural revolution to go with this."

"Yeah, I guess not. Man, those days were something, weren't they?"

Our eyes exchanged memories shared from those magical early days of Haight-Ashbury. Such an unusual time; it's gone down in history as such a thing . . . *unusual*.

Danny and I took a walk on the beach, reminiscing and catching up. He was down visiting his father who was very ill. It felt wonderful to talk with him, someone who knew me when. There were so few people who really knew intimately, who understood how much the Haight-Ashbury experience so profoundly imprinted those of us who were there when all the early action began. We parted friends, as if thirty years had not gone by.

I poured myself and what money I could scratch up into the business, and put all my time into it, nearly 24/7.

Then, unbelievably, I got strung out. Again.

Dilaudid and I were back together and I was up to my old shenanigans.

I ended up selling the coffeehouse after only two years. It's impossible to run a successful business while you're mainly interested in where your next fix is coming from.

Not long after that, Maggie and my old friend Damian showed up. Maggie and I were living apart by then, but still owned the two houses jointly. She had gotten a call from the tenant in our rental house saying she'd better come down and see what was going on. (For some reason, I had shot a bunch of cocaine a couple of weeks before and had talked to Maggie on the phone, which hadn't done much to bolster her confidence in my condition. So, when she got the call, she already knew all was not well.)

By then, Maggie had been deeply involved in the Hollywood Needle Exchange Program, Clean Needles Now, and had seen me coming in to get clean syringes on occasion. This time in my life was awful—in bad shape but refusing to admit I might need some help.

On Thanksgiving Eve, 1995, I lost control of my bodily functions and was living on Pet evaporated milk. Maggie and Damian called an ambulance but I refused to be transported. Finally, one of the paramedics stated I'd have to sign a paper saying that I understood that I would die if I refused treatment. I was hell-bent on signing it and getting everyone out of there. The trouble was, I could not hold the pen, let alone write. That was all they needed. The paramedics put me on the gurney in spite of my vicious

DAMIAN AND MAGGIE, HOLLYWOOD, CA, 1990

protests and hauled me off to Long Beach Memorial Medical Center. Within two hours I lapsed into a coma. I had endocarditis (an infection or inflammation around the inner lining of the heart), as well as double pneumonia, and my kidneys had shut down. My liver was failing, too. Oh yeah, and there was the withdrawal off of all that Dilaudid.

I remained on life support and in multiple organ failure for six weeks. When I finally regained consciousness, I was transferred to Harbor-UCLA Medical Center, where I stayed for another month. Next, I was sent to a rehab for three weeks, then released although I was still not yet able to walk. Debra, an ex-lover of Damian's and mutual friend, offered to let me stay with her. I knew she was always into some multi-level marketing, or other scheme, so I was hesitant to be at her mercy, but I clearly couldn't take care of myself if I was going to be stuck in bed or a chair. Debra also struck me as overly friendly. Unfortunately, I saw no other option. Debra took me to her home, put me in a bedroom and assured me all would be well. She said she'd bring me food, clean clothes, and bedding. Which she did. She was always kind.

One day I heard a bunch of voices from the direction of the living room. I called out, "Debra? Debra? Is that you? Who's out there?" I heard a man's voice, and called out again, louder, "Who's here?" Just then the bedroom door opened and a man and a woman came through the door. Then three or four other people begin to pile into my room.

"What the hell are you doing? Who are you?" I yelled with as much conviction as I could muster, sick and weak as I was.

"Who the hell are *you?*" the guy asked, looking just as shocked and angry as I felt.

"Yeah, who are you and what the hell are you doing here?" the woman chimed in.

"Look, I'm sick and staying here with Debra. What the hell is going on?" It dawned on me that these people didn't seem up to anything illegal. In fact, they seemed to be acting as if they belonged there.

"Debra hasn't paid rent in months," one of them said.

She—and I—had to vacate. Oh fuck. I couldn't believe I had to deal with this as weak as I was. I called a cab and went back alone to Long Beach.

Back home, I could barely get around. I had fashioned a means of getting to my car by grabbing a chair, to the edge of the table, to the end of the kitchen counter. I'd stay there for a moment and sway, then grab the doorknob, swing the door open while still balancing off the counter. Next, I'd stabilize myself with the doorjamb and swing myself out with the screen door where I'd teeter briefly and launch myself a couple of feet down the mildly graded slope to the hood of my car. From there I went hand over hand to the driver-side door handle. I then steadied myself against the car as I swung the door open, grabbed the pillar with my right hand, then the steering wheel with my left hand, slid my left hand down to the armrest of the door while lifting my right leg up and into the footwell of the driver's area. From there I would plop into the seat and rest. Panting, exhausted from the effort, yet fueled by accomplishment, I would wait to catch my breath and try to figure out the most physically conservative way to accomplish my tasks. I'm not sure how I got through it, but I did. I think the humiliation and helplessness I felt at Debra's alleged "home" kept me inspired. Anger and pride were powerful motivators.

Part Seven

I SPOKE TO MY MOTHER every Sunday since I got out of prison. God knows we'd both been through a lot. We talked about buying and selling houses, my relationships, neighbors kind and infuriating (hers and mine), who she ran into at the Winn-Dixie, the raccoons who came begging and knocked on her screen door with the back of their leathery hands at six every evening.

I'd begun to notice her sounding a little less strong, the reports of her activities a little less active. The topics receding into a smaller sphere encompassing not much more than what was happening inside her house and in her front and back yards. She was talking about not driving anymore, about not being as steady, or as agile as she wanted to be.

Everyone with an aging parent, worries. But when you're separated by thousands of miles, you can't be sure if you're interpreting the signs clearly.

One weekend I got a call from my Uncle Billy.

"Neesy? Neesy? It's your Uncle Billy." He always called me "Neesy," his affectionate way of saying "niece."

"Hi, Uncle Billy. What's wrong?" There had to be a problem for him to telephone me.

"It's your momma, Neesy."

I had a sinking feeling as if my stomach had filled with lead and I sat down.

"What? Is she ok? Where is she? Is she dead?"

"No, no, Neesy. She's alright right now. She's just getting old ya know."

"Yeah, so? We all are." I was pissed that he'd frightened me.

"I think she should go into a home. She's having trouble taking care of herself. Drivin' and cookin'—it's too much for her."

"Is she sick?"

"No, she's not sick. But with my wife being ill I can't get over to see Nodie much. She needs some help, I figure."

"Does Mom know you're thinking of putting her in a home?"

"No, Neesy. I thought I'd talk to you first since you're her only child."

"Well, I talk to her every weekend, Billy. It doesn't sound like things are that bad. At least not bad enough to lock her away somewhere."

"I'm just thinkin' we ought to start looking into it, that's all."

"Alright Billy. I'll talk with Mom and see what she wants."

"Alrighty, Neesy. You let me know, ok?"

I hung up and sat on the edge of my bed for a few long minutes.

I took a deep breath and called my mother. We exchanged the usual pleasantries. I heard about the goings on of the small town in Mississippi to which she had moved. I brought up my conversation with Uncle Billy and his concerns. She listened and grew quiet. I asked if she thought she needed some help and she admitted she wasn't feeling like she wanted to keep driving. She was after all, eighty-seven years old.

After I hung up I theorized that she wasn't bad enough for a rest home, but she sure sounded like she needed help. Being in California, there wasn't much I could do from there. My mother had a decent pension from my dad, but that wouldn't go far in paying for someone to be there in the house with her 24/7. I checked into her Medicare and supplemental insurance and found there wasn't much they were willing to pay for either in the way of at-home help. *How the hell do people get by?* I suppose I never thought I, or she, would live long enough for this to become an issue. Yet, here it was.

At least my mother and I had an advantage in that we had each other. I thought of all the times she had taken my desperate, junkie phone calls, all the times she had wired money to bail me out of jail, or help me pay my way out of a jam of one sort or another. She had sewn clothes for my first business venture. She had always simply been there for me, more times than I could count. I was lucky. I always knew that. Maybe now it was my turn to repay that . . . to give something back.

I understood very clearly that I could easily be the one to take care of my mother. But in the South? Oh God, was I really thinking of this? Could I, would I, go back home? I took stock and realized I really didn't have much holding me to the West Coast anymore. I better sleep on this, I thought, although the notion was not filling me with dread. On the contrary, a sort of peace was setting in. I drifted off to sleep with the scent of magnolias on my mind.

The first thought as I awakened the next day: Home. *Home?* For more than four decades, that word for me had not meant a dwelling in the Southern United States, not even a minute. Yes, it was where I was from, as in prior to. As in, *before*. As in, my *past*. As in somewhere far, far away. Yet here I was, with that word—home—reaching toward me with arms like soft branches of Southern Oak, moss-laden and achingly familiar, moist and warm, bayou country, drenched in history, po'boys, pirate lore, and Lake Ponchartrain. All that was comfort and Southern to me, beckoned. I no longer had any aversion. I fell into the invitation. The embrace was complete. I was going home.

On February 26th, 2005, I loaded up my black 4-Runner with my two dogs, ready at last to leave California after all these years. Angel was a rescued German Shepherd that had some neurological disorder that made her unable to walk normally. She basically just went around in a circle, head at an awkward angle, spinning, spinning, and spinning, whenever she wasn't lying down. She was going to be euthanized at the Carson Animal shelter as unadoptable and I scooped her up. I just couldn't let them kill her because she wasn't "normal." She loved to be petted and loved on as long as she wasn't moving. I figured I could at least give her that comfort. The other dog was a lab named Cody that ran into my yard one day and never left. He ended up being so gentle and kind with Angie. Great watchdog, but sweet as could be. This was my little family. I hired one of my tenants to help me drive, and off we headed, south and east towards Mississippi.

It was time. Finally, being clean from drugs, after numerous failed attempts—and one final, success—at rehab, all California seemed to offer me anymore was sorry memories about watching friends die, doomed romantic relationships, and the destruction of drugs. I was done with all that. Even the happier memories of sunnier times when I ran profitable businesses, owned homes and expensive cars, and had once been witness to some of the most powerful music of the century, wasn't enough to keep me there.

PEGGY'S MOM, DRINKING A BEER ON HER FRONT PORCH, 2015

I wanted to go home. Not to Louisiana, my birthplace, exactly. But home to Mom. I needed to, and I wanted to go home and help my mother, one of the two people in the world who had never given up on me—despite my giving plenty of reasons why she should.

Mom, who had been widowed in 1985 after forty-some years of marriage to Dad, lived in a little house that was just right for her alone, but was not going to be big enough for all of us. We traded her house, plus a little more money to get her into a place that would accommodate her emerging needs, which in reality, were *our* emerging needs. I arrived on March 1st and the weather was mild. It was, in fact, splendid. In the South, there is a sweet spot at which humidity feels almost like a touch of kindness on your skin, like you're brushing up against love. I don't think dry air ever feels that sweet. Conversely, when the humidity starts getting up into the ninety percent range it feels especially intrusive, like swapping sweat with strangers.

As March gave way to April, I braced myself for the onslaught of heat and humidity this part of the country is known for. It didn't come. It stayed pleasant. Increasingly warm, but it really hadn't gotten too hot, or humid. May came and it still wasn't too bad. Sitting out on the porch in the late afternoon and early evening became a treasured ritual with Mom. Even in her late eighties, she enjoyed a cold Busch Lite on a hot day. I, still feelin' the sixties, smoked a joint. June and July came, and with it a few quick storms. We lolled through the first couple weeks of August in relative comfort. Then we began to hear news of a big storm. A hurricane that was gaining strength in the Gulf of Mexico. At the store, I got Mom a couple of extra cases of beer. I got the dogs an extra bag of dog food. I grabbed some peanut butter for myself and didn't really worry too much.

"Tropical Storm Katrina Gaining Strength, Expected to Become a Category 2 Hurricane by Nightfall."

The news reports were gaining strength as well. "Hurricane Katrina is now a Category 3. Looking to make landfall on the Gulf Coast." I went back to the store, but there was barely anything left on the shelves. All the canned goods, water, Pet milk, cereal, batteries, fruit—all gone. It looked like locusts had come and eaten everything. All the gas had been pumped and the service stations were closing. There was some kind of foreign energy in the air . . . a sense of panic and urgency. Wow, people sure are over-reacting, I thought.

"Katrina is still gaining momentum and heading straight for New Orleans. At this point, local officials are suggesting evacuation," we heard on the radio.

"Mom, this hurricane looks like it's going to be pretty bad. Maybe we should go."

"You do what you want. I'm not going anywhere."

"Mom, there is nothing left in town—no food, no bottled water—nothing. Everything is closed and the interstate is starting to back up."

"Well then, where would we go?"

I didn't have an answer for her.

Our neighbor Jim was a rocket scientist. Literally. He lived alone and liked to go to the Gulf Coast and spend his weekends and money, gambling at the casinos. He was a nice guy, helpful when he could be, and seemed to have a kindness towards animals that endeared him to me.

"Peggy, Peggy, come here," he said motioning with his hand as he stood in his driveway by the passenger side of his car.

"What is it, Jim?" I said, walking towards him.

"I just want you to know something. It's important."

"What is it, Jim?" I repeat.

"Look here, Peggy," he said as he opened the back door of his broken-down van, "I've set up a triage, just in case we need it. I have mercurochrome, Band-Aids and some gauze. Look, I even have cookies!" he declared excitedly, gesturing grandly as if unveiling a magic trick.

"Cookies?" Apparently, I wasn't getting the full impact of this piece of news.

"Yes, cookies! I also have candy bars! You see, if the storm is real bad, we can come out here and we'll have something to eat. You and your mom are welcome to it. I just want you to know in case you need it," he said with such sincerity and concern.

"Wow, Jim. That's very kind of you," I said mustering up enthusiasm. "Thank you for thinking of us."

"This looks like this is gonna be a bad one. A real bad one, Peggy."

"I know. That's what they're saying."

"You know we're right in the path," he stated.

"No. No, I didn't know that. I thought they weren't sure."

"I looked at the satellite images. We are most likely gonna get hit. Directly!"

"Oh shit! Well, I'm going in. It's feeling awful eerie to me."

"Yeah, well don't forget you and your mama are welcome to anything here in the van."

"Thanks, Jim. I hope it doesn't come to that."

"Me, too, Miss Peggy. Me, too."

I was disturbed by the conversation with Jim. Here was a very smart guy and he was talking about eating cookies and candy bars in his driveway. In his van. The news reports were now saying it was too late to leave and that Katrina might rev up to a Category 4 hurricane, and possibly stronger, by the time she made landfall.

Then it was quiet. Too quiet. I decided to get some sleep. I had only ever been through a Category 2 hurricane and really didn't know what to expect. I thought they were probably overstating the potential and I figured we might be out of electricity for a little while. As I drifted off to sleep I could hear the wind begin to pick up.

At about 6 a.m. I thought one of the nearby trains had jumped the track and was coming straight into the house. The roar was unbelievable. Cody had jumped up on the bed and was next to me, panting.

"Mom?" I called out. "Mother?" I tried to turn the light on. Nothing. I reached into my nightstand and found the flashlight. "It's ok, Cody. You're ok, Boy. Let's go get Mom. C'mon Boy, let's go get Mom." I patted him on his head and rubbed the scruff of his neck. He stuck to me like glue. I shined the light into the hall and towards my mother's room. "Mom? Mom? Mother?" I yelled. The wind was getting louder and the rain beating hard on the roof and coursing down the windows. I could hear things thumping alongside the house, and the chairs scraping along the deck.

"Peggy? Peggy? You up?"

I see her silhouetted in the door frame, making her way toward me. The house began to vibrate, which added to the noise and increasing unease I was feeling. Lightning flashed and the ensuing thunder was lost in the shrieking, roaring tones of the winds which continued to increase in intensity.

Incredibly the storm intensified. The freakish parade of random objects, tree limbs, car parts, road signs, patio chairs appeared and disappeared as the bursts of lightning gave us a freeze-frame editorial through the window. In one of those flashes I watched as one door ripped off a storage shed in the backyard. Then another as the contents of the shed began to swirl around and get carried outside. I felt the ninety-eight-year old house lift slightly off the pilings it was built upon. God-awful scary. If ever there was an instance where I felt a relapse was in order; it was now. I was scared! Yes, a hit of heroin to calm my frayed nervous system sounded really good. Instead, I had to take comfort from knowing that my sweet neighbor had had the foresight to stash some mercurochrome and cookies in his van.

"Mom, the shed doors are gone!" Just then another loud crash. "A pine tree is down! It took out part of the house next door!"

"Well, Dahlin'. What can we do about it?" my mother said, calm as could be.

"We can protect ourselves. But I don't know how long our roof is gonna hold!"

"How're we gonna protect ourselves against a tree?"

Her practicality was annoying me. "You and the dogs are getting in the whirlpool tub; it's big! C'mon Mother!"

"Bathtub?"

"Yes, bathtub. I'm taking your mattress with us!"

My mother stood up and I yanked on the corner of her bed.

"Peggy that isn't gonna help! Why the mattress?"

"Mother!" I yell, exasperated. "I hear the bathtub is the safest place. I'll put the mattress over y'all so you don't get hit with debris if the roof caves in! C'mon!"

I dragged the mattress towards her bathroom, which had been built especially big in case she ever needed a wheelchair.

"C'mon mother! If that tree breaks through, this wind is gonna snatch us up and blow us into the next county! You ever heard of Dorothy and Toto?"

I got mother and Cody situated in the bathtub and leaned the mattress up so it was tipped against the side of the tub. Angel kept circling until I got her into the whirlpool.

Mother protested, "Peggy, I've ne*vah* done this in all my life. Ne*vah*!"

"Well, you ne*vah* been in a hurricane like this either, have you?" I shot back.

"I guess not."

I don't know how long we were in the bathtub, them under the mattress, me on top, but at least the mattress provided the unexpected benefit of muffling the incessant screeching, moaning, growling, shuddering onslaught that was the soundtrack to Katrina's wrath. It somehow helped to soothe our nerves, just the tiniest bit. It wasn't too bad with the blankets, pillows, and all. Sort of like an upside-down bed. Mercifully the endless roar began to abate, the foundation quit trembling.

Tentatively, I eased the mattress off, Cody quickly jumped out. I helped my mother up and out of the tub and went to take a look around. Angel stayed curled up, seemingly nonplused by the whole event. Cody still was glued to my side but was breathing more normally. The roof hadn't been compromised on the inside that I could see. I opened the back door, and Jeezuz! Every tree within sight was stripped bare, that is, if it was standing at all.

There were piles of God-knows-what shoved against the fence, which had miraculously held. The pool I was having built, was nothing more than a gaping, muddy hole that, having breached its own shores, joined the lake that was our backyard. There was hardly a breeze. I closed the door and went back through the house to the front door to see what that side of our lives looked like. Opening the front door, the landscape that had been so familiar was replaced by mayhem. There was hardly a road to speak of. Entire trees with their roots grasping into the air lay, desperate, on their side. Fences, doors and part of what looked like an RV lay tangled amongst matted branches, trunks and copious amounts of mud. I stood with my mouth open and Cody began to whine. He brought me out of my shock.

"You want to go out, Cody? You gotta pee?" I asked. Cody looked up as if to say yes.

"Well, c'mon then" I swung the door open and stepped out onto the porch. Cody ran ahead of me and proceeded to do his business.

I heard, "Peggy!"

I turned to see Jim as he was coming out of his house.

"Well, we made it!" he said, eyes sparkling.

"Yeah, I guess we did. We certainly did!" I began to get excited. Just then the sun broke through and everything seemed like it just might be alright.

Jim went to his van and pulled out a package of cookies.

"Let's celebrate! Want a cookie?" he said, handing me the package.

"Yes!" I grabbed a couple, smiled and handed it back to him.

"God that was something. I thought we were done for. Especially when that tree cut loose," he said, shaking his head as he took in the damage.

"Yeah, me, too."

"I wonder how bad New Orleans is?" he wondered.

"Can't be good."

"No, no I can't imagine it is. God bless 'em."

Jim offered me another cookie. Cody sniffed around but kept returning to lean up against me and whine nervously. I patted him absently as my conversation with Jim turned lively and upbeat, as we began to unwind from the nerve-wracking hours we had just endured in the storm. Then slowly we began to hear what sounded like a train coming down the tracks across the road. We were confused. How could a train be coming when surely there were trees and debris on the tracks? Suddenly Jim looked at me and said, "Oh God, that was the eye, Peggy! The eye just went over us! We're not done! Now comes the worst part!"

"The worst part? The worst part? How can it get worse?" I said, not wanting to believe it.

"On the back side the wind is worse—much worse. It spins the opposite way."

"The opposite way? Jeezuz Jim, you mean this isn't over?"

"No, it isn't. Oh God! We really are in the direct path! That was the eye we've been in . . . oh my God! The *eye*!" That train was getting louder, the roar deep and menacing as it steadily advanced. Jim and I looked at each other, terror in our eyes. "It's coming back, Peggy! Run for your life!" he shouted as he ran toward his house.

So I did. Cody was already at the door, as I scrambled up on the porch. The sky was dark again, the wind whipped past in a huge gust as the "train" headed right for us. I reached the door and Cody bolted inside as a savage current of air tore past me, blowing the door knob out of my hands and slamming against the wall. I grabbed it and shoved it closed from the inside and stood there panting for a moment. I turned to see my mother propped up in her recliner, beer in hand.

"What's going on?" she asked as she took a sip.

"It's back," I said.

"What?"

"The storm. It's back. It's gonna be worse, according to Jim."

"Worse?"

"Yes, worse!" I barked. "I don't know if this house can take it. I don't know if *I* can take it!"

"Well, we've made it so far."

"Yes. But *worse*? Can we take worse? I don't know, Mother."

"We'll see, I suppose," she said and calmly took another sip of her beer.

Jim was right. Katrina's other side was vicious. The sound of a storm like that is unbelievable—imagine not one but several massive freight trains, grinding against each other in your living room, screeching and groaning, scraping and thundering, for hours. In the meantime, the torrents of rain drenched everything. The storm leveled homes. It tossed cars, business signs and flag poles.

It tore the steeples off churches. Staircases and stop signs landed in unfathomable places. Unidentified objects were thrown about like a giant, very angry child in the midst of a tantrum. Then an even greater roar, and a tremendous tearing noise, and the roof over the new bathroom went sailing off into the sky. The gaping hole created a deafening suction against our ears and the volume was unbearable. I grabbed my mother and we held each other, with the dogs pressed up against us, even little Angel, as we fought our way to the other bathroom. We all huddled together in the tub there, and waited another eternity.

Finally, silence. Audible silence. After non-stop, high decibel noise and no electricity—even the hum of the refrigerator is missed when there is no power. We kept trying the lights and then just left the switches how they were, forgetting which way was on and which way was off after the tenth time we flipped them. I tried my cell phone. Nothing.

On the second day, still nothing, and it was getting even hotter. August in the South, the humidity hovering well over 90%. We ate whatever was in the refrigerator and freezer; Jim shared his cookies and we shared our "cold" food. By the third day whatever had been in the fridge was getting ripe and starting to spoil, so we picked through what was still edible and finished that off.

Nights were eerie-quiet, and unbelievably dark. It was however, quite something to see how much light-pollution normally impacts our ability to see the stars at night. With no light for miles in all directions, the stars were a blanket of tiny sparkling crystals embedded in deep royal-indigo velvet. The Milky Way shimmered, a stream of stars undulating in the far reaches of the sky. I was grateful for those moments of peace, for I was still in shock from the beating of the storm.

Jim listened to the radio in his car sparingly and brought us news about our condition, but there was nothing. No one knew about us. All the attention was focused on New Orleans and the horrific circumstances there. Understandably so. A state of emergency had been declared and the federal government promised that "help is on the way." FEMA was allegedly garnering forces and the Gulf Coast had been designated a National Disaster which was code for *we now know where we're going to get the money from.*

We heard that "help" got a bunch of people into the New Orleans Super Dome—with no air conditioning. Too many people, too hot, in a desperate space, locked in. Not good, not good at all. We heard that "help" was now getting them out. We heard the floodwaters were still rising. We heard nothing about us.

Mom had plenty of beer, so she was content. Cody and Angel had plenty of dog food; I had plenty of peanut butter. Jim had run out of cookies. The South had not yet run out of heat or humidity.

Mom kept drinking her beer and by now, a few days into our disaster, the heat had caused her to strip down to her underwear. I had a little pot, so I rolled a joint and fired it up . . . if ever there was a time to chill, this was it!

Some time had passed, I was in utter shock as to what was around us, the landscape looked as if it had sustained a major explosion. The leaves had literally been blown off the trees, what was left of them, save the large pine tree that was sticking out of my neighbor's roof.

I heard a dull roar in the distance. My body reacted with a rush of adrenaline and my mind flooded. "Oh shit, another storm!" It took a full minute or so for me to recognize the percussive sound of rotors that indicated a helicopter was near. The volume increased and moderate dots were visible in the distance. The choppers were flying low, so we could make out the shape of large army helicopters heading towards us. Jim and I leaped and yelled, waving our arms frantically in the air. I don't know if we really knew what we were doing, except that these were the only evidence of outside life we'd seen. The choppers passed directly overhead and headed southwest toward New Orleans.

Dripping with sweat, Jim and I stopped flailing, acknowledging that even if they had seen us, they likely would not have been able to do anything for us. That was the first day I knew for certain we were on our own.

I couldn't drive anywhere as there were entire trees lying across the road. It was too ghastly hot to walk into town on the notion there might be anything: food, generators, something. Help, for Christ sakes!

Day by day we saw more helicopters flying low, but they kept right on going. I was getting more and more tired of the heat. How the hell did people live here before air conditioning? Unless Jim was around, I took to wandering around in my bra and shorts, wiping down with a cold wet rag to help keep the stick and stink off me. Mom still had beer. I still had peanut butter. Cody and my precious little sick dog, Angel, still had dog food. We still had no help. Not quite a week after Katrina brought science fiction havoc to bear upon the people of the South, I began to hear another sound. A different sound—a distant buzzing—throughout the day. It was familiar but too faint for it to be clear. The next day the sound was closer and here we could make out some of our redneck boys, wielding chainsaws, and cutting through the downed trees that sprawled haphazardly out across the roads. Reasonable boys, they realized that without the ability to move around, there would likely be little recovery.

Word got around somehow that there was bottled water to be had. It turned out a church group had headed out from Minnesota when they heard of the devastation, and bless their hearts, I mean truly, bless their hearts, they loaded up and headed south. Determined to do what they could in the name of the Lord. They were the first sign of help we had, and I, for one, appreciated their kindness.

After the roads were cleared, we were able to drive around and see the devastation. On my first foray, out into the post-Katrina world, I found all four doors to the shed. All four of them. They had been blown neatly into a pile on the side of the back road that ran behind our house.

Cody and Angel were low on dog food and it appeared that life as we had known it was not about to return anytime soon. I went into town at first light because I'd heard Walmart had re-opened, even though there was still no electricity anywhere. I was desperate for air conditioning, but the only cool air available was in a vehicle, and the service stations were out of gas. My hope was that I could get in and out before the heat became unbearable. I was not the only one with this idea. The line was already out the door, into the parking lot, and down the frontage road. Gads, this was going to be a feat. The only thing I could do was get in line and hope for the best.

The store had no electricity, therefore no scanners or registers to ring up people's purchases. One clerk would read the barcode numbers off to another clerk who would look it up in an enormous book that contained every single item Walmart carried. Once found, they would bark out the price. All transactions were cash only. I had a total of eleven dollars in my wallet.

By eight a.m. the line stretched as far behind me as it did ahead of me and I had maybe shuffled forward a couple of feet in two hours. By ten a.m. I had moved another few feet. The heat was sweltering. I had brought a bottle of water with me and that was already gone. Noon came and went and by then I was about halfway to the store. By two o'clock, I had reached the parking lot. The sun was relentless and the humidity was nearly enough to swim in. By four o'clock I was willing myself to hold on. I was dripping cold sweat and felt like I was about to pass out. A big teddy bear of a guy in front of me looked me over and said, "You ok, lady?"

"I'm fine."

"You don't look so good. You pale. You sure you ok?"

"I'm kinda getting the chills."

"Maybe you should sit down."

"If I do, I don't think I'll get up."

The next thing I knew there was a man next to me in a uniform.

"M'am, come with me," he said as he took me by the arm to lead me out of the line.

"What are you doing? I'm not going anywhere!" I snapped. Suddenly I became nauseous and horribly dizzy.

"M'am, you've got heat sickness. C'mon over here and sit down."

"I'm not getting out of line! I've been here since dawn. You can't do this!" I struggled, attempting to break his grasp on my arm. I lost my balance and staggered.

"Whoa, whoa, whoa, easy now," he said, pulling me closer to keep me upright. Another man in a medic uniform arrived.

"Captain, this woman is obviously heat sick. She's clammy and drenched in cold sweat."

"I can see that," he said and moved to support me on the other side.

"Let me go! I've been here since the sun came up. I'm not leaving my place in line!" I argued as I tried to break free of their grasp.

"Ok, ok, I understand," said the Captain. "You're not going to lose your place in line." To the other guy in uniform he said, "Get her some cold compresses and wrap them around her neck and head. And get somebody to come help you."

"Alright, Captain," he nodded and took off.

Within a few minutes he was back with another guy and the cool wraps.

"I want you to stay with her. Until she gets inside," the Captain commanded.

"Ok, Captain. Roger that," they said in unison.

"Thank you very much," I sighed with relief. My head was pounding but just knowing someone gave a damn was comforting.

"You're welcome," the Captain replied, and smiled. "We've all been through something here, haven't we?"

"You got that right." I smiled back and nodded. There was a brief moment, where our eyes locked, and a wordless exchange of having shared an extraordinary experience passed between us. I imagine soldiers must feel that way, having shared battle. Most of the people in the world have no point of reference for such an extreme experience. But in that moment, we did.

Inside Walmart I found a twenty slipped behind a card in my wallet, so I now had a grand total of thirty one dollars to spend. My total came to $30.78 for peanut butter, bread, cereal, dog food, a few cans of evaporated milk, and coffee. The guys helped me to my car and I headed home.

When I got home Mom was hysterical. Considering that I had left at daylight and it was now evening, I didn't blame her. She wasn't sure something hadn't happened to me given the circumstances. She couldn't call anyone and couldn't get anywhere. All she could do was worry. For hours. No TV to distract, no air conditioning to comfort. No iced tea to sip on the porch, but she did have her hot Busch Lite and I was glad she did. It seemed to see her through anything.

Day after hot, sticky, miserable day we sat. Clad only in our underwear, my mother and I lounged unabashedly on the front porch, dripping sweat and wondering when, if ever, we might return to some sense of normalcy.

It was about ten days after Katrina had blown through that I heard rumors that there were generators to be had. I got out to Walmart again and thank God it wasn't like the first time. I was able to get a generator and use a credit card. Oh boy, I was able to get a portable air conditioner too! Relief of some nature was in reach; one of our neighbors helped get the generator set up. Once that sucker was fired up, we were able to power some things—the fridge! Glory hallelujah! There were cords going every which way. What a luxury! After sweating and melting for nearly two weeks with no relief, the fan, the air conditioner, and the cool beverages made me almost giddy. Still no telephones or television; however, I'd almost gotten past missing them.

I was humming along, doing the happy dance, when I tripped

over one of the many cords snaking their way to and from the generator. I went sailing and slammed my shoulder into a chest of drawers. Crack! I felt something give and simultaneously a bolt of pain shot through me like a shock as I bounced off the dresser and crashed onto the floor. As I went to push myself up off the floor, I screamed. My left arm useless. There was no support at the shoulder for my hand to brace from. I cursed and rolled to where I could raise up using just one hand and my legs. The pain was excruciating. My mother ran in from the living room when she heard my cursing.

"Peggy, you ok? What happened?"

"I fell, Mom. I think I broke something. I can't move my arm." I tried to show her and instantly regretted it "Shit! Jeezus! Oh fuck, this hurts!" I stood there breathing hard.

"It looks kinda funny," she said as she came to me. "You want an aspirin?"

I turned my throbbing shoulder towards Mom, my entire arm pounding with every beat of my heart.

"I think we need to get you to a doctor," she said and wandered out into the back yard, yelled over the side fence to the neighbor on the other side, Mike. He had left before Katrina hit us, and had returned to find an 80-foot pine tree lodged firmly through his roof. Rain had poured through his ceiling, flooding parts of his otherwise dry house. A week later, he was still working on repairs, crippled as we all were by the lack of services.

Mike popped his head over the fence. Mom explained that I'd been hurt in fall, and asked him if he would go into town and find someone to help. From what we understood FEMA had finally gotten some shelter set up and allegedly had some medical personnel on the scene. I sat out in the living room and waited for what seemed like forever.

Mike made the effort and came back and reported that a medic should be arriving soon. Shortly after, we saw a guy threading his way on foot over the remaining trunks of the trees still too large to move. He practically ran up onto the porch.

"Hi there, I'm Daniel. Who needs help?" he asked, as we invited him in.

"Me." I grunted in pain as I stood up. "It's my shoulder."

"Let me see." He took my wrist gently with one hand and put his other hand on my shoulder.

"Ouch! Shit! Sorry," I said. "Jeezuz that hurts. Ow, ow, ow, owwww!" I howled.

"Ooooh, I bet that hurts," he said as I continued to curse. "Looks like you might have fractured your humerus bone. Maybe your collarbone, too. Basically your whole shoulder. Hard to tell." He palpated along the joint. "The roof blew off of the local hospital, so I can't get you an x-ray or anything. They're totally overwhelmed with trying to help the folks who are on life-support devices."

I understood. "What can you do? Anything?" At this point it was just another issue to be dealt with, in the procession of things to be handled, as a result of the disaster.

"I can try to put your arm in a sling. That's the best we can do. Do you have an old T-shirt you don't care for?" He looked around.

"Yeah, I'm sure I do." I grabbed a shirt from my bedroom and handed it to him.

He bit into the hem at the bottom and then began to tear at it, and in the space of a minute he had created a sling, placed my arm in it and tied it up around my neck.

"There ya go," he said as he stepped back and looked approvingly at his handiwork.

"Well, this gives a little relief. Thank you." I adjusted the knot around my neck a little towards the front so as not to dig in too much. "There. Perfect," I smiled.

"I'm sorry I can't do more, but, well you know, we are all trying to do the best with what we've got to work with," he said as he wiped his brow with the back of his hand. "I need to get going. We're pretty short of people. New Orleans won't let a bunch of people work because they don't recognize the credentials. They wouldn't take me cuz I didn't have a license in Louisiana, but at least I can help here."

"You're kidding?"

"No. Sadly I'm not. I'm an Army medic, and I'm licensed as a Physician's Assistant in Missouri. But people are probably dying over in New Orleans because of bureaucracy." He shook his head.

"From what I've seen here, things are pretty bad. I can only imagine what it's like over in New Orleans."

"It's hard to imagine. What I've seen? It's bad. Very bad. It's not gonna be good for some time," he said as he headed for the door. He stopped on the porch. "Don't move that arm if you can help it. Keep it in the sling as much as possible and it should heal ok."

"Alright. I'll try. Take care."

"You, too." And he made his way back over and around the massive stumps and disappeared up Main Street.

On about the sixth or seventh day post Katrina, we discovered that my mother's telephone worked. I picked it up to check for the umpteenth time, and there was a dial tone. We called over to my Uncle Billy, who lived right outside of town, but his line just rang and rang. We tried several other neighbors and had no luck either. I tried to call out to California and we couldn't get it to ring on the other end. Just silence.

Finally, Uncle Billy was able to come by to check on us and when he heard we had a dial tone he immediately went in and tried calling someone over in Hattiesburg. He got through. This started a cascade of people lining up at our house to use the phone. It didn't seem to be able to connect outside of a limited area and we couldn't call anyone in town because their phones were not yet receiving calls, nor did they even have a ringtone. We couldn't understand why ours worked and others' didn't, but we were glad to help.

Through the trees sometimes I could just make out stretches of Highway 11 which heads north. I stared towards the window and leaned forward, squinting into the night. Through the breeze that swayed the branches of the nearly naked trees a light shimmered. It certainly wasn't a lightning bug. No bugs had survived this storm. Not anything that flew anyways. It felt like I was seeing the equivalent of the Star of Bethlehem, something rare and profound, promising deliverance.

"Come here!" I called to my mother.

"What?"

"You've gotta see this!" I exclaimed.

"What?"

"Look, mother!" I yelled, excitement overtaking me.

"What is that?" She stretched her neck to peer out.

"It's a light, mom. It can't be a star, it's too low."

"Oh, uh huh. It sure is a light."

"That means electricity!"

"Well, I guess it does. One little ol' light in all of our little ol' town."

"It's a start."

"By golly it is. It surely is."

Two days later we had electricity.

There were only three of us in our neighborhood who had opted to stay through the storm, and each of us had obtained generators. But once we got our electricity back on, I was grateful for the relief from the noise. All day and night the chattering, rattling sounds of the little gas engines had chugged, sputtered and created a stark contrast to the palpable quiet we had briefly grown accustomed to after the storm.

Somewhere around the two-week mark my mother's phone rang and startled the crap out of us. I was closest to it, but still had to let it ring a time or two before the idea of being back in contact had penetrated into my consciousness. It was my friend Liz from California. She said she'd been trying to find out anything at all about us—whether or not we were alive and how we had fared. I had been so focused on the day-to-day requirements of life that I had only occasionally thought about the outside world. I figured they probably knew more than we did here in the backwoods of Mississippi. It was clear now that news of this storm was affecting, not only us here in the South, but our nation as well.

I hired a contractor named Jerral whom I had previously employed to do some jobs around the house, to give me an estimate on the repairs and he said he'd be back later to prep for the job. When he returned he came up on the porch shaking his head.

"Miss Peggy, you know where we got your roofing materials a few months ago, 84 Lumber?"

I nodded yes.

"It's gah-won," he drawled "g o n e," in true Southern Style

"Really, Jerral?"

"Yes, Miss Peggy. Nothing left but the cement slab."

"You're kidding." I tried to imagine that.

"No, M'am, I'm not. You know that Toyota dealership in Slidell?"

"It's g-o-n-e, too. Can't even see 'em no more: cars sunk."

I let my breath out in an incredulous whistle.

"Well, let me get on in here and get started." He ambled out toward the backyard, studied the missing roof section a few minutes then glanced over at the neighbor's whose tree still lay across the collapsed north side of his house. I'd followed him out.

"Miss Peggy, you know the bridge that goes between Bay St. Louis and Pass Christian?"

"Yes of course."

"It's gone, too."

"The whole bridge?" My mind could hardly conjure up such an image.

"Gone."

My mind raced with the gravity of what I was hearing. Still it seemed impossible to comprehend. But so were other things. My arm was still in a sling and everywhere I looked I saw a nearly unimaginable alteration of scenery.

"Oh . . . and Miss Peggy?"

"Yes, Jerral?" I look at him apprehensively; I wasn't sure I could take anymore.

"Pass Christian . . ." He cleared his throat. "It's . . ." He cleared it again and drew out his next word. "G-o-n-e."

I sat down, shocked into silence.

✳

About eight months later Mom asked if we could go for a ride over to see the Coast. I said sure and we headed out the next day. We hadn't been anywhere near the Gulf Coast since long before the devastation of Katrina. The news kept reporting that things had gotten much better but nowhere near back to "normal," whatever that may have been before—everything was most certainly changed forever now. We took Cody along for the ride. As we approached the coast, Mom and I were shocked at what we saw. The vistas were nearly incomprehensible. The familiar sights we'd grown accustomed to were obliterated. The two-hundred-year-old trees that lined the roadways had been uprooted and splintered, scattered for miles across the flat, unpopulated landscape. Cody began to pant and then to whine. Whimpering, really. He was obviously agitated. He got down on the floor of the car, then sniffed the air and whined, pitiably. He was shaking and his eyes were wide, to the point where the whites were showing.

"What do you think is wrong with him?" my mother asked. She reached out to stroke his fur, "What's wrong, Cody? What do you smell, boy?"

"I don't know," I replied trying to watch my driving, take in all I was seeing, or more accurately not seeing, and figure out why my dog was acting up.

Cody carried on, increasing his bizarre behavior to the point where he was howling and in a semi-panic, racing now back and forth across the back seat. Mother was trying to soothe him. I stopped the car, thinking perhaps he needed to get out to pee, but he refused to get out of the car and hunkered in the back seat trembling.

"My God Cody, what's gotten into you?" Mom talked to him softly.

"C'mon Cody." I tried again to get him to get out of the car and he reared back, terrified.

"I don't think he wants to pee," Mom said. "Do you boy?"

Cody pressed up against the back seat, shivering.

"Ok baby, it's ok," I said and slid back into the driver's seat. "It's ok Cody, you're ok Honey." I started the car up and returned to the road.

Cody continued with this behavior until we got outside of what had once been the town of Pass Christian. It started to dawn on me that maybe he was reacting to something unseen but palpable. Maybe he was sensing Death. Though most, if not all, the human remains had been dealt with by now, chances were that there were plenty of animals that lay rotting, their undiscovered carcasses tangled tragically amongst the remains of their once happy homes.

Gone.

✳

I'm probably not unique among residents of the Southern states that were rampaged by Katrina in the feeling that I'll never get over that hurricane, never. Yet, crazy as it may sound, if another science fiction storm comes along, I've already decided, I'm staying. Because if it gets that bad, once you leave, you can't get back to your house.

Mother always says, when an evacuation is being discussed in the media, "Well, where would we go?"

"I don't know, Mother. Away from the storm."

"Well, where would that be?"

Had we tried to leave before Katrina, we would have been hard put to do so. By the time we even considered going, we had waited until there was no gas left, and they hadn't yet begun "contra flow"—making the traffic on all roads move in only one direction: out.

Nope, Mom and I agreed: next time, we're sittin' it out again. Anything comes along stronger than Katrina, I figure we're gonna be dead anyway, no matter where we go. I'm just gonna buy a whole buncha shit just like I do every time they say a storm's comin' and I'm hunkering down. I got my generator, I've got my extra gas. I got my canned goods. I got my water supply. I keep Mom's beer supply at 90 Busch Lights at all times. I'm not stopping her. She doesn't get drunk because it's Busch *Light*. Almost like drinkin' water. *I could almost drink one . . . if only I could stand the taste.*

Following Katrina, for 10 years at least, everyone in the area was shell-shocked, and every time there was a storm predicted, people would fall like locusts onto the shelves at the Walmart and Winn-Dixie, grabbing supplies. Hurricane season officially runs from June 1 through November 30, but climate change is changing that. Now we have tornadoes. We never ever had them when I was growing up, nor does my mother, who has spent her entire life, nearly ninety years, remember experiencing a tornado. Climate change makes sense to me. Tornadoes don't all of a sudden, for no apparent reason, decide to stray from Tornado Alley and wreak havoc hundreds and hundreds of miles outside their usual habitat. No. You don't need to be a scientist to figure that out. People have reason to be praying down here in the South.

※

New Year's Day, 2011

"Mom, is your stomach alright?" We'd both eaten the same thing for breakfast and lunch that day.

"It's fine Dahlin'. How's yours?"

"It's not good. I'm feeling kinda green. I'm getting these pains in my abdomen."

"You are? Huh, I'm just fine. I'll let you know if mine gets to acting up."

A while later I asked her again, but she was just fine. I kept going over in my mind what I ate, and the only thing different I had from my mother was some peanut butter. I couldn't recall anyone ever getting food poisoning from that. Maybe it was some kind of stomach bug? I was sweating profusely, and getting chills so I decided to just try to go back to bed and ride it out. I tossed and turned and managed to get some sleep. The next morning found me still sweaty and with the chills. I felt a little better though and went in to get my morning coffee. Maybe I had experienced the worst of it and set about to start my day, when I got hit with a pang in my gut that nearly knocked me to the floor. "Fuck!" I yelled.

Mom called out from her room, "You ok?"

"I don't know," I gasped as I stood up and held on to the edge of the kitchen counter. I heard Mom coming down the hall with her walker and then she appeared in the doorway.

"You look pale, Peggy." She studied me. "Like you gots a fevah."

"I think I do, Mom," I groaned. "Think I'm gonna go back to bed. Need anything?"

"No, you go on. I'm fine," she said, rolling and shuffling her walker in toward the coffee pot.

I put my cup in the sink and, still bent over, made my way back to my room and flopped on the bed. I closed my eyes and for a moment I had some relief. Then came the nausea. "Oh God," I groaned and rolled to my side. The urge to vomit nearly overwhelmed me. I sat up to try to ease the discomfort and broke out in a new rash of perspiration. "Damn," I muttered and went into the bathroom to grab the small wastebasket and put it next to the bed just in case I actually heaved. I propped myself up against the headboard and tried to relax. After several hours, I had not gotten any better, in fact things had gotten progressively worse. I finally called a neighbor to come look after Mom. He took one look at me and called an ambulance which took me to the only hospital nearby. The paramedics put me in a wheelchair and rolled me near the drinking fountain and the receptionist said she'd be with me in a minute. An hour went by, and I was groaning and sweating and shaking in terrible pain. I pleaded with her to please get me in to see a doctor.

"M'am our computers are down, you're just going to have to wait," she explained.

I started begging, desperate. "Please, I am in pain. Pain, you hear me? Please, just get me a doctor. This feels like my guts are being stabbed out. Pleeeezzzeee!"

"M'am you're just going to have to wait," she huffed and turned away.

I was so sick by then that I was nearly delirious from the pain and fever, and it felt like it took all of my effort to just stay conscious. I started looking wildly around and trying to grab the attention of anybody walking by in the hall who appeared to be part of the medical staff.

"Hey, hey, you work here. Please," I said to a young man in scrubs who wandered by a little later. "I'm in so much pain and I'm so sick, please . . ."

He stopped and looked at me. "What are you here for?" he asked.

"I don't know. I'm sick. Like I'm being stabbed in the guts. I'm sweating. I'm shivering. Gaaaawd I'm hurting, please just get me a doctor."

"Have you been checked in?"

"I don't know. I was dropped off by the ambulance and the woman over there said the computer was down and I'd have to wait." I shot her an ugly look.

"Let me see," he said and walked over to the receptionist. As they talked I could see her rolling her eyes and gesturing in my direction. The young guy came back over.

"You're going to have to wait a little while longer," he said and hurried back down the hall.

"Longer?" I yelled after him. "Longer?" I turned to the receptionist. "Are you fucking kidding me? It feels like my insides are going to end up all over your waiting room, and no one has so much as even taken my blood pressure."

She barely glanced in my direction. I looked at my phone. I'd been there four hours by then. I tried to will the pain away and was so exhausted that I was falling asleep for brief intervals. Then I would be startled by another sharp, stabbing pain in my abdomen which would cause me to cry out. I felt like I was in some horrible movie. No one came to me or asked what was going on.

I finally called some neighbors and begged them to come pick me up. They found me still sitting in the wheelchair with my head lying against the water fountain trying to get cool. I was in so much pain I was having a hard time focusing and my vision was fuzzy. I barely recognized Gary and Regina when they arrived. Gary said something about getting me some help but by then I'd had it and just wanted to go home. I don't know how Gary and Regina got me in their car, but they did. Once home and into my room, I passed out.

I kept waking throughout the night in horrible pain. I don't know if I was passing out from the pain, the fever or what. By morning I was writhing in agony, having a hard time even thinking. I felt like I was on fire, yet freezing. The searing, stabbing sensation in my abdomen had spread and I couldn't even pinpoint its origins anymore. Regina called to see how I was doing and didn't like what she heard; Mom was getting worried, too. Gary and Regina decided to call for an ambulance again. I was just coherent enough to refuse going to one and insisted they take me to another hospital. Thank God they did!

I saw the blue glow of the Emergency Room sign as the paramedics slid me out of the ambulance and wheeled me through the automatic doors. Medical people swarmed upon me as soon as I arrived, and immediately got me into a room, placed an IV in my arm, and drew some blood. One of the nurses started to palpate my abdomen.

"Does it hurt when I press?"

"It hurts worse when you let go," I said gritting my teeth.

I heard her say to one of the guys, "It looks like it's her appendix."

The doctor arrived and asked me how long my symptoms had been going on.

"At least a couple of days."

Next, someone wheeled me down the hall to the x-ray room, then right back to my room. The next thing I know there was a flurry of activity. The doctor said, "It's your appendix. You need emergency surgery now. We're afraid it has burst, and you definitely have sepsis. It appears the infection may have spread throughout your body."

"I guess that's bad?"

"Very bad. We're going to do our best to help you."

Everything was grey and foggy. I felt like I was floating through tendrils of thick misty fibers. Wisps of gossamer clouds hung overhead, clinging to my consciousness. Through the veils a muffled voice droned in a rhythmic chant. At first so far away. I wasn't sure if it was coming closer or if I was moving towards it. I drifted on.

"Per istam sanctam unctionem et suam piissimam misericordiam adiuvet te dominus."

The light flickers. The grey mist retreats as a large dark specter appears, menacing, looming over me.

"Gratia spiritus sactii, ut a peccatis," the voice booms.

I recoil, screaming in horror. The Grim Reaper! Oh my God, it's the Grim Fucking Reaper!

"Get out! Get the fuck out! Get away from me! Get the fuck away from me," I yell as loud as I can. "Get the fuck away from me. Get away!" I'm flailing my arms and kicking while cursing with all my might. I see the Grim Reaper lift his "skirt" and leap straight up into the air and high-tail it away as my words continue to pelt him in the back. "That's right, get the fuck away from me! Get away! Mother fucker, go!" More light is making its way into my field of vision. More contrast, more color.

I hear a woman's voice approaching me. "Peggy! Peggy! Calm down, you have to calm down." Hearing my name gives me pause.

"Who are you?" I ask, trying to focus.

"I'm your nurse. Angie. You're in a hospital. You've been in a coma."

"Whaaa?" I'm suddenly feeling very, very tired.

"You're ok. Let me just check you out."

I feel her hand on my face as she lifts my eyelids one at a time. I have a hard time keeping them open, but I try. "How long have I . . . what happened?" I'm trying to piece things together and not doing a very good job. I realize also that I'm in pain, a lot of pain, especially in my torso.

"You had emergency surgery. Your appendix burst and you went into shock. You had quite a bit of poison throughout your system," she says, gently. "You almost didn't make it."

"Huh," I grunt and vaguely recall feeling very sick, visions of ambulances and hospital waiting rooms. I touch my stomach and my hand moves over some unknown terrain. I move my hand more slowly and feel an indent in a straight line right up the middle of my torso with short, flat, metallic ridges crossing it. "Geezuz, I've been gutted." I murmur and breathe a deep breath.

"Yes, M'am, you very nearly have," says the nurse as I fell back to sleep.

A familiar voice breaks in "Neesy, Neesy?"

"Uncle Billy?" I struggle to awaken again.

"Neesy, you alright?"

"I don't know," I say, my voice all thick and weak. "Guess I'm better than I was."

"You shouldn't have spoken to the Priest like that," he says.

"I shouldn't have . . . what? What Priest?"

"The Priest was here earlier. I sent him to pray for you, to give you your last rites."

"You sent a Priest? For me? Why in the hell would you do that?"

"For your soul. We thought you were dyin', Neesy."

A-ha, the Grim Reaper. "I thought it was the fucking Grim Reaper, Uncle Billy! When I opened my eyes, I saw some scary guy dressed in black hovering over my bed, chanting in a language I don't understand. Why wouldn't I think it was the Grim Reaper?"

"Neesy, you do understand that language. You're a Catholic. You grew up with . . ."

"I am not a Catholic any more, Uncle Billy! That mutha fucking priest about killed me from fright! You about killed me trying to save my God damned soul! Never, ever do that to me again!"

"Ok, Neesy calm down. You're sick. You just rest now, Neesy."

"Yeah, I'm sick and almost dead thanks to your priest." I just have to get that last dig in.

"Well, I'm gonna go now, Neesy and let you rest. God Bless you. I'll come back tomorrow."

※

I RAN INTO SOME TROUBLE

I was in a coma for over two weeks. My friend, Taren, came to see me often and said my arm was so swollen it was five times its normal size. My legs were enormous too. Tubes, stretched in multiple directions, horribly distended my torso. Sometimes I fought against the tubes, perhaps feeling like I was being devoured by a Giant Squid. There was so much poison in my system they had to create holes in a myriad of places to drain the infection out of me. The sepsis was so bad my organs shut down and the doctors had to do extensive "cleaning" of my abdominal cavity. I awoke with an incision that ran from my bra line to my panty line. Over the next couple of days I learned what condition my condition was in.

Not good.

"It seems we got most of the sepsis cleared out. But there's been some damage. Your kidneys aren't functioning. In fact, they're shut down," one of the doctors explained.

"Shut down?" I asked, "As in temporarily or . . . ?"

"You need a kidney. Both of yours aren't working. When the infection is in the system as long as yours was, you go into shock. It shuts down your organs. Your liver recovered but your kidneys haven't."

"Can I get on a donor list?" I didn't like the way this was going.

"No. Unfortunately, due to a number of factors, combined with your age, they most likely won't give you one."

I had just turned seventy, three months before.

"What if I get a donor?"

"Still don't think they'll do it."

I turned indignant. "How the hell can all these rich celebrities get a new liver? *And* more than once? A bunch of drunk rich people can get new organs. You're telling me that I can't? If I had the money I'll bet I could buy one. No. Nope. No. I'm not accepting this. There has to be a way."

"I'm sorry. There isn't. You're going to be on dialysis for the rest of your life. Which will probably be about five years."

"Are you telling me I only have five years left to live? On dialysis, no less? Kill me now."

"No, M'am I can't do that."

"It was a figure of speech, kinda. I wasn't really asking you to off me," I said, trying to take in this new and unpleasant information

"Five years, huh?"

"Yeah, five years."

There was only one person I wanted to talk to about my health at that moment.

"They say I'm going to die in five years! Endure the fucking dialysis in the meantime?" I exclaim, exasperated. "This is fucked up, Maggie. Really fucked up."

"You've forgotten who you are," Maggie said, quietly.

"What do you mean? I'm seriously dying here. As we speak."

"Like I said, you've forgotten who you are. Look, I've seen this movie before," she paused for a moment. "I swear if they ever drop another atomic bomb it will be you, Keith Richards, and the fucking cockroaches left on this Earth." Maggie laughed. "Remember, you survive everything."

I knew she was talking about my long stay at Harbor-UCLA.

Maggie continued. "Double pneumonia. Endocarditis. It's like your mama said, 'Y'all get to healing before you even know you been cut'. You've got this, Peg. Don't let them make you forget who you are."

"Yeah well, hmmmph. We'll see . . ."

"Just don't forget."

※

Two weeks later, I was sitting in my hospital bed awaiting the arrival of the guy who took me for my tri-weekly appointment with the dialyzer.

A nurse appeared at my bedside.

"Where's my chariot?" I asked, not seeing my special "let's go get dialysized" wheelchair.

"Not today. No orders today."

"But it's Wednesday. I go Monday, Wednesday, and Friday."

"I know, Peggy. No orders today, though."

"You know I hate sitting through that crap, but I'm not quite ready for the alternative. Shouldn't you check to make sure they didn't just forget? I mean, it wouldn't be the first time information got lost in a hospital."

"I'm sure, Peggy. I double-checked the orders myself before I came in here."

"Huh. Well, I hope it's not a mistake."

Friday comes, and a nurse arrived and took my vitals.

"No chariot today, Miss Peggy. You're not on the schedule."

"No. Something is wrong. It's Friday, and I haven't had dialysis since Monday. That's four days. Four days. You guys have been telling me I'm as good as dead in five years even *with* dialysis, now suddenly I'm not on the schedule? This is bullshit. I'm not liking this. Somebody is fucking up."

"Well, your numbers have changed."

"My numbers? Changed how? *What* numbers?"

"Apparently, they've been steadily changing. Improving. Your blood work is looking good."

"How good?"

"Much better. We aren't certain why, but your creatinine levels are moving into the normal range."

"As in I'm getting better? As in my kidneys are working now? When was someone going to tell me? I mean, c'mon, it's my life on the line here."

"Like I said, we can't be certain. It just may be a temporary anomaly."

It wasn't. Day by day my kidney function improved. The doctors were alternately incredulous and skeptical. They had never seen such a rapid turnaround. They had written me off in five years, designated me to a life of dialysis, gloom and doom, and within a couple of weeks all that was reversed. I was nearly as surprised as everyone else. When I had told Maggie about my prognosis, she wasn't surprised, and reminded me that years ago when I had all those other medical problems, I had been on dialysis then, too. I'd actually forgotten, but I realized that I should not have allowed myself to succumb to the medical professionals' ideas of what I was capable of. Should not have accepted that their diagnosis was my truth. I *had* accepted it and wallowed in my certain miserable demise. Then I remembered.

I remembered beating the odds before. Survived decades of the kind of addiction that killed so many others. Survived prison.

Survived the worst financial disasters, terrible emotional upheavals, and the grief, guilt, and heartache that accompanied the loss of so many friends, cut down in their prime. I may not have survived with my bank account, my pride, or much else intact. But here I was.

I remembered I still had my mom to care for. I still had my dogs. I still had my mind. I remembered. I remembered who I was. I remembered the impossible was possible. Again.

Epilogue

AS WHAT I THOUGHT would be months rolled into years—12 to be exact—I cared for my mother and led a quiet life. I had my dogs, my weed, and I was generally happy. Mom, on the other hand, was slowly facing her own internal war, and toward the end, her dementia was winning. As she lost her faculties, I tried to just love her more. It's odd, how life works in circles—how I wound up, back home on the bayou, finally got my head straightened out, as Mom began to lose hers.

Our conversations flipped in somersaults. I think back to all the blurry, blustery days, and being swept up in a storm of my own making. As I search now for the silver lining in those storm clouds, the synapses of Mom's brain search for one another, not from her own abuse, not from overdoing it, loving too hard, being too loud, or living too much. Just from life. Just . . . life.

❇

I get home from shopping at the Winn-Dixie like I do nearly every week. I can see into my mother's room once I've entered the living room. Up against her bed, catawampus and mangled, I see her walker. Just then I hear her.

"Peggy? Peggy? Peggy!" I drop my groceries and hurry into her room. There she is, sprawled out on the floor, one of her hands desperately grasping at the sheets, trying to pull herself up.

"What happened?" I got on my knees to try to help her up.

"I don't know," she says, perplexed.

I can see a goose egg forming on her forehead, partially hidden by her hairline.

"What do you mean you don't know?" I ask, my voice somewhere between frustration and worry.

"I don't. I just know. I'm on the floor."

"What were you doing? Or trying to do?"

"I don't know." The now-familiar bewildered look appears on her face. "You gonna 'hep me up, or not?"

"Of course." Then I add, "Are you hurting anywhere?"

"Yeah, my side hurts, but I can move my legs, see?" She kicks her legs a little.

"You think anything is broken?"

"How would I know?"

"I would think you would. You've fallen and broken both hips, both arms and by now you are pinned together like the bionic woman."

"I am?" she says, puzzled.

"Yes, you am," I say as I help her up.

"Oh." Her little face searches mine. "Oh..." Then she asks, "What's your name?"

"Peggy."

"No, your last name?"

"Caserta."

"That's the same name as my daughter."

"I am your daughter."

"Then why don't you call me Mother?"

"I do. I call you Mother all the time."

"So that means you're my daughter." She seems satisfied by this.

Then she asks, "Well, where's Peggy?"

✺

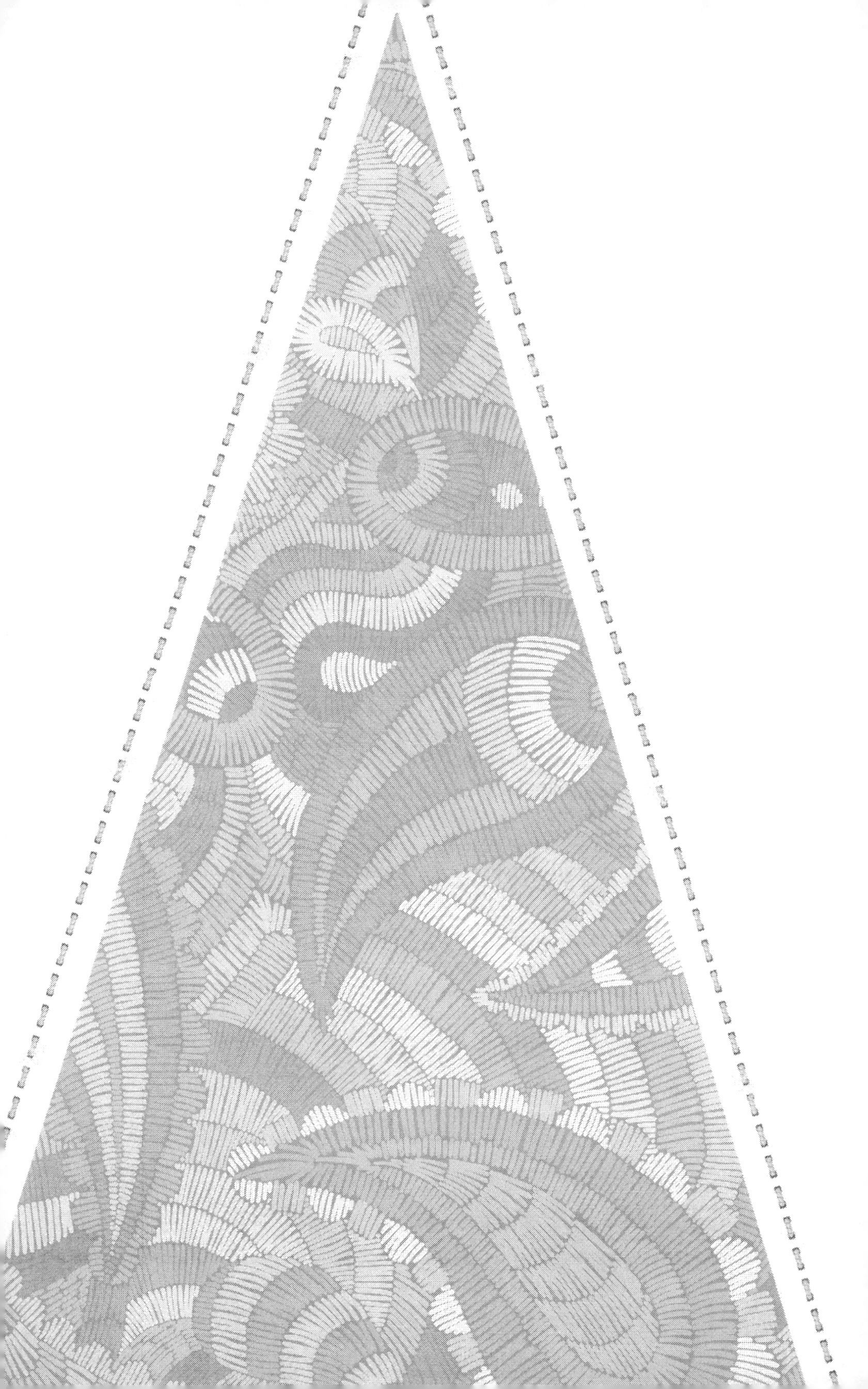

Acknowledgement

After years of insults, along comes a Karen Anderson and acknowledges, in a public forum, what was *my* voice and what wasn't in that first book, giving me a chance to exhale and try again. Beyond thanks to Karen of Kona.

※

NOTES

[1] If you don't believe me, compare Peggy's story with Achilles Tatius over-the-top 2nd century classic *The Adventures of Leucippe and Clitophon*—and he wasn't chewing on anything stronger than *tana* leaves.

[2] Associate Professor of Sociology and Sexuality Clare Sears from an interview SFSU Feb 2015 (https://news.sfsu.edu/when-cross-dressing-was-criminal-book-documents-history-longtime-san-francisco-law)

[3] From LS&Co. Archives: "One particular shop, Mnasidika, was run by a woman named Peggy Caserta from 1965 to 1968. It was at her shop that she met Janis Joplin. Jimi Hendrix also came out of the shop rocking his infamous style—bell bottoms and a vest. Peggy's story is included in a National Register of Historic Places draft application detailing Peggy's connection to Levi Strauss & Co. It's said that she convinced the company to change its production lines to manufacture the hot new bell-bottoms taking over The Haight. Though we are unable to verify Peggy's role in the lore, I can confirm that LS&Co. launched its Orange tab line, and Lot 646 bell-bottom jeans, in 1969." (http://www.levistrauss.com/unzipped-blog/2017/04/levis-link-haight-ashburys-hippie-headquarters/)

[4] "Herb Caen, *the San Francisco Chronicle's* columnist, strolled into Mnasidika one day and was struck by these unique new bohemians. They needed a name, and Caen supplied it. He took a little-known slang term and launched it into perpetuity: 'hippies.'" (https://www.vanityfair.com/culture/2012/07/lsd-drugs-summer-of-love-sixties)

[5] Purchase Country Joe McDonald's "Feel like I'm Fixin' to Die" on Amazon: http://amzn.to/2ACgqWb or read the lyrics: http://bit.ly/2AFlwzd

Made in the USA
Las Vegas, NV
13 January 2025

20ed576f-c3a6-48ee-8d76-5675fd4642deR01